P9-CDO-220

ONE HUNDRED PERCENT GUILTY

How an Insider Linked the Deaths of
Six Children to the Politics of
Convicted Illinois Governor George Ryan

BY

ED HAMMER

Retired Captain, Department of Police,
Illinois Secretary of State's Office

with DAVE MCKINNEY,
CHICAGO SUN-TIMES SPRINGFIELD
BUREAU CHIEF

FOREWORD BY
REVEREND SCOTT WILLIS

Copyright © 2010 Ed Hammer
All rights reserved.

ISBN: 1439260672
ISBN-13: 9781439260678

Library of Congress Control Number: 2009910328

TABLE OF CONTENTS

FOREWORD

It has been a plan of mine to reread the novels that were assigned in high school and college from back in the 1960s. While reading, one line stood out from Sinclair Lewis's book *Babbit,* speaking of the main character who dealt in real estate: "he followed the custom of his clan and cheated only as it was sanctified by precedent..."

Corruption in government comes with consequences. It may be in the raising of taxes to pay for shady deals; it may be the loss of confidence in the institution of government itself; but most importantly, and tragically, it can mean the loss of lives.

Putting an unsafe and illegal driver at the wheel of a semi-truck in exchange for political contribution is criminal. To quash the incendiary evidence of corruption is unconscionable.

I think that most people would agree, but have little chance to make an impact for truth, justice, and change. Yet there were people who fought for the truth to be known, risked their careers to see justice prevail, and hopefully will live to see needed changes made.

Ed Hammer, Russ Sonneveld, and others investigated an accident that caused the deaths of six children. They began to uncover corruption. Whistle-blowers courageously came forward; Joseph Power, a brilliant and unrelenting lawyer, pursued the truth; and a team of federal prosecutors led by Patrick Collins prevailed in court to prove cover-up and graft.

From his own personal experience, Ed Hammer recounts for us the environment and the workings of the criminally corrupt politics in the Illinois Secretary of State's Office under George Ryan during the 1990s. He gives us an insider's look at the pattern of corruption, of the custom "sanctified by precedent" yet lowered to unthinkable depths.

Duane Scott Willis

ACKNOWLEDGMENTS

From the time I began my career as an investigator with the Illinois Secretary of State Police Department and attended graduate school at Governors State University until well past my retirement, there were many co-workers, supervisors, mentors, and friends who so positively impacted my career that I feel they all have contributed to this manuscript.

I have had several partners, including Inv. Willie Granberry, who was my field training officer, and Inv. Tom Henderson, who worked with me to shut down South Side automobile chop shops posing as licensed junkyards. Both of these officers loved their job, setting the right example for the new rookie. Later, along came Inv. Jim Murphy. Although he came on the job after me, he taught me more about basic policing than the academy. After being assigned to the auto theft investigation squad, I partnered with Inv. Jim Rader. Like all good partnerships, we began to instinctively know each other's thoughts. Long hours on surveillance, undercover assignments, and practical jokes are only a few of the things we shared to bring about that close link. When I was assigned to work with the FBI on a case, I was introduced to Inv. Steve Streder. Ten years younger than I, he brought an energy and enthusiasm that I have kept to this day.

Also, I want to recognize Inv. Mary Beal's efforts during certain covert investigations, a skill not all police officers have. Likewise, Inv. Keith Lake risked his career and reputation by fighting those who held the power. Sgt. Mike Hogan gets special kudos for being my final backup when I was working on this project.

Special Agent Russ Sonneveld's contribution was essential to telling this story. He not only was my partner during the reign of George Ryan, but our subsequent lengthy conversations—in person, by telephone, and via email—refreshed my often fragile memory. More often than not, the purpose of these discussions was simply to vent our frustrations. I, however, found them to be a valuable aid in recalling facts.

Sgt. Pat Dowdle was my sergeant when I was a rookie. I was then his boss when he was assigned to the Department of Inspector General. Under Dean Bauer's command, Dowdle and I worked as partners. Pat had a reputation for finding conspiracies where none existed. However, with the Ryan organization, he did not need to look far to find a real one. Pat also brought humor to all around him, a necessary release valve for public corruption investigations.

Many supervisors were supportive; something that often is not the norm. Major Art Hartmann was old school but always encouraged me to do the right thing. I would especially like to thank Inspector Jim Redenbo, who was never angered by my confrontational style and welcomed a difference of opinion. Master Sgt. Denny Meyer and Commander Chuck Doerr with the Bi-State Auto Theft Unit task force gave me the work ethic and experience needed to successfully supervise a squad doing complex long-term investigations.

ASA Pat Quinn and ASA John Feeley, as well as Investigations Supervisor Ralph Dewitt, Inv. Bill True, and Inv. Rich Kopekin from the Office of the Cook County State's Attorney, all played critical roles in the investigation worked jointly by our agencies.

FBI Agent Jim Davis, Postal Inspector Basil Demczak, and DOJ Investigator Don Norton were the valued Feds that were my friends during the peak of the corruption investigations and remain so to this day. There were scores of assistant United States attorneys that worked on Operation Safe Road. The case was so complicated and lengthy that it demanded a team effort. I did not interact with all AUSAs on that team. However, I did work directly with Patrick Collins and Zack Fardon. Their part in seeing this historical case reach fruition is now infamous. Just as famous nationally as he is locally was U.S. Attorney of Northern

Illinois Pat Fitzgerald. I am more than grateful that he allowed his prosecutors to run with the ball.

Paul Green, one of my graduate professors, provided me with some advice when I first began writing this manuscript. Paul's experience with writing about local politics was a valuable asset I sought out. I attended Paul's classes more than twenty years ago, but the lessons I learned remained with me throughout my career in public service.

I sought out Dave McKinney early on to become a partner in this project. Our meetings were encouraging to me and his input was a major part of the final product.

Last, but most definitely not least, I want to thank Scott and Janet Willis for their support, input, and consideration. I would not have finished this manuscript without it.

DEDICATION

This book is dedicated to Ben, Joe, Sam, Hank, Elizabeth, and Pete.
I hope their story will bring better awareness of the consequences of
corrupted power.

It is also dedicated to Katie, Lauren, and Eddie.
They will always be my inspiration to seek justice.

INTRODUCTION

*Live in such a way that you would not be ashamed to sell
your parrot to the town gossip.*
                                                    —*Will Rogers*

George Ryan knew all about fake licenses before he was elected
secretary of state, but he denied it. "This skullduggery that went on, and
this crookedness that went on, happened on my watch. I was the secretary of state when it happened. I have taken the hit for it pretty well...
Was I involved in selling driver's licenses to people illegally? Hell no,
I wasn't. I didn't have anything to do with it. Would I have tolerated it?
Hell no, I wouldn't tolerate it. Not in a second would I have put up with
that had I known it was going on... To say I was responsible personally
for it—absolutely unfair." These were George Ryan's own words on
March 9, 2000, when confronted by reporters questioning him about
truck drivers who paid bribes to obtain their Illinois commercial driver's
licenses and the fatal traffic accidents caused by some of those illegal
drivers.

Two years later, when Lawrence Warner, his close friend and
confidant, was indicted, and Ryan was asked by reporters if he was Official A named in Warner's indictment as the person that shared part of

$2.8 million in kickbacks, he responded in his brash baritone voice, "I don't know. I don't believe I am. I don't think I am."

Eventually Ryan too was indicted. A jury of his peers, Illinois citizens, found him guilty on all counts: one hundred percent guilty. Judge Rebecca Pallmeyer sentenced him to serve six and a half years in a federal penitentiary. The afternoon of the sentencing, WGN radio talk show host John Williams was taking calls on the topic of Ryan's sentence. Callers were voicing their opinions as to whether the sentence was fair or unfair. I listened and became angry. Some callers said that Ryan had not done anything different from many other Illinois politicians. Other callers said it was business as usual. Several said six years was too harsh for the crime of awarding contracts to friends in exchange for gifts and campaign donations. One caller said that the fatal crash in 1994 resulting in the deaths of Scott and Janet Willis's six children should not be considered in the sentencing. The caller inferred that Ryan could not be connected to or held responsible for the crash.

I called in too and got through to Williams's producer. He put me on the air. I told Williams that I was an investigator for the internal unit responsible for investigating employee corruption in the Secretary of State's Office during Ryan's tenure. I then told Williams and all his listeners that Ryan was responsible. We investigated many cases of corruption, including the illegal sale of commercial driver's licenses for bribes. One of those CDLs went to Ricardo Guzman, the truck driver responsible for the fatal crash. George Ryan and his top investigator covered up and halted those investigations. I told Williams that Ryan deserved a much more severe sentence. I was angry. I was there when it happened. It was my job to stop the corruption.

This book is my recollection of the conspiracy by George Ryan and his cronies to obstruct justice and the related events. I was a cop whose duty was to root out state government employee corruption. Little did I know that these investigations would take me to the top, testifying against my immediate boss, the inspector general, and his boss, George Ryan. It includes my accounts of the licenses for bribes scandal, the federal case known as Operation Safe Road, and the record-breaking trial that was a tragic but historic event. The story traces my personal experiences as a special agent/internal investigator with the Office of the Secretary of State Department of Inspector General. I look at how the external forces surrounding the events viewed the corruption and lusted the power gained through the politics. The ultimate tragedy resulting from this complacent view was the deaths of the six Willis children and other nationwide highway deaths. The book looks at the prosecutors who took on the daunting trial. It also describes where Scott and Janet Willis are today. Finally, it concludes with Ryan's trip from his home in Kankakee to federal prison in Wisconsin.

"If he knew six kids burned up, he wouldn't care and would cover it up." According to Kenton Manning, retired sergeant of the Illinois

Secretary of State Police, these were the words of Jack Pecoraro, the chief of the Secretary of State Police and a George Ryan appointee. The man Pecoraro was referring to was George Ryan, his boss. It was 1997. Manning and Pecoraro were in the chief's office. They were discussing Manning's lawsuit against Ryan, Pecoraro, and other top managers of the Secretary of State Police. Manning was suing for an unlawful job action against him, followed by a departmental conspiracy to cover up that action. From the time Ryan took office, he and his appointees engaged in a series of cover-ups that culminated in Ryan and several of his top aides being indicted on federal charges of obstruction of justice. Some of the obstructions appeared to be minor incidents meant to protect the public image of George Ryan. He wanted to be governor of Illinois, and petty political drivel was not going to get in his way. However, there was a consistent pattern to these cover-ups resulting in a series of criminal conspiracies. The most serious included the cover-up of the connection between the licenses for bribes scheme and the deaths of six innocent children in Milwaukee, Wisconsin. Once authorities began to unravel the scheme, twelve other highway deaths nationwide were connected to the issuance of Illinois commercial driver's licenses for bribes, with the bribe money going to the Citizens for Ryan campaign fund.

Ryan's ties to corruption go back even further than his tenure as Illinois secretary of state. Robert Cooley, the Mob attorney turned FBI informant, alludes to it in his book *When Corruption Was King*. He says in October 1988, he and Johnny D'Arco, the former state senator convicted of extortion, were cooking up a kickback scheme with state lobbyists. They would pay a friendly lobbyist fifty thousand dollars to help get some favorable legislation passed, and then the lobbyist would kick back five thousand dollars to each of them. The lobbyist would also report receiving the entire fifty thousand dollars to the IRS, thereby preventing D'Arco and Cooley from having to pay taxes on their cuts. D'Arco told Cooley that one of the friendly lobbyists was Ron Swanson. Swanson, a former state senator himself and a close friend of George Ryan, was convicted in 2003 for kickback schemes in connection to the George Ryan scandal.

In 1998, when the scandal became full-blown after a bust by the United States Postal Inspection Service (USPIS), Ryan continued to deny his connection to any wrongdoing, stating he knew nothing about the issuance of any false driver's licenses. This was just one of the many deceptions Ryan and his allies engaged in from 1991, the year he was elected secretary of state, through 2002, when he vacated the Illinois governor's mansion in shame.

After Democrat Jerry Cosentino and Republican George Ryan won their respective party's nomination for secretary of state in 1990, all the investigators in the Chicago Office of the Secretary of State Department of Inspector General as a unified group decided to get behind George Ryan. I was one of those investigators. As a matter of fact, I was their boss. We enjoyed our appointments to the Secretary of State Department of Inspector General, a law enforcement entity responsible for investigation of public corruption within the Office of the Secretary of State. Because of Illinois politics and bureaucracy, most of the agents not only believed they would lose their assignment, they believed they could lose their jobs altogether if Cosentino was elected.

Most of the investigators had been assigned to the Department of Inspector General for at least seven years and believed that, because of a series of previous personnel actions taken during that period of time, they would not be allowed to return to their old positions in the Secretary of State Police if a newly elected secretary of state wanted to replace them in the Department of Inspector General. We feared that if Cosentino was elected, he more than likely would either get rid of the Department of Inspector General or put his own people in it. We believed he was corrupt and had organized crime connections. The former would later be proved true with a federal fraud felony conviction.

I was not in fear of losing my job. When I was promoted to Secretary of State Police sergeant in 1987, my assignment to the Department of Inspector General was only supposed to last two years, followed by either a position as a uniformed district sergeant or a supervisor over an auto theft investigation squad. In 1989, when my two years were almost up, the then inspector general, Jim Redenbo, asked me to stay one more year. His explanation was that I was doing a great job supervising the Chicago office of the Department of Inspector General, and he said Jim Edgar wanted me to stay. I do not know if this was true. I never met Jim Edgar the entire time he was secretary of state. I never really cared for the assignment either. A lot of the SOS employees, police officers included, disliked the special agents of the Department of Inspector General. They felt we were out to get them. Some felt that we were a political tool used by the powers that be to rid the office of political enemies.

I never felt this was true during Edgar's tenure. We were questioned from the top down about our actions as to why we were pursuing or not pursuing certain investigations. Some of the cases we worked involved the political friends of the secretary and some involved his enemies. Our briefings and explanations to Jim Redenbo were never questioned. They were based on professional law enforcement criteria and that always seemed to be acceptable to the Jim Edgar administration. If one of his political allies got caught up in an internal investigation, the punishment usually fit the crime. If it was a serious infraction, but a noncriminal violation, Edgar asked the violator to resign.

I handled one case in which a Vehicle Services Department facility manager, a Jim Edgar political appointee, sexually harassed a fifteen-year-old female. He allegedly invited her into his private office while her parents were conducting business in another part of the facility. According to the young girl's account, while she was in the office alone with the middle-aged manager, he made sexual advances toward her and even got down on the floor in front of her in an attempt to suck on her knee. Witnesses saw her run out of the office crying. I investigated the incident and believed the teen was telling the truth. Unfortunately, there was no physical evidence or witnesses to what occurred behind closed doors. It was the manager's word against that of the fifteen-year-old girl.

I heard rumors that the manager had resigned his previous job because of sexual harassment complaints. So I decided to question all the females less than thirty years of age working in the facility, about nine women, and asked them if the manager ever hit on them. They all replied that he did. Redenbo asked me what I thought we should do, since there was no actual evidence of the harassment of the young girl in the manager's office. I suggested we ask the manager to resign from the Secretary of State's Office, and if he refused, then fire him. His resignation would avoid litigation and public embarrassment for all, especially the teen.

The manager was ordered to come to the Secretary of State's Personnel Office in downtown Chicago. There he met with the director of personnel, the director of the SOS Vehicle Services Department, and me. I did the talking. When I told him he was being asked to resign, he immediately was beside himself. He complained, "I cannot believe Jim Edgar is doing this to me!"

I responded, "Jim Edgar is doing you a favor. You are lucky you are not being arrested on a battery charge." I told him the young girl's father was outraged about the incident and that he, the manager, should be grateful it wasn't going beyond a simple resignation. In my mind, I was wondering if the manager might be afraid of retaliation by the girl's father. He was Italian, and he lived and operated a business in a Chicago suburb that was known to be a Mob town. I didn't know if the father had Mob connections, but felt that if the manager believed the girl's father was connected, he more than likely would resign rather than face the wrath of the Mob. The manager did resign that day, and Jim Edgar successfully rid his office of a sex pervert.

I thought that if George Ryan was elected, passing the baton from one Republican to another Republican would go smoothly. I would retain my supervisory role and we would continue to remove the corrupt and sullied employees from the Secretary of State's Office without any interference from higher-ups. In other words, I thought Ryan would let us do our jobs. Up to this point, the feedback I received from Edgar's administration was that our investigative techniques were successful and acceptable. So in the process, all the agents and I looked for an issue that might give Ryan an advantage in the election. By September 1990, Cosentino was ahead of Ryan by seventeen points in the polls. Historically, driver's licenses were a hot issue. Identity theft was yet to be defined as a crime. For that matter, the term "identity theft" had yet to be coined. Based on our experiences in the Department of Inspector General while investigating fraudulent driver's license cases and input from the other members of the IG unit, I wrote a proposal. Through a political connection of Special Agent Pat Dowdle, we then submitted the proposal to the Ryan campaign.

The proposal, addressed to then Lt. Governor George Ryan, suggested the adoption of a law enforcement program by the Office of the Secretary of State, with Ryan making that program part of his campaign. The written proposal defined how driver's licenses were feloniously used by various groups such as illegal aliens, drug dealers, perpetrators of fraud, those convicted of drunk driving, and underage drinkers. I also described how fraudulent driver's licenses could impact public safety by presenting a menace to safe drivers on the state highways. I further identified how an aggressive law enforcement policy by the Secretary of State's Office on fraudulent driver's licenses would be supported by various public interest groups and agencies, including Mothers Against Drunk Driving (MADD), financial institutions, and law enforcement officers. I concluded the proposal with the statement: "Adoption of this by any one person would establish that person as a forerunner in an untouched area showing sensitivity to the needs of his constituents."

January 18, 1990

Lt. Governor George Ryan
State House, Room 214
Springfield, IL   62706

Dear Lt. Governor Ryan:

The purpose of this letter is to make you aware
of a serious need in the State of Illinois to adopt
a law enforcement program directed at the investigation and prosecution of the fraudulent use of the
Illinois Drivers License and Illinois Identification
Card.

(Beginning of letter of campaign proposal to secretary of state candidate Ryan)

Pat Dowdle used a behind-the-scenes Republican activist, Dick
Anderson, whom he had known for more than twenty years. He would
find a way to get the proposal to Ryan. They had worked together in
1968 to get Richard Ogilvie elected governor of Illinois, as well as on
other campaigns of Chicago area Republicans. Having a behind-the-
scenes guy eliminated the chance of the proposal not reaching the top of
the Ryan campaign. Anderson got the proposal to Roger Bickel, Ryan's
friend and chief counsel. Dowdle and I met with Bickel in the lieutenant
governor's office at the State of Illinois Building in downtown Chicago.
Bickel read the proposal and loved it.

Later, in October 1990, Bickel contacted both Dowdle and me to
advise us that George Ryan was going to announce the submitted program in a press conference in Springfield. Bickel told us that Ryan had

invited us to attend the announcement. I was a little apprehensive about attending a political event of this type while employed as a law enforcement officer. I telephoned my boss, Inspector General Jim Redenbo, and asked his advice. He told me it would not be wise and suggested that Dowdle and I not attend. Ryan eventually made the announcement of the fraudulent license enforcement program and Dowdle and I were not there. We did hope it would get Ryan elected and that he would use our proposal as the Illinois secretary of state. He was elected, but we never heard about our program again.

Something more disturbing occurred while I participated in a transition team after Ryan won the 1990 secretary of state election. Redenbo called and told me that I had been asked to participate in the law enforcement committee for the Edgar to Ryan transition. The meeting was held at the State of Illinois Building in November shortly after the election. Various issues were discussed at the meeting, two of which I had a great deal of experience with. The first involved the numerous requests made by law enforcement officers for duplicate photos on driver's licenses to aid in criminal investigations. Illinois did not keep duplicate photographs of driver's license applicants. Even though other states were keeping duplicate photos on file, the other members of the committee felt there were an insignificant number of requests by law enforcement to justify the costs. I had no ammunition to disagree with them, just my gut instincts based on thirteen years of experience.

The second issue was more serious. While Jim Edgar was secretary of state, a routine assignment of the Department of Inspector General special agents was background investigations on new employees of the Secretary of State's Office. The combination of low wages and political patronage often brought applicants with backgrounds of arrests and convictions on charges of theft, drug possession, and even sexual assault. Applicants were put to work before their fingerprints cleared a check through the Federal Bureau of Investigation. An employee could be working for several weeks before we discovered that he had been convicted of a serious felony and had failed to disclose this on his application. One employee that was hired and assigned to a job that included handling large amounts of cash had been convicted on two separate occasions of theft from his previous employers. He eventually was fired, but not for lying on his state employment application. He was fired for stealing cash from the Secretary of State Public Affairs Office located at the Cook County Circuit Court building.

Another employee was hired under an assumed name, and when his fingerprints were returned from the FBI, it turned out he was wanted for an eighteen-year-old warrant from the Chicago Police for auto theft. Furthermore, the old auto theft case involved Steve Ostrowsky, an organized crime chop shop proprietor on South Chicago Avenue. Further investigation on the new employee also revealed that he had been convicted in Miami on a federal U.S. Customs case of smuggling guns. He was hired to give driver's license exams before all this was discovered. I discussed these specific incidents with the transition committee, but no one else seemed to be concerned. One member of the committee whose name I do not recall even suggested that the practice of background investigations might be discontinued under the new Ryan administration. It was a sign of things to come.

Ryan was now the secretary of state. Months before he was inaugurated, he was made aware of the danger to the public of fraudulently issued driver's licenses. He was in a position of public trust, a trust that included safe roads and safe drivers. The next eight years proved that he had little regard for the public's safety. His priorities were money and power.

Some people might think or say I wrote this book because I am biased. Those alleged biases might include a bias against Republicans, a bias against the George Ryan political organization, a bias against political patronage, or even a bias against Illinois-style politics. My response to those opinions would be an emphatic no. Before George Ryan was elected Illinois secretary of state, I had no personal feelings against him or the Illinois Republican Party of which he was a member.

I consider my political leaning to be independent and middle of the road. I vote for the candidate that I believe has the most integrity, even though I may not agree with that candidate on all the issues. I am more concerned that he will carry out his duties within the guidelines of our Constitution, laws, and values. I am conservative on some issues and liberal on others. Unlike most police officers, I am opposed to the death penalty, which some may say is a liberal Democrat point of view. In fact, George Ryan was the most powerful Republican in Illinois, but he too opposed the death penalty.

I believe Ryan's stance regarding the death penalty was that he was openly opposed to it in order to win liberal support. Likewise, he needed to take the heat off himself for the corruption allegations he and his cronies were facing. This was supported by the fact that on January 30, 2000, the *Chicago Sun-Times* ran an exposé about money stolen from the Naperville driver's license facility in 1994 while Ryan was secretary of state. It was alleged that the facility manager stole the money to contribute to Ryan's campaign. It was also alleged that Dean Bauer, Ryan's inspector general, covered up the investigation of the theft and that Ryan was aware of this. On January 31, 2000, the day after the incriminating article appeared, the then Governor Ryan publicly announced that he was placing a moratorium on the death penalty. In his press release, Ryan said, "I believe many Illinois residents now feel that same deep reservation." It sounded like an attempt to win sympathy!

The fact that I agreed with Ryan on the death penalty issue would not have been enough for me to support him for governor. His 1998 gubernatorial opponent, Glenn Poshard, was a strong supporter of the Second Amendment right to bear arms. This is generally a Republican or Libertarian position. Downstate Democrats would likewise be pro Second Amendment. Yet Poshard was a Democrat needing votes from downstate and the gun control advocates of the Chicago area. I agreed with Poshard on this issue, but this one issue was not enough for me to support him. I did support Glenn Poshard for a more important reason: he was Ryan's opponent. George Ryan had no integrity.

From the time the Department of Justice began investigating George Ryan and his political organization, I often heard comments from friends and co-workers that it was Illinois politics as usual, and there was nothing wrong with things like patronage or kickbacks. Thus Ryan and his cronies were not committing any crimes.

For this reason, let me address patronage and how I view it. Let's say you own a small business and you need to hire one person for the business. You have two applicants who are equal in all aspects. One is some stranger you know nothing about except what is on his submitted application and resume. The other is your wife's brother to whom you bear no grudges. Who are you going to hire? Your brother-in-law is qualified, a good guy, and the brother of the closest person in your life. Of course, logically, you hire the person you already know and trust over the stranger. Is this patronage? Is it nepotism? Or is it common sense? If one believes in the philosophy that government needs to run like a business, then my premise is acceptable. Furthermore, some of our greatest leaders, like John F. Kennedy and Ronald Reagan, had family or close friends appointed to positions of confidence.

When patronage becomes unethical, or even possibly unlawful, is when individuals are placed in positions for which they have no qualifications. The impact of unqualified employees is one reason for the high cost of government services. Unqualified people doing government jobs mean ineffective service resulting in delays, waste, and ultimately higher taxes. Add to this disservice the fact that there was a quid pro quo relationship to the hiring of the unqualified employee. Government job applicants paying money or contributing to individuals or their campaigns to get the jobs is beyond unethical; it is illegal. In some cases, it may even be extortion. Not only does this conduct impact the government services, it raises questions of trust and integrity.

Then there are kickbacks and paying money to government officials in exchange for services or contracts. This was the biggest known form of corruption in which Ryan and his cronies participated. Like patronage, requiring a private business to kick back money to political campaigns in exchange for products or services used by the government costs the taxpayers more dollars. It inflates the cost of the product and passes that added cost on to the citizens in the form of higher taxes.

Shaking down a license applicant for money in exchange for issuing a driver's license when the applicant is not qualified is a public safety issue. Shaking down applicants for commercial driver's licenses and allowing unqualified drivers behind the wheel of eighty-thousand-pound rigs is even more serious. Imagine if the surgeon about to do open-heart surgery on you had paid a bribe to some government hack for his medical license because he could not pass the state medical board exam. Wouldn't you be concerned for your health and safety? And so it was in a bribery case called Operation Safe Road.

Unqualified truck drivers paid from one hundred fifty dollars to one thousand dollars to Office of the Secretary of State driver's license examiners in exchange for passing them on both written and road exams. Issuing them a CDL authorized them to drive eighty-thousand-pound tractor-trailer combinations, sometimes carrying hazardous material, on state highways and interstates. A family lost six children as a result of negligent driving by one of those unqualified truckers who paid a bribe to an examiner at the Chicago south suburban McCook commercial driver's license testing facility.

The more I worked for Ryan, the more unethical conduct I saw and heard about. As a police officer, my job was to investigate those crimes without bias. My co-workers and I assigned to the Department of Inspector General did just that. The outcome was that George Ryan, our boss, was found guilty by a jury in federal court on twenty-one separate charges. He was not found guilty of politics as usual. Nor was he found guilty of some vague ethical violation of some administrative rules. Ryan was found guilty of receiving gifts in the form of cash and vacations in exchange for state-favored contracts. He was found guilty of not reporting those gifts as income to the Internal Revenue Service. Most importantly, Ryan was guilty of obstruction of justice. When hard-working, honest investigators uncovered employees engaged in theft, shakedowns, and bribery, Ryan led a conspiracy to cover it all up.

CHAPTER 1

Fighting Crime with the Secretary of State

When men are pure, laws are useless; when men are corrupt, laws are broken.
—Benjamin Disraeli

Little did I know that sometime during my career as a cop I would become the nemesis of the governor of the State of Illinois. Growing up in the Chicago area, I learned at a young age that in Illinois politics corruption was par for the course. Often, cynics referred to Cook County as "Crook County" and followed the remark with a sardonic laugh. During my lifetime I have witnessed several local, state, and federal politicians getting taken down by the Office of the United States Attorney. Before I turned twenty-one, two Illinois governors ended up in federal prison. Both the pundit newspaper columnists and the players in local politics called it politics as usual.

I was interested in politics as far back as I can remember because my father always talked about it. It was probably his Irish Catholic roots. Dad was a Barry Goldwater Republican. He believed that the government should not be involved in an individual's everyday life. He was opposed to high taxes, government regulation, and political elitism. Even though he was drafted at the age of twenty-nine, three months before the attack on Pearl Harbor, he was also opposed to the draft. He fought in the South Pacific and received a Bronze Star for his heroism at Guadalcanal. He was one of those from the greatest generation.

My father returned from the war and worked in the steel mills for thirty-nine years afterward. He made sacrifices every day for his family in south suburban Chicago. He was a man of the highest integrity. He never swore or used violence to solve a problem. Dad was my hero.

My father hated corrupt politicians. I remember conversations with him when I was a kid. Politics were a frequent topic of discussion at the dinner table in our house. Even at extended family gatherings, we talked politics. My mother, father, sister, and I participated in these verbal exchanges with aunts, uncles, and cousins. All opinions were welcomed and shared.

Dad often criticized the Richard J. Daley machine and the patronage army Daley exploited in order to maintain his political power. Dad enjoyed talking politics, but the abuses and corruption in local politics made him angry. Dad grew up during Prohibition when there was a very fine line between organized crime leaders like Al Capone and political leaders like "Big Bill" Thompson, and I am sure this influenced his thinking. My father believed convicted politicians like Tom Keane, Otto Kerner, and Dan Walker deserved their very public demise. Dad's opinion of Governor Jim Thompson, whose reputation was gained from prosecuting these people, was likewise less than approving. Dad would say Thompson's public persona of the shining knight and crime buster was a façade. To my father, Thompson, like most Illinois politicians, lusted after power and abused it to keep it.

Despite Dad's political leaning, he cried the day John F. Kennedy was killed. As the Vietnam War escalated, the discussions my father and I had became more polarized. I was against the war, pro labor, and anti big business. But, much like my father, I hated corrupt politicians.

Dad did not want me to be a cop. He loved me so much that he never wanted me to be in harm's way. I hated the thought of working in a nine-to-five office or some dark, dingy factory. I liked excitement, and I liked the streets. Despite the differences between us, Dad respected my decision to be a cop and was very proud of me. He cried the day I graduated from the police academy, and then it was my turn to be his hero.

I started with the Secretary of State Police Department (SOSPD) in 1977. Alan Dixon was the secretary of state. One needed a political sponsor to get the job; in other words, it was patronage. It did, however, require testing and a certain level of physical fitness, and I passed both requirements. I was trained at the Illinois State Police Academy, and most of the members of my SOS Police class wanted to be professional law enforcement officers. Those who didn't failed the training.

I began my career in uniform, conducting administrative inspections of junkyards in the south suburbs of Chicago. The purpose of the regulatory inspections was to control the sale of stolen vehicle parts. Mr. Dixon wanted to be the U.S. senator from Illinois and closing the

3

blatant and notorious organized crime-controlled junkyards and chop shops in the area was a surefire way to get name recognition.

In 1981, I was assigned for a short time to the SOSPD Internal Investigation Division. During that time, we cooperated with ABC Channel 7 and the U.S. Immigration and Naturalization Service, which were probing corrupt Secretary of State's Office employees taking bribes in exchange for issuing driver's licenses to illegal immigrants.

I then was assigned to the Auto Theft Investigation Division, recovering more than one million dollars' worth of stolen vehicles and arresting several well-known car thieves. In early 1983, I was assigned to a multi-agency auto theft task force known as the Bi-State Auto Theft Unit, or BATU. We operated primarily in southern Cook County, Will County, and northwest Indiana. We conducted two long-term sting operations that netted more than 150 vehicles and 130 arrests.

On November 1, 1987, I was promoted to sergeant. Two weeks later, I was assigned to the then Department of Internal Affairs. On the day I started, Secretary of State Jim Edgar changed the name of the office to the Department of Inspector General. The newly formed department's responsibilities included rooting out inefficiency, examining employee policy violations, and investigating criminal official misconduct. It was composed of auditors and investigators. The investigators, like me, were either reassigned from the Secretary of State Police or were other individuals with certified police backgrounds.

4

Inspector General Jim Redenbo was an Illinois State Police deputy director on leave and had an impeccable reputation and credentials.

I was immediately promoted from the rank of sergeant to special agent in charge and was responsible for overseeing a team of seven investigators and two support personnel. We investigated Secretary of State's Office employee corruption in northern Illinois. Applying the standard investigation techniques I used while with the auto theft task force, including surveillance, informants, and electronic overhears, resulted in a highly successful team operation.

In January 1991, after Edgar was elected governor and Ryan defeated Cosentino to become secretary of state, I was privileged to attend the FBI National Academy Program in Quantico, Virginia. While I was there, I was pleasantly surprised to learn that Ryan had appointed Ron Gibbs, a retired FBI agent, as the new inspector general.

I graduated from the National Academy in March and returned to my assignment in the Department of Inspector General, only to have my high expectations immediately turn to disappointment. I found the new inspector general to be very incompetent, either because he didn't care about our important function of rooting out corruption or possibly because he was showing signs of dementia. Either way, the message to me was clear that George Ryan did not care about government corruption or about appointing competent professionals to positions of authority.

One of the first things on the new administration's agenda was to remove me from any supervisory authority. This was done despite my prior obvious successes and the fact that I recently had graduated from the most prestigious police command officers academy in the world. As a matter of fact, I now believe that it was done because of my reputation of successfully rooting out malfeasance within the Office of the Secretary of State. And Ryan's cabinet feared the methods the IG team employed under the Edgar administration. I asked for a transfer back to the SOS Police Department. The transfer was denied, and to this day I do not fully understand why.

The first recollection I have that the office was going to be run as a political force of corruption was a telephone conversation I had with Roger Bickel, Ryan's general counsel and personal friend. Bickel wanted to know if I could furnish him with a list of employees that had supported Cosentino in the fall election. He also wanted to know if I knew how many attorneys contracted their services to the Secretary of State's Office. I cannot tell you for a fact, but I believe the first request was made to retaliate against the employees that supported Cosentino and the second request was a source of political contributions—kickback money from contracts awarded. That phone call occurred shortly after I returned from the National Academy in April 1991.

Ron Gibbs was replaced by Dean Bauer as inspector general after only one year of service to Ryan. Bauer was a former Kankakee

County deputy sheriff, chief of police of the City of Kankakee, and, like me, an FBI National Academy graduate. Most importantly, he was Ryan's friend. I was initially impressed by Bauer's credentials, only to be disappointed many times by his lack of integrity.

The purpose of the Secretary of State Department of Inspector General was to root out employee corruption. The department was started in 1987 by Jim Edgar.

Edgar first became known statewide when he was appointed to the position of secretary of state by Republican Governor James Thompson, replacing Alan J. Dixon, a Democrat. When Dixon left to take his seat in the U.S. Senate, Thompson had the constitutional authority to fill the vacated position. Edgar was a loyal Illinois Republican that came with little or no baggage. At the time of his appointment to secretary of state, Edgar was Thompson's legislative liaison. Edgar was considered a social moderate, but a fiscal conservative.

Once he became the constitutional officer known as the secretary of state, Edgar began a ten-year career there with a reputation of professionalism. He cut waste and for the most part demanded that his staff perform their respective duties proficiently. Prior to Edgar taking the job, the Secretary of State Police Department was known as the Secretary of State, Division of Investigation. The officers wore uniforms with patches designating the same and their job title was investigator. Many were political appointees going back to the 1950s and 1960s under

Secretaries of State Charles Carpentier and Paul Powell. Those particular appointees cared little about law enforcement, unless it had to do with the Feds going after them for shaking down car dealers, body shops, or other state licensees regulated by the Division of Investigation.

Edgar took a department comprised of more than two hundred men and trimmed it down to 172 officers, renaming it the Department of Police. The uniform patches and marked squad cars reflected the name change. The badges referred to the investigator as "officer." This was done to clearly represent to the public that the organization was a professional law enforcement arm of the Secretary of State's Office and to prevent any confusion that these men and women in uniform could write traffic tickets and make arrests.

Edgar also appointed a career law enforcement administrator, Dave Watkins, to oversee the new department. Watkins, a wounded Vietnam veteran, was elected sheriff of Warren County while attending Western Illinois University. According to a story Dave Watkins told me, he ran for sheriff on a whim. Another student in one of his college classes dared him to run, so he did. Edgar felt he needed a "cop" instead of a politician to lead the department. Hiring and promotions emphasized merit over political connections. Because of the department's responsibility to protect the Capitol Complex, the state's first bomb squad and SWAT unit were formed. Physical fitness was demanded, with disciplinary action used against those who did not meet the standard.

Early in his tenure, Edgar formed the Department of Internal Affairs. It consisted of investigators on loan from the Department of Police, and some investigators laterally transferred from other police agencies. These investigators performed probes into allegations of criminal conduct by employees of the Secretary of State's Office for acts like bribe taking and official misconduct. The department chief was Jim Redenbo, later named inspector general. Although Redenbo and Edgar were college chums, Redenbo's appointment was based on professional qualifications and not cronyism.

One of the biggest cases of corruption Internal Affairs took on involved the Chicago South Driver's License Bureau located at 9901 South Martin Luther King Drive. Several employees inside the bureau were alleged to be selling fake driver's licenses to area drug dealers. It was later learned that one of the main purposes of the fake licenses was to launder the drug profits in bank accounts under aliases used by the drug dealers.

Before I was assigned to Internal Affairs, I assisted the Will County Metro Area Narcotics Squad in a bust of Dante Autullo. Dante was a former car thief that had graduated to the level of drug dealer. Along with kilos of cocaine in a Tupperware container and a bundle of cash in a Burger King bag, Dante was busted with several driver's licenses in different names. When I eventually ended up in Internal Affairs,

I learned that Dante's source of the fake driver's licenses was employees at the King Drive facility.

On November 15, 1987, I was promoted to sergeant within the Department of Police. Two other officers in the Chicago area were also promoted. One officer was assigned to the district uniform division, another officer was going to supervise an auto theft investigation unit, and the third's destination was Internal Affairs. The promotion board consisted of a contract psychologist, SOSPD Chief Dave Watkins, Chief of Internal Affairs Jim Redenbo, and SOSPD Chicago District Commander Art Hartmann. I was pretty confident that I was going to get the promotion. After the promotion interview with the board, I knew my destiny was Internal Affairs. I could tell by the way the promotion interview went. Jim Redenbo made eye contact with me several times and seemed to take a liking to me during the interview. I also had the experience of the auto theft task force, which was operated under the direction of ISP. As a result, I had an ISP way of doing police work and it came through during the interview. Redenbo liked that.

Consequently, I started with the Department of Internal Affairs on December 1, 1987. My first love was auto theft investigations. It involved organized crime and gangs. Chasing criminals is why I became a cop. However, I thought that Internal Affairs possibly was the fast track to the top, and I was going to make the best of it.

On the same day I was assigned there, the department was merged with Internal Audit and given a new name. It was now the Department of Inspector General, and Jim Redenbo was the first inspector general. The department was not only responsible for rooting out employee malfeasance, but with the new internal auditors it also was looking for inefficiency and waste.

The investigation of the employees at Ninety-ninth and King Drive was already ongoing and was close to reaching fruition. My first task, however, was to get to know my staff.

The veteran cops in the unit included Frank Murphy, Ralph Richter, Gerry Woods, and Dan Gilman. They were all on assignment from the SOS Police. Special Agent Kelly Holmes was the rookie in the unit. Later Pat Dowdle, my old sergeant, would be assigned, as well as Steve Streder, my former partner and best friend. JoAnn Robertson was our only support person. We occasionally had temporary secretaries when JoAnn went on vacation or leave. By my insistence, we eventually hired Carolyn Miller as our second full-time support person.

Frank Murphy was a DuPage County Republican. I only had few prior occasions when Frank and I worked together. Throughout our time in the Department of Inspector General office, it became apparent to me that Murphy was a functional alcoholic. He routinely was intoxicated at social events. Often he smelled like alcohol at work. One night in 2001, I received a call from an old friend, Dave Tikus. I hadn't spoken with him in a long time, so his calling me was a surprise. Tikus was a state police lieutenant, and he was calling me to inform me that Murphy had been arrested for driving under the influence while in his state squad car. Murphy was not under my command, so I referred Tikus to Murphy's supervisor. At the time of the arrest, Murphy was assigned to the state police's financial crimes task force and we had not spoken in three or four years. He retired shortly after I heard about the DUI arrest and I do not know if he was convicted. Despite his political involvement, Frank liked the thrill of investigating corrupt employees. Frank was loyal to me as a boss, at least until the time George Ryan appointed a new inspector general.

I had worked with Ralph Richter on several investigations. He was from my district, and while I was in uniform we worked together on some innocuous licensee administrative cases. Ralph was smart but terribly cerebral. Oftentimes his reports reflected information that was not relevant to the cases. Ralph always followed orders to the letter. That sometimes worried me, in the way one might worry why Nazis blindly followed Hitler.

Gerry Woods was a good cop but was antsy. His investigations and reports were detailed and complete, but despite a bond between us, Gerry wanted out of the Department of Inspector General. Almost everyone has a limit to the type of investigations we conducted and Gerry reached his. He transferred out two months after my arrival.

Dan Gilman was from Streator, Illinois, and definitely country. He spoke with a downstate Midwestern accent, played in a country music band, and had conservative leanings. He was in the Illinois National Guard and his military background was reflected in his job ability and efficiency.

Kelly Holmes was not a cop before being hired by the Department of Inspector General. Her father was the chief of police of Springfield City. She had not attended a police academy and failed the state-required fitness test when we tried to put her through the Cook County Sheriff's Metro Academy. Despite these shortcomings, she worked hard and was very intelligent and loyal. She left after she became pregnant.

Pat Dowdle was brought on about a year after I took over. He had been injured a couple of times on the job and was sent over from the SOS Police because he was not capable of passing the mandatory fitness test. I guess the bosses felt you did not need the same level of fitness for internal investigations. Pat was my boss when I was a rookie. He was also a friend. I always believed that as a boss you must be fair to all your underlings because someday they may be your boss. Pat was more than fair to me, and now I was his boss.

Dowdle was special. He was conservative and had gotten his job through the Republican Party back in 1971. Prior to that, he was a Cook County Sheriff's Office deputy under Republican Sheriff Joseph Woods. When Democrat Secretary of State Paul Powell died in office, Republican Governor Ogilvie appointed fellow Republican John W.Lewis as secretary of state to fill the vacancy. Most people know the stories of money-filled shoe boxes found under Powell's bed. The office was filled with Powell's like-minded friends, and Lewis attempted to clean house. The SOS Police was filled with hires from both Powell's and Lewis's time, and fortunately most were from the latter. Pat was from that time.

Dowdle was an enigma. He was loyal to his party roots, loved politics, accepted the political way, but hated waste and corruption. Sometimes that seemed like a conflict. Whatever the case, I could always count on Dowdle. He was like one of those little dogs that bites your leg and won't let go. When he sank his teeth into a case, he would not let go.

Steve Streder and I were typical partners. Back in auto theft investigations, he was assigned to me as a subordinate to work an organized crime case with the FBI. The FBI case did not work out, but they kept us working at their secret off-site location. We no longer assisted with the FBI cases but worked our own cases. We kicked butt. Like me, Steve was a risk taker, but even more so.

Most police officers, especially administrators, don't like change. They will continue to do things the old way because that's the way things are done. Not Streder. He was not afraid to try new ideas and take some risks. We immediately became friends, resulting in the end of the boss-employee relationship and the beginning of a partnership. That almost cost me a promotion at one point, but it never mattered.

When Streder put in for a vacancy in the Department of Inspector General, it was between him and another good friend and former partner. I asked Jim Redenbo to make the decision because I did not want to be put between the two friends.

Steve did high-risk cases, meaning they either involved undercover work or upset some political crony. He loved it, but eventually quit police work due to the pressure of the Ryan administration.

Walter Jackson was a thirty-year police veteran when he was assigned to the Department of Inspector General. Like Dowdle, he worked for Sheriff Woods before coming to the Secretary of State Police. He had years of experience in auto theft investigation, with a smooth-talking style that won over several street contacts and informants. Many didn't even realize they were talking to the man when they gave up information. Redenbo preferred college-educated agents, and Walter was only a high school graduate. However, he spent his first few days in the office hanging about twenty-five law enforcement in-service certificates and diplomas behind his desk. Walter never had to prove anything to me. I knew what he could do, and he always did it for me.

JoAnn Robertson, the office secretary, made me shine. I am not a very organized person and JoAnn kept me organized. She ran an efficient office on my behalf and, typical of people in that position, often angered the other staff. She also was loyal to me. When Ryan brought new people in over me, she no longer answered to me but remained a fighter for the cause of justice. The U.S. Attorney's Office owes a lot to JoAnn for her assistance provided to them in the George Ryan Operation Safe Road Case.

Carolyn Miller was hired by me as a part-time secretary. As soon as she started, I wanted to make her full time, and I received resistance from both the Edgar and Ryan administrations, the reason being that she was not politically connected. She learned her assignments rapidly and brought both humor and a calming effect to the office.

Carolyn was African American, and when George Ryan's people from Kankakee arrived in the office, they barely acknowledged her presence. I often sarcastically reminded Carolyn and a few other associates that Kankakee has three *K*s in it.

(Carolyn Miller at work in Hillside IG office)

(Director Dave Watkins and Hammer at Sergeant's promotion)

(Gillman at Hillside IG office)

17

(Hammer at police inspection)

(Hammer in Hillside IG office)

(Jackson and Gibbs at Hillside IG office)

Eventually they made Carolyn full time, but acted as if it was a favor to me.

Springfield was the other office in the Department of Inspector General. As I mentioned before, I respected Jim Redenbo, and Springfield was the geographic location from which he operated. I frequently had to attend to meetings in the Springfield office. It oftentimes was like stepping into a foreign land. The downstate department's culture was so immeasurably different from Chicago. The Springfield agents' caseload was much lower than the Chicago area agents' caseload. Springfield agents' cases were less crucial by Chicago standards. As a result, their pacing was slower, their tolerance was lower, and their attention to minute details was much higher. Of course, that attention was to the low-level employee policy violation cases. High-level employee misconduct was much more tolerated in both Springfield and Chicago. However, Edgar himself only tolerated it if it did not bring him adverse public attention. If there was bad publicity for Edgar as a result of a high-level employee, or even the potential for bad press, the wrath of the inspector general came crashing down on the employee.

Besides Jim Redenbo, the Springfield office consisted of a deputy director, one special agent in charge, and three special agents. They also had a much larger support staff. Jim Burke was the deputy director. He was a former Sangamon County Sheriff's Office deputy and very political. Burke was a very likeable person, but his political loyalties were his priorities.

Bob Vasconcelles was the special agent in charge. Vasconcelles was a former Springfield City police officer. What he lacked in education he made up for with his gift of language. Redenbo relied heavily on Vasconcelles, but I did not trust him. When Ryan dissolved the department in 1995, my instincts proved right. On June 1, 1995, all the employees of the Department of Inspector General were either fired or transferred to their prior assignment within the Secretary of State's Office. Vasconcelles was fired because he had no prior assignment with the Secretary of State's Office. However, he had a new state government job the next day, working at Central Management Services under the governor's office. State election records show he contributed to both Ryan's campaign ($650) and Edgar's campaign ($750). From these contributions, it made sense that he might know in advance of the plan to purge the Department of Inspector General office and shortly thereafter be gainfully employed. That purge eventually resulted in an obstruction charge for Ryan.

Rick Cox was a special agent formerly with the Illinois State Police. It was reported to me by friends in Springfield that Cox always spoke negatively of me. Why he did not like me, I didn't know. I could only guess that he was jealous because Redenbo made me an SA III and he was an SA II.

There also was Special Agent Tony Klassing. He was formerly with the Sangamon County Sheriff's Office. When he talked, he reminded me of Chester Goode from the 1960s TV show *Gunsmoke*. You might remember Chester as the deputy with a limp played by Dennis Weaver. He was known for calling out his boss's name, "Mr. Dillon! Mr. Dillon!" in a Southern accent as he hopped along after Marshal Matt Dillon, played by James Arness. To me, Klassing's accent sounded more Southern than Midwestern. Klassing hated everything about Cook County and Chicago. He believed we were all corrupt, even the agents in Chicago.

Later Jim Redenbo hired Mark Lipe from the Illinois State Police. Lipe was hired for his surveillance technology expertise. He was, overall, a great cop.

Jim Redenbo's secretary was Barbara Schwartz. Her husband, Jim Schwartz, was a political heavy with Edgar, and the director of Central Management Services. Barbara was another person I did not trust.

Like my instincts with Vasconcelles, I was later proved right about her. Although she was not fired in June 1995, she too had to be aware of the purge of the Department of Inspector General office. State election records show that she and her husband contributed $1,650 to Ryan's campaign and much more to several other Republican causes. She also had a close friendship with Vasconcelles.

Once Edgar was elected governor, Redenbo, Burke, Cox, and Klassing all eventually left the Department of Inspector General. Redenbo went back to ISP as an assistant deputy director. Burke and Klassing obtained jobs at the Illinois Department of Transportation. Cox resigned, and I don't know what he went on to do. From the Springfield staff, Vasconcelles, Schwartz, and Lipe remained.

Most of the time, the Chicago and Springfield staffs worked separately. Occasionally we worked together, but in most of the internal investigations the staffs mistrusted each other for a variety of reasons. Egos often got in the way because one individual wanted credit for successful cases over another. Likewise, when a case went sour, somebody wanted to pass the buck.

The Edgar period had its ups and downs. Looking back on my twenty-five years as a cop with the Office of the Secretary of State, the Edgar tenure was the best time in my career. I was allowed to do my job with little interference. I was promoted to sergeant and then special agent in charge. We had a lot of fun in the Chicago office and occasionally a few laughs with the Springfield crew. We weren't pre-pared for what was about to begin with George Ryan's election as secre-tary of state in 1990. Steve Streder used to say we were spoiled. I guess "spoiled" meant that our bosses tolerated us living up to our sworn oath within a limited extent.

In 1990, George Ryan was the lieutenant governor and he wanted to be governor. Jim Edgar wanted to be governor too, and the Republican Party nominated him. Ryan resented that, probably feeling it was his inheritance to the royal throne. Ryan became second fiddle to Edgar and accepted the nomination for secretary of state. Secre-tary Edgar had quite a number of people doing a professional service for the Illinois taxpayers. Ryan didn't care. He wanted his people and only his people managing the Secretary of State's Office. At the time, I thought it was because Ryan hated Edgar Republicans as much as he hated Democrats. That was naïve. He was putting his people in control because he was going to use the office as a gold mine for his campaign war chest and lavish lifestyle. Ryan wanted only people he could trust not to rat him out.

By its very nature, the Department of Inspector General han-dled sensitive cases. Enemies of the person holding the office look for wrongdoing in order to embarrass the secretary and thereby quash any political ambition. The Department of Inspector General is a public ser-vice department that protects the integrity of the office on behalf of the taxpayers. It also, however, allows the secretary to give the appearance that he cares about public integrity and deserves to be elected. Ryan's spin on the office would become entirely different. He attempted to use it to clean house of his enemies and cover up the malfeasance of his loyalists.

CHAPTER 2
Ryan's People Take Control

Power does not corrupt men. Fools, however, if they get into a position of power, corrupt power.
—George Bernard Shaw

The Secretary of State's Office employs more than three thousand people. Most of those jobs are political patronage. The office also regulates the automobile industry, the securities business, the trucking industry, and corporation registration. Most people interact with the office on a routine basis because it also oversees the driver's license bureau and the Department of Motor Vehicles. The Secretary of State's Office is the official record keeper for the State of Illinois. All this makes it a major source of revenue for the state and, more importantly, gives the secretary and the bureaucracy he oversees an awesome amount of power. This power has the potential to be exploited for both political and economic gain.

George Ryan was chomping at the bit the day he was sworn in as Illinois' thirty-sixth secretary of state. The only things that would be in his way were some honest cops with little tolerance for politicians and zero tolerance for corruption.

In 1990, Illinoisans were poised to elect a new governor. The Illinois Constitution also allowed for the election of attorney general, treasurer, comptroller, and secretary of state. In some states, those positions are appointed by the governor. In Illinois, they are constitutionally elected positions, which often simultaneously put party opposites or political rivals in statewide positions of power. Edgar was the Republican pick for governor. Neil Hartigan, the state's attorney general, was his Democratic opponent. Edgar had a reputation for being Mr. Clean; however, in the fall of 1990, Hartigan made accusations of a cover-up within Secretary of State Edgar's Department of Inspector General office.

In a hearing before the Illinois Attorney Disciplinary Commission, Phil Igoe, an attorney facing disciplinary action, made a statement that alerted Hartigan. Igoe was accused of surreptitiously obtaining a list of drivers whose licenses had been revoked for driving under the influence convictions. He then solicited these individuals to represent them in hearings before the Secretary of State's Office. A complaint was brought before the commission for this unethical conduct. The accused attorney was formerly with the Secretary of State's Hearing Division. He had resigned, and the facts of his resignation came out in his statement before the disciplinary commission. Igoe had mentioned to an attorney contracted by the Secretary of State's Office that he would like to go into private practice. That attorney, contracted to represent the state in DUI hearings, asked Igoe how much he needed to start his private practice. Igoe replied forty thousand dollars. The contracted attorney gave Igoe a forty-thousand-dollar gift and Igoe resigned his position with the

Office of the Secretary of State's Administrative Hearings Department. The next day, the contractual attorney took Igoe's former position with the Hearing Division.

Hartigan cried conflict of interest. Igoe and his replacement previously had been under investigation by the Department of Inspector General. It was Special Agent Dan Gilman's case. During the course of the investigation, the Department of Inspector General became aware of the forty-thousand-dollar gift during a witness's interview. The interview was conducted by Dan Gilman, Jim Burke, and me. Upon completing the interview, Burke told me he personally was going to follow through with the investigation because now it involved a department director. The department's director had to be aware of the hiring of Igoe's replacement after Igoe received the monetary gift. Burke stated he felt that since it involved a high-ranking Edgar appointee, protocol required a higher-ranking investigator to follow through. Of course, Burke also was the deputy director in the Department of Inspector General and an Edgar appointee.

Well, that was in September 1989. A year later, Burke had not followed up on the case like he said he would, through September 1990. I was responsible for writing a monthly memo to Redenbo summarizing the status of all open cases. Since it was Gilman's assigned case and he was under my charge, the monthly updates included references to this case. From September 1989 through September 1990, Redenbo was reminded monthly that Burke needed to complete his promised follow-up. Hartigan called this a cover-up.

Hartigan was able to get the chief judge of the Cook County Courts to appoint a special prosecutor. Joe Hartzler, later famous for being part of the prosecution team of the Oklahoma City bomber, Timothy McVeigh, was the special prosecutor. All the special agents involved, including me, were subpoenaed to give a deposition to the special prosecutor. Edgar hired the high-priced law firm Sidley and Austin to represent him at these proceedings, with the bill going to the taxpayers. The Sidley and Austin attorney prepped me before the deposition and kept reminding me that he was my attorney. I knew better. He was Edgar's hired gun.

When I arrived at the deposition, I discovered that internal affairs investigators from the Illinois State Police were part of the special prosecutor's team. Jeff Vlcek was one of them. Jeff not only graduated from Western Illinois when I did, we graduated from the ISP academy in 1977 at the same time. He was a fellow cop and a friend, and now he was at this deposition. He was a cop I respected, and he mutually respected me. I was embarrassed that I was about to be deposed over an allegation of a cover-up and a cop friend was there.

During the questioning, Hartzler asked me why I never took the information of Burke's failure to complete the investigation to a higher authority, especially since nothing had been done in a year's time.

I answered that I trusted that Inspector General Redenbo would always take the proper action. I could not offer an explanation of why Deputy Director Burke had failed to take action. After the deposition, I made a pledge to myself. Never again would I allow a boss to fail to take action on an allegation of any impropriety without going to an outside authority. The pledge was for both ethical and practical reasons.

In the end, the special prosecutor's official statement criticized the inspector general for not presenting our reports to the state's attorney, but concluded that no one in the Secretary of State's Office was criminally responsible for any cover-up. I viewed that conclusion as a form of Monday-morning quarterbacking. The special prosecutor reached the same conclusion I did, based on my years of experience. Why would I present a case to the state's attorney if, based on my professional opinion, there was no proof of a crime being committed? After this dog and pony show, I resolved that if there were any cases in the future that might involve political finger pointing, I would present the case to the appropriate prosecutor. I would not allow some political battle to affect my integrity or professionalism.

At the same time this inquiry was going on, George Ryan and Democrat Jerry Cosentino were involved in a battle for the coveted secretary of state position. Early polls showed Cosentino ahead by as many as seventeen points. Cosentino carried a lot of baggage related to his reputation. Ryan was doing his best, using Cosentino's tarnished reputation to gain points in the polls. Most of us in the Department of Inspector General office wanted to see Ryan win. Pat Dowdle and I had submitted our plan I mentioned earlier and felt it would help Ryan get elected.

Prior to the election, Larry Hanzar, an auditor for the Secretary of State Vehicle Dealers Bureau, was accused of shaking down a car dealer licensee. The auditor told the licensee that his application for a used car dealership would be approved if he contributed to the Jim Edgar campaign for governor. I posed undercover as the applicant and paid the auditor five hundred dollars cash. During the undercover meeting, the auditor bragged that he could get me a low number car dealer license plate for an even higher amount. After the undercover contact with Hanzar, a surveillance team followed the auditor and watched him deposit money into his bank account.

Shortly after the November election, I contacted the Public Corruption Bureau of the Cook County State's Attorney's Office to review the case on the auditor. The assistant state's attorney assigned to the case wanted us to make another contact with the auditor, this time equipped with a consensual overhear order (COH). The order gave us permission from the court to record the conversation.

A recording serves as a strong piece of incriminating evidence, even stronger than a confession. It is a tool commonly used among undercover drug investigators and works just as effectively in public corruption cases. It is a tool feared by most politicians. That is why it requires a court order in only a handful of states, including Illinois. The majority of states do not require a police officer to obtain a warrant to electronically record an undercover conversation.

This time I contacted the auditor by telephone, telling him that I met a friend at the auto dealers' wholesale auction who wanted to obtain a low number vehicle dealer license plate. He told me the price was now higher as a result of campaign debts Edgar had to pay off. It would now be $1,200 for a three-digit plate. Hanzar agreed to meet with both of us.

At the meeting, Hanzar bragged about his various political connections. He stated that his job was safe under the newly elected George Ryan because Ryan liked guys like him. Walter Jackson, the agent acting as the car dealer friend, paid Hanzar $1,200 for a three-digit plate number and Hanzar stated he would be in touch with us later. Both Jackson and I were equipped with recording devices, and I was equipped with a transmitter that sent the conversation to our surveillance team, where the conversation also was being recorded. This gave us three separate recordings of the same meeting. After the completion of the undercover transaction, the surveillance team again followed Hanzar to his bank.

Upon returning to the Department of Inspector General office, I contacted the assigned assistant state's attorney. He wanted us to do one more undercover meeting before making an arrest. This last meeting would also have a consensual overhear order.

I telephoned Hanzar and told him my friend Jackson wanted a two-digit dealer plate. I tweaked the story by saying I thought Jackson was into stolen cars and had plenty of money. I also said Jackson felt that the two-digit plate number would impress his car thief associates. The auditor said it would cost three thousand dollars. I responded that Jackson had already paid $1,200 and only would owe him $1,800. Hanzar responded with, "Yeah," but sounded hesitant, as if he meant three thousand dollars more. I guess he decided that three thousand dollars total was enough.

The next meeting, Jackson met with Hanzar by himself. Jackson was equipped with both an electronic recorder and a transmitter. We planned that since it was now December, once Jackson had passed the $1,800 bribe to Hanzar and said, "Merry Christmas," the surveillance team would move in to make the bust.

All went smoothly. Walter and the auditor met and Hanzar made incriminating conversation. He enthusiastically accepted the bribe and Walter wished him a merry Christmas. Our unmarked cars swept in on Hanzar's vehicle from five different directions. Hanzar was taken into custody, and Special Agent Steve Streder was assigned the job of interviewing and interrogating him.

I will never forget Hanzar's first words when he was brought into our office for booking. He said, "What are you guys doing? We are all on the same team." He told Streder that it was his boss, Robert Hickman, who had ordered him to solicit the bribes in exchange for Hanzar approving the car dealers' license applications. Hanzar apparently was under the impression that it was perfectly acceptable for an employee of the state whose salary was paid by our tax dollars to accept bribe money in exchange for certain routine state services and then contribute that bribe money to a political campaign. Nevertheless, we asked Hanzar if he would telephone Hickman and have a conversation about this matter. We also asked Hanzar if he would agree to electronically record this conversation. To save himself from doing some time at a state correctional facility, Hanzar reluctantly agreed.

There was one catch. We needed the state's attorney's approval to go to a judge for a consensual overhear order. Streder telephoned the assistant state's attorney assigned to the case and told him what Hanzar had told us. The ASA refused to give us the go-ahead for a new order. He said we had our man and enough evidence; there was no need to go any further.

Streder was steaming hot. He told the ASA that the reason he did not want to go further with this hot political case was because he was afraid that Governor-elect Edgar would ruin the ASA's career. The case ended with Hanzar's arrest. Edgar later was sworn in as governor and appointed his good friend Robert Hickman as the director of the State Tollway Authority. A few years later, the FBI would have a public corruption case on Hickman. He ended up embarrassing Edgar and pleading guilty. The one big difference between Edgar and his successor, Ryan, was that Edgar distanced himself from his cronies who got caught with their hands in the state's cookie jar. Ryan would eventually try to cover up for his greedy cronies.

Following the Hanzar case, I took a three-week vacation that included a trip to Disney World. Both my family and I needed the trip. After returning from Florida, I was scheduled to attend the FBI National Academy Program in Quantico, Virginia. My wife was in her third trimester of pregnancy with our third child and I would be gone for eleven weeks. Our son was in third grade and our daughter was in first grade. This would not be an easy time for any of us, but it would be a booster shot for my career and would eventually pay off.

Ask any graduate of the FBI NA program and he or she will tell you it was a highlight in his or her career. I was grateful for the honor of being picked to attend the FBI NA and thoroughly enjoyed my eleven weeks in Quantico. However, I was leery about being gone during the political transition of Edgar to Ryan.

I left Chicago on a Saturday morning in January 1991 at about six thirty a.m. There was already ten inches of snow on the ground, and my eight-year-old son was shoveling at the end of the driveway. His actions were both incredibly adult and childlike at the same time. He was trying to hide the tears. Daddy was leaving for eleven weeks, and he was going to miss him. My pregnant wife, my six-year-old daughter, and my son all stood at the end of the driveway in the blizzard as I drove off to meet a caravan of seven other Illinois police officers driving to Quantico, Virginia.

Two days later, we arrived at the academy. Quantico was great. The weather was much milder than Chicago, and the fellowship that followed was even better. There were 230 law enforcement officers from around the United States that were picked to attend this class, and about another twenty from Canada, Japan, Austria, France, Spain, Uruguay, Hong Kong, and Singapore. It was like attending college, a spa, and boot camp all at once.

The FBI can take credit for making what can be a very difficult ordeal an exemplary lifetime experience. Your education and training are advanced. You become more physically fit. You develop lifelong friends and contacts, all while you are being paid and advancing your career.

My first bit of bad news from the job back home was in a telephone call from my partner and friend Steve Streder. He and I talked about twice a week while I was in Quantico. We talked about personal stuff, but he also kept me apprised of the goings-on in the office. This late January telephone call included a description of the new boss, Inspector General Ron Gibbs. Streder said he was an older guy and seemed like a pretty good guy.

I immediately became concerned about his age. As you may remember, I mentioned earlier that I believed Gibbs was in the early stages of dementia. This was not my immediate concern. Rather, I was worried that the generational differences might result in conflict in trying to do the job effectively. My experience thus far in the field of law enforcement was that the majority of older police commanders preferred the status quo and often resisted any changes or innovative thinking. This was my bias based on my experience and Gibbs fit the profile.

Next, I learned that Gibbs was a retired FBI agent. I thought this would be good because it would mean he would be professional and not be affected by the political tides. That was immediately negated when Steve told me that, upon his retirement, Gibbs had become an under sheriff in a Louisiana parish. If there is one state where political corruption impacts the effectiveness of law enforcement, it's Louisiana. My first thought upon learning what Gibbs's last job had been was that he was a "Boss Hog"!

Being the savvy employee that I was, when it came time for graduation from the FBI NA, I invited Gibbs. I invited former Inspector General Redenbo too, but he was unable to attend because of commitments to his new deputy superintendent position with the Illinois State Police. I also extended token invitations to both Jim Edgar and George Ryan, figuring that they were too busy in their newly elected positions. Besides, I was nobody to them and would have been shocked if either had accepted. Despite the fact that I did an excellent job in the Department of Inspector General uncovering employee corruption, I was nobody because I was not a large contributor to either politician's election fund. But the new IG could use the time to get away from the office and rub elbows with some of his former associates from the FBI.

Gibbs did just that.

Despite her obstetrician's recommendations, my pregnant wife flew to Washington, D.C., to attend the FBI NA graduation ceremonies. I thought I would feel somewhat comfortable with that fact knowing that my boss, a lifetime law enforcement officer, was flying with her and would kind of look after her. After all, cops are trained in basic first aid, and that training includes childbirth. When my wife exited the plane, I was no longer comfortable. She got off the plane first. Although she had met him before the flight, he had made no effort to sit by her. She even felt that he was attempting to avoid her. Well, she survived the flight, the graduation, and the drive home with me without any birthing complications. The experience, however, gave me an idea of what kind of cop Gibbs really was not.

He walked around the academy rubbing elbows as expected. He bragged to the FBI agents on staff about his new job. He sometimes expounded on what the position was. I was getting the real picture. He was a self-centered old-timer with no heart. I was probably right about the resistance to any innovations. The signs of dementia would begin to show after we got back home.

My first day in the office after graduation, I received a telephone call from my Springfield counterpart, Bob Vasconcelles. I was pretty sure while I was at Quantico that the Springfield staff of the Department of Inspector General would have their heads so far up the new IG's butt that it would take a team of highly skilled surgeons several days to remove them all. The phone call was the first piece of evidence to prove I was right. Vasconcelles told Gibbs that the fairly decent 1988 Chevrolet Caprice that Redenbo had assigned to me to take to Quantico was to be brought to Springfield and was now being assigned to Special Agent Tony Klassing. I was to take a 1985 Caprice with 183,000 miles on it back to Chicago for my use. It was minor stuff, but symbolic of what was to come.

I decided to prepare a list of ideas and recommendations to present to Gibbs when I brought the car to Springfield. I was naïve and idealistic enough to believe that he might listen and even implement one or two items on the list. The most significant idea was that the new secretary of state might want to propose legislation regarding the duties and responsibilities of agents in the Department of Inspector General. Up to this point, the law provided the secretary with the power to appoint investigators to enforce provisions of the Illinois Vehicle Code, and those investigators would have the authority of peace officers. No statute ever addressed our duties to enforce the criminal code, particularly when it came to official misconduct and bribery.

Likewise, the statute referred to the SOS Police appointments as investigators, but there was no language for the job titles of agent or special agent. This led to some confusion within and conflict between the Department of Inspector General and the Department of Police, as well within the entire Office of the Secretary of State. With our own house confused and conflicted, the courts and the public were confused too. My suggestion to Gibbs was simply a matter of clarification so that we could better serve the public.

After going over my recommendations, Gibbs gave me a civics lesson. He hypothetically asked me if I knew how legislation was passed. He said first a crisis had to occur and then a law was passed in reaction to the crisis. Hallelujah! Now I could tell all my graduate school professors in public administration how it really worked. Gibbs was right. The George Ryan administration caused a major crisis of government corruption, and as a result, today we have a new law that gives the secretary of state the authority to appoint special agents under the direction of an inspector general. Furthermore, these agents' duties are to investigate corruption within the Office of the Secretary of State. My suggestion was made in 1991. The law was passed in 2001. Let me hear an amen. I was a visionary. And actually, to the best of my knowledge, the Secretary of State's Office had been conducting these types of investigations since 1981, twenty years before the law was passed.

Shortly after this civics lesson, I received a phone call from Gibbs telling me that the department was getting a new deputy director and he would be working in our Chicago office. The new appointee was

Spencer Leak, former director of corrections for Cook County Sheriff James "the Reformer" O'Grady. The Republican O'Grady lost his re-election bid for sheriff in 1990 for failing to live up to his promise to rid the sheriff's office of corruption. His own under sheriff, James Dvorak, went to prison for shaking down sheriff's employees for political contributions to the O'Grady campaign. Although Leak had no experience or training in enforcement or investigations, he had plenty of administrative experience running the Cook County Jail under an allegedly corrupt sheriff. He also was a political heavy. His father owned and operated a funeral home on the South Side of Chicago that had a reputation for burying assassinated drug dealers and gangbangers.

Leak was actually quite likeable. However, now he was a boss over me in the Chicago office. As a matter of fact, the first item on Leak's agenda was to take all my supervisory duties away and reassign me to field investigations. That was his right as George Ryan's designee; however, it did not make sense. We were doing an outstanding job of tracking and eradicating corruption on all levels. Our success was under my leadership. The fact that Leak was a likable guy probably cost him his job within his first year as deputy director of the Department of Inspector General.

My first taste of what the George Ryan organization was going to be like came in early 1991. I was at the FBI National Academy in Quantico, Virginia, from the first week of January through the third week of March. Upon returning to our Hillside office, I took charge of investigating a sexual harassment case. Normally I did not like to work noncriminal cases, but since 1987, when I was promoted and transferred to the Department of Inspector General, I generally assigned the sexual harassment cases to myself. They usually were as complex to investigate as a criminal case. If the employee was guilty of violating the Office of the Secretary of State's employee policy regarding sexual harassment, there was a high potential of that employee being discharged. If the complaint was not adequately resolved, then the Secretary of State's Office faced serious litigation in the federal courts. No elected public official wanted the publicity from that type of action. Ninety percent of the time, the subject of a sexual harassment complaint was a male supervisor. I took on these cases when I was first assigned to the department due to their sensitive nature. I wanted to assure the people responsible for my assignment as special agent in charge, Jim Redenbo and Jim Edgar, that they had promoted the right person for the job.

The first sexual harassment case under the Ryan administration came within days after I returned from Quantico. Before this case, there were subtle hints of corruption. Roger Bickel, Ryan's new general counsel, called and wanted me to furnish him with a list of supporters of Ryan's defeated Democratic rival, Jerry Cosentino, who worked for the Secretary of State's Office. Bickel also wanted to know how many attorneys had contract work with the SOS and how much money they made, an obvious potential source for political fund-raising. I was not capable of answering those inquiries because I did not have that information readily available. If he had asked me to gather the information, I would have refused, but he didn't.

Then there was Ron Gibbs, the new inspector general, and his incompetence and possible dementia. What kind of political leader would hire Gibbs for a position responsible for the integrity of three thousand employees who handle cash, securities, titles, and contracts? None of these subtle hints of corruption involved Ryan's direct interference until the first sexual harassment case.

I was contacted by telephone by Liz Vogt, an assistant general counsel assigned to the secretary's Springfield office. I had worked with Vogt in the past. She was a holdover from the Edgar administration and had a tough-as-nails approach to prosecuting employee policy violations, especially sexual harassment. Vogt advised me that three female employees of the Business Services Department had filed complaints on their new boss, a middle-aged male. The department's function was to register and maintain records of corporations, nonprofit corporations, limited partnerships, limited liability companies, and limited liability partnerships, as well as other business-related information. The department maintained a database of all these records and a telephone line manned by personnel to assist public inquiries for information from the database. Both the Chicago and Springfield offices employed personnel to answer calls at their respective locations. Historically, most of the telephone personnel were female. Their new boss in the Chicago office was a middle-aged male whose prior management experience was that he had owned and managed a ladies' shoe store in a north suburb of Chicago. He was a Ryan campaign worker who was hired and given the management position as a reward for his campaign contribution. I do not know why he left the women's shoe business.

Vogt asked me if I could pick her up in the morning at Meig's Field, the small airport (now closed) located on Lake Michigan near downtown Chicago. She was flying in on the State of Illinois plane, which routinely flew between Chicago and Springfield and carried passengers that had high-up state jobs or important state business.

When I was first promoted to special agent in charge in 1987, Redenbo asked me if I wanted to fly the plane when I traveled to Springfield on Department of Inspector General business, since I traveled to Springfield at least once a month. I declined because it was a one-hour drive in rush-hour traffic to Meig's Field from my home and then an hour flight to the capital. I lived in the southwest suburbs, and the drive to Springfield took about two hours and forty-five minutes in my state squad car. I preferred the drive. By doing so, I missed out on rubbing elbows with Illinois political fat cats who took those flights. On Liz Vogt's flight into Chicago the next morning was the newly elected secretary of state, George Ryan.

I picked her up at Meig's Field that morning but saw no sign of Ryan. I did not see a limousine or bodyguards, the usual signs that one of the state constitutional officers was nearby. Liz climbed into my unmarked Chevrolet Caprice and immediately started to tell me about a one-sided conversation she had been having with the good old boy, Ryan. She said she had been seated right next to him, and he had stated in a matter-of-fact tone, "Make this go away." Vogt explained to me that Ryan was alluding to the sexual harassment complaint on his newly hired crony.

Liz said she told Ryan, "I can't do that. This is serious, and it can snowball into a more serious litigation against the Office of the Secretary of State." She explained to him that if the complaint was not adequately responded to, the victim employees could go to the federal Equal Employment Opportunity Commission and file a charge. They could hold public hearings and levy large fines.

According to Vogt, Ryan retorted, "Aw, come on, this is no big deal."

"Let me do my job, Mr. Secretary," she answered, and the conversation ended.

Vogt grinned as she described the conversation she had had with Ryan on the plane ride. I was not sure if the grin was due to the fact that she was uncomfortable with Ryan's request. She appeared to me as the type of woman that was angered by sexual harassment and employees that created a hostile workplace. She could have felt it was only a harmless expression of Ryan's displeasure with this type of complaint, a common attitude for old-fashioned bosses. Ryan came from a generation where employees did not speak up about these types of problems. They were supposed to be grateful they had jobs. So just shut up and do your job.

Whatever Vogt felt, she did not say, nor did I ask. I, on the other hand, worried that this might be a sign of things to come. The two prior secretaries of state for whom I had worked had occasionally stepped in and asked for consideration on behalf of a friend on cases of a less serious nature. I worked a handful of sexual harassment complaints while Jim Edgar was secretary. He may not have liked the fact that I was investigating employees he hired, but to my knowledge he never stepped in and attempted to interfere with a sexual harassment case I investigated. All the ones I worked under Edgar's term resulted in disciplinary action against the subject. They did not go away.

Liz then described to me the nature of the sexual harassment complaint. The Business Service Department's manager allegedly had made lewd remarks and leering gestures toward three female employees. Vogt and I conducted interviews of the three female complainants at the downtown Chicago office of the Personnel Department. I do not recall the specific remarks, but I remember one of the females saying that when she bent over the office drinking fountain, she saw her boss staring at her derriere. I did not justify the supervisor's behavior; however, after meeting with the complainants, I felt that two of the three did not fit the profile of workers that complain about sexual harassment. Those two were tough, streetwise women who routinely used four-letter words in their speech like a longshoreman would. The one who told us about the leering gesture was dressed in a tight blouse and skirt. She was popping out of the top and showed more than enough skin from the bottom.

The third woman was different. She was attractive and dressed professionally in a pair of dark slacks and a dark turtleneck sweater, with a thin gold chain around her neck. She was soft-spoken, speaking in a tone that reminded me of a mother talking gently to her children. If we had to take this case to a hearing, she would have been the most credible witness. In order for a sexual harassment complaint to be valid, the victim of the harassment has to feel that she was harassed or the subject of the complaint must be creating a hostile environment. All three women stated they felt they were being harassed. In my opinion, the supervisor was creating a hostile environment through his innuendos and mannerisms.

Assistant General Counsel Vogt and I next interviewed the subject of the complaint, the manager of the Business Services Department telephone information line. He was a middle-aged man, thin, with a pointed face. He was neither handsome nor ugly. He wasn't what I would call a lady's man either. He was, however, abrasive and cocky. He tossed his political connection around quite freely and was angry at Liz Vogt and me for questioning his authority. He told us how hard he worked to get Ryan elected secretary of state. He denied that he had sexually harassed his subordinates in any way. He admitted that he complimented female employees for dressing attractively. He also stated that some females dressed provocatively, implying that men would leer at a woman who dresses in such a manner.

I did not feel this was a clear-cut case or easy to prove. I didn't doubt that the manager was capable of sexual innuendos. He was brash and arrogant throughout Vogt's and my interview. If he had been my boss, I would have found him to be a very difficult person to work for. I felt at least two of the complainants were using the sexual harassment complaints to attack a jerk of a boss. The third employee would have to testify against her boss at a hearing if he were disciplined and challenged the disciplinary action. I did not want to put words in her mouth like "hostile environment," and her description of the harassment was not as detailed or precise as that of the other two complainants. We had two poor witnesses with details and one good witness with inferences. It would be a difficult case to prove.

Assistant General Counsel Liz Vogt and I discussed our interviews. I told her that I would write the facts as they were told to us and submit my reports up the chain of command, which was standard operating procedure. It would be the Department of Personnel's decision combined with Vogt's input that would decide if the Business Services Department's manager would be subject to disciplinary action. I do not recall if he was disciplined. He may have received anything from a verbal warning to time off. I believe the one female that wore the tight clothes was transferred to another department. There were a variety of possible reasons for the transfer. It could have been due to the harassment complaint. It could have been for political reasons. It was even possible that she legitimately bid on a different job, resulting in a promotion and transfer. It wasn't important to me anymore.

As time passed, more serious cases of employee misconduct were reaching my desk, including bribery for licenses. I was more concerned now with the fact that Ryan or one of his politically appointed cronies might interfere with later felony investigations.

CHAPTER 3
Good Guys and Bad Guys

Pride goeth before destruction and a haughty spirit before a fall.

Proverbs 16:18

In the summer of 1990, Special Agent Steve Streder and I developed an informant who was going to purchase fictitious driver's licenses from a former Secretary of State's Office driver's license bureau employee. A fictitious driver's license is one issued when the applicant furnishes a false name or other false information. Applying for a fictitious license is a felony. An employee who aids the applicant in the false application process has committed the crimes of conspiracy and official misconduct. If the applicant gives the employee money for the license, then the employee has committed the crime of accepting a bribe.

The suspect former employee of this case had been fired a few years earlier for similar violations of employee policy, but was never convicted of crimes connected to his official misconduct. He allegedly still had contacts inside the driver's license bureau's facility at Ninety-ninth and Martin Luther King Drive. We had the informant equipped with a recorder supported by a consensual overhear order so that he could record the conversation in a meeting between him and the former SOS employee. The informant was also given two hundred dollars cash in marked U.S. currency to make a down payment on the fictitious driver's license. The purpose of marking the cash was to use it as evidence of intent if we later busted the suspect with the cash. Also, that same cash might be passed on to another conspirator, and he or she might likewise be busted with the cash. The two hundred dollar amount was minuscule compared to many drug deals and what undercover officers spend on these types of deals.

Our informant was to meet with the former employee at a house just a few blocks from the Ninety-ninth and King facility. I contacted Inspector General Gibbs by telephone just prior to the meeting. I briefed Gibbs on the operation, including advising him of the court order recording device and the two hundred dollars. He did not seem fazed by the briefing, and that made sense, since this was a pretty routine investigation for us. It definitely seemed routine for a seasoned FBI agent like Gibbs.

Our informant met with the former employee while Streder and I monitored the encounter from our vehicles. After meeting with the target, the informant briefed us on the conversation he had with the targeted employee. Details were lacking from our snitch, but it was too soon in the investigation to be concerned.

Shortly after the meeting, I made a telephone call to Gibbs to update him on the case. He was livid. He angrily told me that I had never advised him of the consensual overhear order. He also was angry that we had spent two hundred dollars on this deal and did not get any tangible results. I was miffed. I was expecting a pat on the back. Working these types of investigations for the previous four years had netted quite a bit of success. I later realized why he was angry.

Up to this point, I still had a professional relationship with Ryan's general counsel, Roger Bickel, and even respected his professional position in the Secretary of State's Office despite his earlier politically based telephone call to me. The day after my telephone briefing with Gibbs, I called Bickel. The purpose of the call was to advise Bickel of Gibbs's outburst directed at me. I was concerned that I might have broken some new policy under the Ryan administration and wanted to be sure I was following procedure. Bickel seemed genuinely concerned. In particular, he showed distress over Gibbs's failure to recall my first briefing with him. The second telephone call to Gibbs was slightly over an hour after the first call. Bickel asked me to advise him prior to any future arrests, warrants, or consensual overhear orders. I considered his request a minor annoyance, but did not believe it would negatively impact our operation. I now believe that Bickel was actually bothered by the fact that we were aggressive investigators who might use our technical skills to incur the demise of Ryan's cronies and maybe even Ryan himself. If Bickel was kept advised, at least he could prevent this demise.

Streder was working on a series of investigations that involved the manufacture and sale of fraudulent driver's licenses. Fraudulent driver's licenses were those manufactured at home, in a college dormitory, or in a rental garage. In other words, counterfeit. Most were sold to teenage drinkers who used the fake licenses to purchase beer, wine, or hard liquor. Some were sold to criminals to commit identity theft crimes.

The Illinois driver's license in 1991 was primarily a Polaroid photograph. The typical way to counterfeit the document was to manufacture a poster board backdrop using some basic drafting and graphic arts skills for the lettering in the logos. The subject whose license was being made then stood in front of the part of the poster that had the blue driver's license field background. A Polaroid photo was then taken with the subject standing in place. A specific distance from the camera to the subject had to be determined to duplicate the actual state documents to scale. Once the photograph was taken, the counterfeiter had to cut or trim a rectangle to the exact shape and appearance of the Illinois driver's license. Up to this point, the steps were easy. Any high school student who had taken a drafting or graphics art class could complete the steps.

A more complicated step followed in order to complete a fake document allowing the subject and his buddies to purchase alcohol. The photograph had to be sealed with a lamination that contained security features. Many attempts were made to duplicate these features. More often than not, these false licenses were caught by the cops, the bars, or honest liquor store clerks. The arrested usually ratted out the source of the shoddy workmanship.

There was a better way to make a counterfeit, and oftentimes it involved an insider in the Secretary of State's Office. Once the Polaroid-based document was counterfeited, it could be sealed with an actual state laminate containing the security features. Employees within the Secretary of State's Office could be responsible for stealing and selling the lamination to business associates, thereby aiding and abetting the underage drinkers or identity thieves. At least, the investigators in the Secretary of State Department of Inspector General office believed that this had occurred. The lamination itself included a hologram that was impossible to duplicate, and that was why it was valuable in the counterfeiting process. Also, it did not contain a control or inventory number, which made the Secretary of State's Office employees less accountable for it.

Streder developed a confidential source who could introduce Streder to a suspect that would sell authentic state laminations containing a hologram security feature. To the best of my recollection, this was the first criminal case in which George Ryan interfered. Through the snitch, Streder arranged a meeting with the lamination supplier in Algonquin, Illinois, at a new car dealership.

Most of the Department of Inspector General Chicago unit participated in the undercover operation, including Spencer Leak. The plan was that Streder would meet the suspect inside the car dealership. Leak, Agents Richter, Murphy, Gilman, Dowdle, and I watched outside as the deal went down. Once the suspect received the marked cash from Streder, he would walk outside, followed by Streder, and we would all move in for the arrest.

This was the type of assignment most cops wished for, an undercover buy followed by a buy bust. It was fun. These assignments usually gave all the participating cops an adrenaline high. We all felt the anticipation, and not just for the bust. There were all the "what ifs." What if the suspect doesn't have the goods? What if he also has drugs or a gun? What if he resists or runs? Every time a cop makes a buy bust he anticipates these things. Whether it's a paper crime or a drug deal, these are all possibilities and we would have to be prepared. It raises the heart rate, increases perspiration, increases the flow of adrenaline, and keeps you alert.

The deal went down without a hitch. Streder went into the car dealership and made the buy. He signaled to us that the transaction had gone down, and before we could rush into the car dealership, he had the suspect in custody. There were no injuries, no drugs, and no guns. The suspect went peacefully and was taken to the Algonquin Police Department for processing. Streder would do the booking, and I would conduct the interrogation.

The interrogation method I used involved a one-on-one conversation with the suspect and no other officers present in the room. There would be no desks, barriers, dividers, and no note taking. The point of this style was to develop a rapport with the suspect. You appear to empathize with him to the point you might even offer a scenario he could use to justify his unlawful conduct. Once he does this, he has confessed. You ask him to agree that you type up this scenario, and then he signs it. Since you're now such good friends from the rapport you developed, he agrees to sign. He is probably better off doing this than lying or refusing to talk.

This suspect went for it, hook, line, and sinker. He verbally admitted that he had unlawfully obtained the laminations, then sold them to Streder, and was about to agree to sign a typed statement when Agent Richter burst into the interview room.

"Secretary Ryan called. He said he talked to the suspect's attorney. Ryan ordered us to stop the interrogation."

I was outraged by Richter's foolish actions. I ran out of the interrogation room and chased Richter down the hall.

"What the hell are you talking about?" I angrily inquired.

"Leak spoke with Secretary Ryan on the telephone. Ryan told Leak that the kid's lawyer called and demanded that we stop the interrogation," Richter responded.

I located Leak in another room and demanded an explanation. He reiterated Richter's statement. I told him it was contrary to standard police practice. Leak advised me that it was an order coming from Secretary Ryan himself.

Despite what you might see on TV shows like *Law & Order*, a lawyer cannot arbitrarily decide to walk in on a confession in progress. A suspect in custody has a right to refuse to answer questions and has a right to have an attorney present during questioning. He is told this when he is read his rights, the Miranda warning. He may waive his rights and agree to answer questions or talk to the police. He also may waive the right to have an attorney present during questioning. If he does waive these rights, he may later, at any time, stop answering questions or demand an attorney. No one can call or come into the station or have someone call on the defendant's behalf and demand that the interrogation stop. The subject must make this demand himself. Not even his mommy can do this for him. Nobody can do this for him. His mouthpiece cannot do this for him. The secretary of state, George Ryan, the suspect's legal adversary in this situation, cannot and should not do this for him. Besides, why would a criminal suspect's mouthpiece call George Ryan directly? Why wouldn't Ryan advise the attorney just to come to the station? Was there a political connection? This was not one of the "what ifs" we planned to encounter; our boss telling us to stop doing our job, our legal duty; our boss running legal interference for a felonious suspect.

This was as if a Chicago cop busts some scumbag drug dealer, and then the scumbag's attorney reaches out to a political boss to interfere with the arrest. It is as if the attorney calls Mayor Daley. Then the mayor calls the commander of investigations and orders the commander to stop interrogating the scumbag drug dealer. Well, this may or may not happen in police departments like Kankakee, but it definitely never happened before to me in my fifteen years with the Secretary of State Police. I was furious.

I researched the issue of Ryan ordering the end of my interrogation of the suspect with the general counsel and legal adviser for the Springfield FBI office. He advised me that the interrogation should have continued until the suspect revoked his waiver by demanding an attorney or refusing to answer any more questions. The legal adviser also cited case law, which I used in a memo to Leak. I believed it was my duty to point out to my boss an operational mistake that might have cost us a case. What I actually was doing was telling the boss in a professional but surreptitious manner that he was an idiot. Nevertheless, I am certain that was one of the first of many black marks on my unofficial employment record.

The information furnished by the suspect selling Streder the laminates led us to the son of a vice president of a division of General Binding Corp. Polaroid Corp. subcontracted to that particular division to manufacture the driver's license lamination containing the hologram. Streder and I arrested the vice president's son for selling laminations stolen from the General Binding plant and transported him to the DuPage County Jail. Waiting for us there was the vice president of General Binding

Corp., the father of our suspect. Our suspect, working for his daddy at the factory, stole the laminates right out from under his daddy's nose.

If I were a big shot with a company that had a million-dollar contract with state government and found out my teenage son was stealing from the factory, and that it could cost the company the contract and me my job, I would be pissed. The VP was pissed all right—pissed at Streder and me. The kid admitted to us that he was stealing and how he was doing it, but it was us, the cops, that were at fault for picking on this poor privileged child. Yes, support your kid, but place the blame where it belongs. If your kid is stealing from you, what else is he doing?

Shortly thereafter, I learned more about Polaroid's contract with Illinois to manufacture and supply the implements used to make the driver's licenses. The contract was about twenty pages long and contained no security clauses. It did, however, have a clause that prohibited subcontracting; i.e., General Binding Corp. Other states have similar contracts one hundred pages long containing multiple security clauses. I even called California's Department of Motor Vehicles to obtain a copy of its suppliers' contract and compared it to Illinois'. That contract was close to two hundred pages. It made sense that Polaroid Corp. also was a large contributor to George Ryan's campaign fund. State election board records showed that Polaroid contributed $4,700 to Citizens for Ryan. They also contributed $2,361 to Edgar's campaign.

We also toured the GBC lamination manufacturing facility. There were no guards. A large portion of the factory workers were youthful summer helpers and immigrants. A person from either group could certainly have had an unlawful interest in fake IDs.

Polaroid sent two representatives from the corporate security office to review the findings of our General Binding Corp. case. They were typical corporate security people. They acted like experts but really knew little about the law and the impact of counterfeiting on public safety. Their two biggest concerns were, of course, protecting their own jobs and protecting the corporation for which they worked.

Shipment of the laminates to the Office of Secretary of State driver's license facilities was not secured. Usually, if a facility needed more laminates, they were shipped via United Parcel Service. Under Illinois law, possession of laminates by an individual was a felony. They were considered contraband because they could be used to counterfeit licenses, which in turn could be used to perpetrate more serious crimes. Laminates had a street value of as much as one hundred dollars each. A case contained one thousand laminates, with a street value of one hundred thousand dollars. You would think they should have been delivered by armored car. The actual manufacturer's value was somewhere between two cents and twenty-five cents. If UPS lost a case of laminates between the factory and the driver's license facility, the Secretary of

State's Office, Polaroid, and General Binding considered it a twenty-dollar loss. You must remember this was pre-9/11 thinking.

In the end, the Secretary of State's Office, Polaroid, and General Binding agreed with the investigators of the Secretary of State Department of Inspector General. They would now manufacture laminates with an inventory control number. The factory would keep a record of all products shipped based on the numbers. The shipper would be responsible for accurately shipping specifically numbered laminates to specific driver's license facilities. And the managers of the respective driver's license facilities would be responsible for numerically matching laminate inventories.

The total cost to the taxpayer was about a nickel per lamination. This procedure was followed until 1995 when, suddenly and quietly, it was stopped. By 1998, the new digital license was in use and Polaroid no longer held the contract. What mattered in 1991 was that we did our job with no public embarrassment to either Ryan or his campaign contributor, Polaroid.

Then, in November 1991, our team began an investigation of a subject counterfeiting Illinois driver's licenses from a garage on the Northwest Side of Chicago. This investigation was indicative of how serious the counterfeiting of driver's licenses could be. This time, Streder and I mutually developed an informant. He was a peripheral player with the Gangster Disciples (GDs), a Chicago street gang. Through his gang affiliation, the informant knew a guy on the Northwest Side that would sell counterfeit driver's licenses. That guy was selling fake licenses to both local underage drinkers and South Side Gangster Disciples. The GDs were using the counterfeit licenses to establish fake identities and purchase new cars with no money down using fraudulent credit histories. Our snitch went to a counterfeit license mill operated from a residential garage on the Northwest Side and purchased a counterfeit driver's license for five hundred dollars cash. We obtained a search warrant, recovered the counterfeit manufacturing implements, and arrested the seller.

The day after the bust, Spencer Leak arranged a news conference for Ryan in our office. WBBM-TV, WMAQ-TV, WLS-TV, WGN-TV, and WFLD-TV were all there. Ryan sat at a desk and read a press release while the cameras rolled. Ironically, while Ryan stated how he would use the Office of the Secretary of State to fight identification fraud, boxes of Polaroid film could be seen on the desk where he was sitting. This was purposely done by some of us IG agents to send a message that one of the flaws in the Illinois driver's license system was Polaroid, Ryan's corporate buddy. I doubt that anyone watching the TV news understood, but we felt it was both ironic and humorous.

After Ryan read his prepared statement, a reporter asked a question. I don't recall what reporter asked, nor do I recall what the question was. Ryan was unable to answer and he fumbled through his words.

Ryan was good at reading prepared statements, but always fell apart when reporters asked impromptu questions. It seemed as though he wanted one of us to help. We were standing behind him like so many good cops do when they are part of the team that makes the bust, resulting in TV news coverage.

Streder spoke up and answered the question. If there was a way I could have stopped him, I would have. Ryan turned and looked at Steve Streder with an evil eye. Man, I thought, Streder was dead.

The next day in the Department of Inspector General office, Leak called both Streder and me into his office. He told us that some front office people wanted to know why we had made the bust. We were supposed to investigate our own Secretary of State's Office employees and this case did not involve any. We told him we believed the laminations used by our suspect in the counterfeit driver's licenses case came from a Secretary of State's Office in-house source. We also briefed Leak that it was standard operating procedure to build a case on the outside to lead to the source on the inside.

(Dowdle, Streder and Hammer on counterfeit driver's license raid)

Streder's next step was to arrest the credit manager at the car dealership for selling the new cars to the Gangster Disciples. Streder believed that the credit manager ran credit histories on individuals and then advised them which ones had a good credit rating. The GDs then knew what fraudulent identity to use. The Gangster Disciples used a good credit history matched with a counterfeit Illinois driver's license to buy a new car. It was an organized conspiracy. Digging into all aspects would reveal the Secretary of State's Office inside source of the laminations for the counterfeit Illinois licenses being used by the conspirators. The cancer inside the Secretary of State's Office would be found and removed. We would do our job, and it was good police work. It was just a plan, and all the investigative steps were not yet completed.

Inspector General Gibbs telephoned Streder and ordered him not to make the arrest. Streder faxed a memo to Gibbs, asking him, "Please do not obstruct my arrest." Gibbs called back and Streder was promptly ordered to General Counsel Roger Bickel's office.

Bickel ordered Streder to turn the case over to the Secretary of State Police's auto theft investigation squad, supervised by Sergeant Dennis Serafini. Both Streder and I disliked Serafini immensely. We felt he lacked the people skills necessary to be a successful supervisor. He was rude and often callous. He hated us as well. Streder loathed the idea of giving this case to Serafini. We were never able to complete the investigation and find the inside source of the counterfeiter's laminations.

If Serafini was able to determine the source of the stolen laminates, he never shared that information with the Department of Inspector General investigators. Wittingly or unwittingly, he did the Ryan people's bidding, and the internal investigation went unsolved.

At the meeting, Bickel was in his shirtsleeves. When Streder arrived, he followed suit. He removed his jacket, exposing his weapon, a state-issued 9 mm semiautomatic. The 9 mm was safely secured and holstered on his belt. The next day Bickel inquired if the Department of Inspector General had a policy about agents exposing their weapons in front of civilian employees. The inquiry was made with Leak to determine if Streder could be written up for a violation of policy. Making an issue out of a plainclothes police officer taking his jacket off and exposing a secured weapon in a meeting with supervisors was a stance that sounded like one a liberal anti-gun person would make. Upon hearing of this inquiry, I began using a phrase among close friends to describe Bickel and other similar types. That phrase was "pro-law-enforcement, hypocrite Republicans." Illinois was full of them, especially Ryan's camp.

Law enforcement officers generally are conservative and, as a result, more often Republican. Likewise, many Republicans appear to be pro-police, pro-law-enforcement, and pro-law-and-order. In actuality, there are crooked Republican politicians that hate cops, especially if the cops lock up one of their corrupt cronies. After the convictions of the

Republican staff of Ryan, including Scott Fawell, the chief of staff, it is understandable why they would take an anti-law-and-order stance.

The informant in the Northwest Side counterfeit case used five hundred dollars of his own money to purchase the fraudulent license from the suspect. He volunteered to do this because he was certain the deal would go down, and he was aware of our concern based on the previous case on the South Side involving the lost two hundred dollars. The plan was to pay the informant back after the case was successfully completed. As a result of the informant's efforts, we obtained a search warrant, arrested and indicted the suspect, and recovered a sizable amount of incriminating evidence. The informant was entitled to the reimbursement.

I was responsible for maintaining the confidential source fund checking account. Each check issued required two signatures. To ensure that there would be no repercussions, I asked Leak to cosign the check to the informant. He agreed, but telephoned Gibbs to clear it with him first. Gibbs okayed the check, and the informant was paid. Later Gibbs called Streder and me on the carpet for violating a policy that stated we were not to use personal funds to pay for undercover operations. The intent of the policy was directed at agents, mandating that agents would not use personal money to pay informants. Three paragraphs later on the same policy page, it stated that confidential funds could be used to purchase evidence in a documented case. This was essentially what we did.

We paid our informant for evidence he purchased, and we did not use our personal money. The investigation Gibbs initiated on Streder and me was one of many forms of subtle harassment conducted by Ryan's people to discourage us from doing our lawful duties.

I believe it became apparent to Bickel that Spencer Leak and Ron Gibbs could not control the agents in the Department of Inspector General. Two months after the press conference, both Leak and Gibbs were removed from their positions in the IG office.

Gibbs was relegated to a do-nothing position within the Secretary of State Police. The chief of the SOS Police was Jack Pecoraro, a Ryan appointee, who had begun his law enforcement career with the Chicago Police. Through his father's connections, Pecoraro was able to obtain a cushy assignment, earn his law degree, and move up and out of CPD. He became the general counsel with the city of Springfield Police Department and, from there, earned his clout with Ryan. After being elected secretary of state, Ryan made Pecoraro the SOS Police chief. Gibbs was given an office in the SOS Police headquarters where Pecoraro kept a careful watch over him. It was a much better assignment for Gibbs than being inspector general. He played a lot of golf and caught up on his naps.

Spencer Leak was also reassigned. He was taken out of law enforcement altogether and placed in the Vehicle Services Department. Need I remind you that these reassignments were not due to any corrupt acts by either Gibbs or Leak. Nor were they made because either appointee was incompetent. Gibbs and Leak were reassigned because Ryan probably believed that neither one of them could control the renegade agents of the Department of Inspector General.

Along came Dean Bauer. I was fooled at first by the change. Steve Streder begged Roger Bickel for some professional direction during their meeting after the Northwest Side arrest. I thought the replacement of Gibbs and Leak was a response to Streder's plea. Like me, Bauer was an FBI National Academy graduate. Getting accepted by the FBI National Academy program required a background check by an FBI agent and passing certain physical and professional criteria. Bauer also was the former chief of police for the city of Kankakee, Ryan's hometown. At the time, I put aside the fact that the right political clout might get one through the appointment process to the National Academy. I also was naïve enough not to realize that the political climate of Kankakee may have been directly related to Bauer's political and personal relationship with Ryan. Nevertheless, I wanted to believe the Department of Inspector General, responsible for the integrity of the Illinois Secretary of State, was about to be fixed. Was I fooled!

Bauer was a lifelong friend of the Ryan family and handpicked by Ryan for the job of quashing corruption. Bauer had attended Kankakee High School for three years and then joined the United States Coast Guard. He was discharged after serving only two months. He then went to work for a chemical plant in Joliet before joining Illinois Bell as a repairman. At some point while he worked there, he also became a deputy for the Kankakee County Sheriff's Office. In 1965, he quit Illinois Bell, and eventually Sheriff Elmer Nelson appointed Bauer his chief deputy. When Bauer first became Ryan's IG, there were rumors that back in his deputy days he routinely spent his shifts in the Kankakee strip bars and lingerie shows. A former deputy told me that he was drafted and sent to Vietnam because he was outspoken against deputies being forced to contribute to local Republican political campaigns. Bauer also served on the local draft board during this time. The deputy said that, after being honorably discharged as a combat veteran, he had to file a lawsuit to get his job with the sheriff's office back.

Then in 1970, Tom Ryan, mayor of Kankakee and George Ryan's brother, appointed Bauer the city's police chief. The outgoing chief, Tom Maass, had just been elected Kankakee's new sheriff. Bauer remained in that position until 1985, when Democrat Russell Johnson was elected mayor. He then went to work as a safety director for one of George Ryan's biggest contributors, Azzarelli Construction. Owned by John Azzarelli, the company was fined two hundred thousand dollars for bid rigging on state road contracts. It also donated ten thousand dollars to Ryan's campaign for secretary of state.

In 1991, Dean Bauer first went to work for the Office of the Secretary of State in the Accounting Revenue Department as a collector under Georgia Marsh, another Ryan appointee. Bauer's job was to check mileage on trucks that were issued mileage registration. If the trucks' owners did not pay their mileage fees, Bauer would attempt to collect the past due fees, or seize their license plates. It was an assignment that, under all the secretaries of state, historically was known for also collecting campaign donations. Bauer served Ryan in this capacity for two months before becoming his second inspector general.

Shortly after Bauer's appointment, Joe Jech was appointed Bauer's chief deputy director. Jech was retired from the Internal Revenue Service internal inspections. His job there was to oversee investigations of IRS employee incompetence and corruption. Overall, Jech's administrative skills were superior to Bauer's. However, in my opinion, Jech was a spineless bureaucrat with very little political savvy. Someone higher up was pulling his strings, and he almost never appeared motivated to do the ethical thing. Rather, his administrative decisions seemed as if they were based on his survival in his new political career.

Bauer, on the other hand, was not very bright. He had years of experience in Kankakee-style politics. I do not believe his decision-making process contained much forethought. He believed the purpose of his position of inspector general was not to root out corruption or protect Illinois citizens from waste of taxpayer dollars. Bauer believed his job was to be blindly loyal to George Ryan. He believed the purpose of the inspector general and his investigators was to protect Ryan from public embarrassment. I will go so far as to say that Bauer believed part of his job was to protect those that engaged in extortion on behalf of Ryan's campaign for governor.

While all this petty nonsense was going on, the state employee's union was trying to get Ryan to honor a wage agreement on a contract signed by Edgar, his predecessor.

Ryan would comply with the contract only after he made some cuts. He directed each department head to evaluate his or her respective departments and remove positions based on least seniority. Streder was targeted by Bauer to be laid off, based on Ryan's mandate. He was given two weeks' notice and a pink slip in March 1992. He was not the lowest senior police officer in the Secretary of State's Office. He had twice the time on the job that several of the officers in the Department of Police had. They were protected by the Fraternal Order of the Police, the union. Streder gave up his union protection when he took the assignment with the Department of Inspector General. The pink slip was a slap in his face. No other officers had put their lives on the line during their career to the degree Streder had. Before his assignment with the IG, Streder worked as a full-time undercover operative and bought stolen vehicles, guns, and drugs from street gang members coming from Cicero, the South Side, and Gary, Indiana. Now Bauer was going to lay Streder off because he was a competent cop.

Streder had had enough. He began researching business opportunities. Bauer withdrew the pink slip before the two weeks' notice was up. It didn't matter. Like many disenfranchised undercover officers do, Streder quit and went into business for himself.

Bauer got what he wanted. He was able to rid the office of a cop that could cause the Ryan people problems. Streder was eventually replaced. New blood was being brought into the Department of Inspector General, politically appointed as special agents. This was not so unusual, since the Office of the Secretary of State is very political. The Department of Inspector General should be composed of law enforcement professionals and be free of political hacks. In my opinion, most police agencies are not free of political appointees, whether the Illinois State Police, the Cook County Sheriff's Office, or the Chicago Police. For that matter, the FBI and the U.S. Secret Service have their share of politically connected and loyal employees. In this sense, the Illinois Secretary of State Department of Inspector General was no different from the others.

As I observed the little day-to-day corruptions in the IG's office, I was suspicious of any new blood brought in under the patronage of the Ryan organization. My instincts told me that new blood was brought in to report to higher-ups the corruption the honest cops in the IG were uncovering, and thereby giving the higher-ups the opportunity to obstruct the investigation. First, they put a retired state trooper in as a contract computer expert. He had served on Ryan's bodyguard detail while Ryan was the lieutenant governor. His executive security experience did not give him the credentials to conduct public corruption investigations or the computer expertise for which he allegedly was contracted. When I got the opportunity to observe him working, I could see that he barely could figure out how to operate a fax machine. Once an agent completed a report and turned it in to Bauer or Jech, the report was given to this new contracted expert to fax it to Bickel. I think it took him two weeks to learn how to work the fax machine without other office staff assistance.

Next, they hired a private investigator and gave him the same credentials as an IG special agent. IG special agents were supposed to be sworn police officers, meaning they had to complete a minimum amount of training set forth by the Illinois Police Training Board. Private investigators were licensed by the Illinois Department of Professional Regulation, but did not have to obtain the same certification as sworn police officers. The contracted investigator should not have been issued the credentials of a special agent.

The private investigator was assigned to work with me on a case that involved an allegation on Carl Catuara, son of mobster Jimmy "the Bomber" Catuara. Catuara was a manager at a Chicago driver's license facility and was alleged to have unlawfully helped a man living in Lake Point Towers, a luxury downtown Chicago high-rise, obtain a driver's license. I don't recall the man's name or the reason he was not eligible for an Illinois license, but I remember we arrested him and he worked out a plea bargain. It seemed to me we should have worked him to snitch on Catuara, but it never went that far. I know I did not trust the private investigator the two or three days he worked with me on the case. Neither he nor the retired trooper was around very long and their contracts were not renewed.

Two new agents were hired for the Chicago office around the same time. They were Elwyn Tatro and Russ Sonneveld. Tatro first started appearing in Dean Bauer's private office. On the occasions Bauer called an agent into his office for a conference, Tatro would be sitting in there. Bauer never bothered to introduce him to any of the veteran special agents. I remember walking in and discussing cases with Bauer. As we talked, this swarthy-looking character would be giving me the once over, yet he never spoke. After several months of this, suddenly this silent observer was introduced to all of us as the newly hired special agent, Elwyn Tatro. Nothing was relayed to us about his background, but the rumor around the office was that he had worked for a short time as a Kankakee County Sheriff's deputy and later became a commercial truck driver. We believed he was receiving a pension for his years of over-the-road experience.

When it came to report writing, one of the most important skills of a professional criminal investigator, Tatro missed the mark by a country mile. I don't believe anyone in the office actually witnessed him writing an investigative report. Talk in the office was his wife wrote his reports for him.

A more serious concern was Tatro's integrity. It was eventually learned by federal prosecutors looking into the Secretary of State's Office that Elwyn Tatro was making money on the side from poker machines placed in Kankakee area bars while employed by the Secretary of State's Office. Generally, what comes to mind when one thinks of poker machines in bars is illegal gambling and organized crime. The machines are placed in licensed liquor establishments for the entertainment of the patrons. They are operated similar to home computer poker games. You play poker against the computer. Like your home computer, there is no payoff when you win. However, when you play in a bar, if the machine has been placed there for the actual gambling experience, there will be a payoff. To play, a person might insert a five-dollar bill into the machine, and the monitor will display one hundred points, or five cents each, in the lower left corner. The player then works buttons on a console to play hands of video poker. Points are awarded based on various combinations. The machines don't pay winnings directly, as many casino slot machines do. Instead, players receive tickets from a dispenser to verify the number of accumulated points. They take them to the bar or a bartender to verify the points. Points are then redeemed for cash. The customer playing the poker machine notifies the bartender or another employee of the business of his win and then the customer is paid in cash. Losses are collected by the bar and a percentage goes to the poker machine's owner; i.e., Elwyn Tatro or the Mob.

There are some cases where the bar owners do not want a poker machine in their establishment, but they are forced to keep one and pay collections based on Mob-style strong-arm tactics. Video poker is highly addictive, and the profits are enormous. Odds are unfavorable to the player, and taxes are not paid on the profits. According to federal court documents, Tatro had been placing the machines in bars around Illinois since 1980. Placing the machines in bars is not illegal in Illinois. Making the payoffs is. He was never charged with a crime related to the poker machines. He would, however, eventually be subject to questioning by federal authorities regarding his relationships with George Ryan and Dean Bauer.

The other new agent, Sonneveld, would turn out to be from the other side of the criminal justice spectrum. Bauer and Ryan would in due course regret bringing in an honest cop as part of the team.

CHAPTER 4

My New Partner, the Good Cop

Associate yourself with men of good quality if you esteem your own reputation, for 'tis better to be alone than in bad company.

—*George Washington*

Russ Sonneveld was hired by the Illinois Secretary of State Department of Inspector General in February 1993. He had a strong law enforcement background, bringing with him more than twenty-three years of experience. In 1970, Sonneveld started as a Forest Park, Illinois, police officer. He later joined the Chicago Police Department, where he worked both patrol and investigations. He left CPD to work for Elk Grove Village, Illinois, as both a patrol officer and a detective. Sonneveld eventually became an investigator with the Division of Internal Investigations in the Illinois State Police. There he was promoted to area commander. Eventually he took a leave of absence from ISP and took on the assignment of chief investigator for the medical section of the Illinois Department of Professional Regulation. Sonneveld worked in the medical section for seven and a half years. There he met Nancy Ryan, George Ryan's daughter, who would eventually help him get into the SOS IG department. After working with Professional Regulation, he had a brief stint with the Illinois Department of Public Aid before he left state government. Sonneveld tried a private enterprise for a year before he decided to return to his area of expertise, busting the bad guys.

In 1992, Sonneveld decided to contact his former acquaintance from Professional Regulation, Nancy Ryan. Sonneveld sought out George Ryan's daughter to assist him in obtaining a job under Ryan in the Secretary of State's Office. Sonneveld applied for the position of special agent in the SOS Department of Inspector General and was granted an interview. In the interview process, he was asked about his knowledge of government employee official misconduct and bribery. His knowledge and experience apparently got him the job. He was assigned to work in the Northern Illinois office located in Hillside. His job assignment was to root out corruption within the Office of the Secretary of State under the direction of Ryan's number-one corruption buster, Inspector General Dean Bauer. At least that is what Special Agent Russ Sonneveld believed.

Up to this point, I did not know Russ Sonneveld personally. I had only heard of him through professional channels. I had a slight distrust for cops that achieved positions of command in highly politicized environments. He had been through a roller-coaster ride of police command assignments. Now he was being brought in by the very obstructionists that wanted to halt the work of the investigators attempting to live by their oaths. Needless to say, I was more than apprehensive to work with the new kid on the block.

By my analysis, Sonneveld is a very private person. He took that privacy into official duties. In order to carry out the duties of an investigator, it is often wise to discuss only the aspects of your cases necessary to effectively resolve the issues. When Sonneveld first started working in the office, our conversations were limited to those necessary aspects and the typical office niceties. We eventually became partners and friends. I do not recall when I began to trust him. When asked, Sonneveld likewise did not specifically recall when that trust became mutual.

Cops like their coffee. They often will sit down and talk about events and people they have in common over a cup or two. To the best of both of our recollections, this was how we got to know each other better. The office building where the Department of Inspector General office was headquartered had a small cafeteria where we took our breaks. Russ Sonneveld, Pat Dowdle, and I would meet there for a morning break and exchange stories. "War stories" is a common expression cops use among each other when talking about incidents, arrests, or other job-related occurrences. They are often funny. They may express job-related cynicism. Sometimes they may be a form of braggadocio, expounding on an arrest or case that might have involved danger. In any event, the stories are a way cops can develop professional and personal bonds. If the bonds are strong enough, they can last a lifetime.

The bonds between Sonneveld, Dowdle, and me became strong. Dowdle was a veteran police officer dating back to the 1960s, serving as a deputy under Cook County Sheriff Joe Wood. Wood was a Republican. Dowdle was one of the few Chicago Republicans from the Bridgeport neighborhood. Because of this, he not only rubbed elbows with his boss, he was friendly with Republican Governor Richard Ogilvie and his wife. Dowdle even talked about his attending the 1968 Republican National Convention, getting past Secret Service agents and meeting Richard Nixon.

Sonneveld was raised in the Chicago South Side neighborhood called Roseland. His father was active in local politics and worked for state senator Ron Swanson. Little did we know that while we were doing all this bonding, the former state senator was conspiring with Ryan in money-making schemes that would rip off the Illinois taxpayers. When Sonneveld became a Chicago cop, he worked the Roseland neighborhood.

I too had roots in both the sheriff's office and Roseland. My uncle, Joe Lux Sr., had worked for the Cook County Sheriff's Office since the 1940s and retired in the 1970s. My Uncle Joe's and Pat Dowdle's paths crossed many times. I attended a Catholic high school in Roseland, Mendel Catholic Prep. The nearby area of 111th and Michigan—often referred to by the locals as "the Ave"—was a regular hangout for me in the late 1960s. My cousin, Joe Lux Jr., like Sonneveld, was also a Chicago policeman. My cousin was assigned to the Roseland area, and he and Sonneveld knew each other.

Sonneveld, Dowdle, and I also talked about organized crime guys like Billy Dauber, Albert Tocco, Richie Ferraro, and Timmy O'Brien. These were South Side mobsters who were into chopping cars and murder. We all worked cases that involved these now deceased thugs and often tested each other on our knowledge of who's who in the South Side Mob. Because of my years in the auto theft task force, I interacted with law enforcement officers from several other agencies, especially the Illinois State Police. It turned out that Russ Sonneveld and I mutually respected some of the same people from ISP. From these kaffeeklatsches, our trust and bonds grew and we started working as a team. Like Tatro, Sonneveld was politically appointed by Ryan. Unlike Tatro, Sonneveld was a good cop.

The first case Sonneveld and I worked together was a burglary at the Secretary of State facility located at 5301 West Lexington Avenue, on Chicago's West Side. This specific area of the city where the facility is located is known as "the Island" because the cities of Cicero and Oak Park are tangent on all four sides of the neighborhood. The West Side of Chicago is a high crime area with a full share of drive-by shootings, drug dealers, gangbangers, pimps, and prostitutes. With the notorious crime-ridden and Mob-controlled Cicero on the border, it was no surprise that this particular SOS facility had its own portion of the area's crime. On any given day, three thousand to six thousand people entered the West Side facility to do driver's license or vehicle registration business with the Secretary of State's Office. There was anywhere between $750,000 and $1 million in the building at any time.

We also felt, considering the high crime area, that there would be an attempt to do an armed robbery there. I often suggested to higher-ups that the facility cashiers receive the same training that bank tellers receive from the FBI. The SOS Police called the West Side facility "the war zone." We had two officers assigned to foot patrol there during its business hours. Most of the SOS Police District 1 arrests came from that assignment. When it was closed, the facility was equipped with both a burglar alarm system and a security guard. Despite that, a burglary was reported by a driver's license examiner supervisor shortly after opening on a weekday morning.

No alarms were activated, and there were no reports made by the security guard. It was immediately suspected that it was an inside job; therefore, the inspector general was assigned the investigation. Originally, Dowdle and I were sent over to the West Side facility to begin the investigation. My initial instinct was to suspect a facility maintenance manager because of his alleged ties to the Cicero Mob. Shortly after beginning the investigation, I was proved wrong. The burglary occurred from a locked room located in the driver's license camera area.

Once a driver's license applicant completed the application process, paid the fees, and was tested, he was sent to this area, where his photograph was taken and his driver's license was issued. The cameras being used were large Polaroids mounted on suitcases. Before the applicant's photo was taken, a computer card printout was generated with the applicant's identifiers (name, birth date, and address) on it. That card was placed into a clear plastic security plate that contained the driver's license security features as well as the Office of the Secretary of State's logo and George Ryan's name. The applicant's photograph was taken once the security plate was placed inside the camera. The photograph was then removed from the camera and sealed in the lamination containing the hologram. As a result of the multitude of thefts of plastic laminations, they were kept in a locked roomed next to the camera area and inventoried on a daily basis.

The employee that initially reported the incident worked in the driver's license camera area as a supervisor. Upon arriving at work in the morning, he saw what at first looked like several pieces of crumbled and broken Styrofoam on the floor around the cameras. Looking up, he saw several ceiling tiles ajar. His suspicions were that the locked room had been accessed by going through the ceiling, over the wall, and into the room. No inventory was taken until Agent Dowdle and I arrived. We entered the room where there were four unlocked metal cabinets about five feet tall and four feet wide. Inside the cabinets were shelves stacked with boxes of the laminations. Each box contained one thousand laminations. There were now six missing boxes, for a total of six thousand stolen laminations. They were valued on the street at as much as one hundred dollars for each lamination, which meant the street value of the stolen items was six hundred thousand dollars. The actual manufactured value was only about two cents each, or one hundred and twenty dollars. Looking further around the room, I found a footprint on top of one of the cabinets, confirming that the thieves came in from the ceiling.

Since the supervisor would have observed any attempt to access the room during business hours, the burglary had to have occurred while the facility was closed. We had the facility manager call the two nighttime security guards and they came in for questioning. One of the two guards was a nineteen-year-old from Elmwood Park. He had recently been discharged from the Marine Corps for medical reasons after serving only six months. This was his first job since being discharged. He was also attending classes at Triton College in River Grove. Dowdle and I began questioning him in the supervisor's office. During the questioning, I asked him if he had a fake license to buy beer and get into bars. This was a routine question in cases involving fake licenses and underage drinking. Besides, the theft of the laminations was more than likely intended for the eventual purpose of manufacturing fake licenses for underage drinkers.

The teenage security guard said he didn't have one. I then asked him if any of his friends had one. He replied that the friend that had just driven him to the facility had recently been busted by the Melrose Park Police for possessing a fake license. We called the guard's buddy into the office and began questioning him. He confirmed that he had been arrested by the police for possessing the fraudulent license. With further questioning, he admitted that he bought the fake from a guy named George, a fellow student at Triton College. He went on to describe the seller as a husky Italian guy. The kid described the same guy we had busted in 1992 for making counterfeit licenses in the garage on the Northwest Side and selling them to the South Side Gangster Disciples. What the kid didn't realize was that he had made himself and the security guard suspects in the burglary of six thousand driver's license laminations. We finished questioning the two and let them go. We did not have enough evidence to arrest them then, but now we knew where and what to look for.

The room that was burglarized was secured and treated like a crime scene. Pat Dowdle and I left so Dowdle could begin writing reports on what we had thus far. I later returned with Sonneveld. He and I contacted the Chicago Police and requested that a crime scene technician (CST) be sent to the Chicago West Secretary of State facility. The CST could check the crime scene for fingerprints, shoe prints, or any other latent evidence left behind by the burglars.

Chicago crime scene technicians are sworn police officers that receive additional training in recovery of both overt and hidden evidence. They are assigned to the CPD Area Divisions. The officer sent to work with us was from CPD Area 5, in which the SOS Chicago West facility is located. Shortly before his arrival, a building engineer gave us some additional clues to the crime. A ceiling tile on the other side of the Driver Services Department appeared to be damaged. There was no explanation of why that tile was damaged. The broken tile was in the middle of a large room with a roped-off area for lines of people to wait. The lines led to a service counter where driver's license and identification card applicants initiated the application process with a public service clerk. The engineer had an industrial ladder on wheels used to access light bulbs and wiring. The ladder could extend all the way to the ceiling tiles and even touch them. The engineer kept the ladder stored on the east side of the building and only removed it from storage when he needed it. He stated that he never moved the ladder in a manner that would have damaged the ceiling tile.

What the engineer believed was that the ladder was moved to the west side of the building to use as a means to access the room where the laminations were stored via the ceiling. Furthermore, he believed that while the thieves moved the ladder, either to or from storage, they broke the ceiling tile with the top of the ladder as they passed that area of the facility.

The engineer's theory gave more credence to the fact that it was an inside job. As I mentioned before, the facility was guarded by a night watchman when it was closed. Moving a ladder from the distance the engineer suggested meant the ladder would have passed through three wings of the building and traveled a total distance of about two hundred and fifty feet. There was no way a night watchman would miss that, since his primary station was smack in the middle of this path.

Upon the arrival of the CPD crime scene technician, we explained to him the circumstances of the burglary we knew up to this point. He first checked the ladder for fingerprints and found none. Then he followed the theoretical path of the ladder to the locked room for the laminations. He began to search the room for latent fingerprints and other possible signs of hidden evidence. After about twenty minutes, he told us that the room had been wiped clean of prints. We pointed to the disturbed ceiling tile in the lamination room. The ceiling was about eighteen feet high. The technician said, "How do you expect me to get up there?" We told him he could use the engineer's ladder. He coarsely responded, "I ain't goin' up there," and abruptly left.

Sonneveld then told me he was a trained crime scene technician and he could examine the ceiling area. Our only drawback was that the SOS IG department had no crime scene kit. The kits are equipped with brushes and different types and colors of powders to dust surfaces for suspected prints. Who would ever think that George Ryan investigators would ever have a need for such a sophisticated piece of law enforcement technology? We went into the manager's office to ask him for assistance. We knew he was on a local suburban fire and police commission and hoped he might have some influence on that suburb's chief to lend us their kit. In my time with the Secretary of State Police, we were always mooching equipment from other PDs.

With the facility manager's help, we were lent the suburban police department's kit. With it, Sonneveld climbed the engineer's ladder to the ceiling of the burglarized room. Crime scene technicians must have the patience and concentration of a surgeon, looking for the tiny lesions otherwise missed by the untrained eye. With only a flashlight to illuminate the path of the burglars, Sonneveld painstakingly searched the ceiling tiles and tile supports for loops and whorls of fingerprints left behind.

After about ten minutes, he shouted down to me, "I think I got something!"

My heart began to race. It always did when I knew I had evidence that would prove a case beyond a reasonable doubt. Fingerprints could do that. I shouted up at him, "You got something?"

Russ said, "Yeah, I think so. Give me a minute." I could see through the opening in the tiles that Russ made to get up above the ceiling that he was wearing latex gloves and was dusting powder with an evidence kit brush across one of the metal supports. The support appeared to have a slight kink, which later proved to be significant as the investigation progressed. Russ shouted back down, "I got a hit!" He came down the ladder holding the tile support with his latex-gloved hand. He showed it to me. "I got one print on the inside crease of this.

See it." He held the support in front of me and carefully pointed to the dusted fingerprint without touching it.

I was impressed. I had worked with crime scene technicians before. Usually they were Illinois State Police guys that I called to help me make a case of possession of a stolen vehicle after recovering a stolen car. At least half the time there were no identifiable fingerprints inside or on the car. Never did I have a partner who located an incriminating print.

We still had to see if it matched a suspect, but this was a big step in making this case.

Sonneveld's diligence strengthened the bonds we were developing, and my respect for him as a cop was growing. Normally the crime scene tech takes a lift of the dusted print using a special clear fingerprint tape, placing the lift on an evidence card that allows one to clearly see the latent print in the crime lab and courtroom. You can't remove walls and drag them into the trial, but the tech can testify to his observations and bring the latent print with him. This time, because the tile support was a narrow twenty-four-inch piece of metal, Russ did not need to take a latent print.

Together we took the ceiling support to the nearby Broadview ISP crime lab. It was Russ's discovery, but I had a need to be close to the evidence and participate in the process. After all, the excitement of making a case was one of the reasons why I loved being a cop.

Logging the evidence into the crime lab required filling out a report, including our case number and evidence exhibit number. The ISP lab technician then assigned the lab's own report and exhibit number. The crime lab technician took custody of the bar. There, the fingerprint would be examined to see if it matched that of any criminal in a nationwide database. To speed up the process, we furnished the names and birth dates of the suspects we believed might have been involved. We gave the technician the night watchman's name, the name of his friend who had driven him to the interview, and a third subject's name. The third subject was the codefendant with the driver in a prior arrest. We obtained his name from checking the driver's arrest record and cross-referencing the list of arrest reports to see who the driver's criminal associates were. We also gave him the name George Dzierzynski. I believed Dzierzynski was the guy who the security guard's driver described to Dowdle and me as the person who sold the driver the fake ID for which he had been arrested. The ISP technician told us it would take several weeks to get the final report of the lab's examination.

Sonneveld and I were done for the day and went our separate ways. On the way home, I received a telephone call from Secretary of State Police Deputy Chief Jerry LaGrow. I always felt LaGrow was strange. It was difficult to communicate with him. He was a former Chicago Police drug investigator that had made his way into the Secretary of State Police through its former chief, Dave Watkins. Jim Edgar hired

LaGrow after he led the Peoria area drug task force. Most of the people in the Secretary of State Police whom I considered allies did not like Jerry LaGrow. He supported me and was somewhat responsible for my promotion to sergeant. He liked that I was an aggressive and persistent investigator. However, he did not like subordinates to challenge him, and I had a reputation for challenging my bosses. His talking style was short and direct. In person, when he spoke, he usually looked right into the listener's eyes, as if asserting a canine-like dominance over the listener.

Fortunately, I did not have to deal with the dog show over the telephone. LaGrow said he had heard from Dean Bauer that I was working a case involving the burglary of six thousand driver's license laminations. He asked if I had any suspects. I told him about the night watchman, his friend, and the codefendant buddy. I also told him that I believed there was a connection to a punk we previously arrested, George Dzierzynski. Offering no explanation, he said Dean Bauer had authorized him to order me to work with Lt. Mike Juliano on a case that might be related. Juliano was a Secretary of State Police District 2 investigations lieutenant. District 2 covered all of northern Illinois, with the exception of Cook and Lake counties. I had not worked with Juliano much, but my old police academy partner, Larry Ciposwski, had. Word was, Juliano was a pretty decent guy to work for.

LaGrow then asked me, "Who is this trooper guy?"

I answered, "Russ Sonneveld."

LaGrow barked, "You trust him?"

"Well," I said, "he has a lot of experience. He was with Chicago Police before he joined ISP."

LaGrow now growled, "You trust him?"

I said, "Yeah."

"Look," LaGrow snarled, "I trust you, and I'll take your word if you think he is a good cop, but I don't know him. He's from ISP. So be careful what you say around him. Call Juliano. Keep me advised." LaGrow then ended our phone call.

I was both confused and angered by the conversation. I wondered if LaGrow was trying to play me. Did he not trust Sonneveld because he might go mouth off to the ISP on how incompetent the SOSPD was? Was LaGrow now part of the Ryan culture of corruption and thought I was too? Was he afraid Sonneveld might rat on us? Was LaGrow just playing super-secret spy? Some cops liked to do that, and actually believed they should not share information with other police. Or could this just have been LaGrow's way of displaying his authority? Regardless, Sonneveld was now a partner. Partners not only share all the information on cases, they often share personal information. It was officially a bond of trust.

I called Juliano. He asked, "Eddie, do you know this guy, George Dzierzynski?"

I told the lieutenant that Steve Streder and I had busted Dzierzynski in 1991 for counterfeiting Illinois driver's licenses for the

Gangster Disciples in a garage on the Northwest Side of Chicago. I also told Juliano that Sergeant Joe Gabuzzi later busted Dzierzynski in a motel room in Rosemont with an official driver's license camera taken in an armed robbery from the Niles, Illinois, driver's license facility. The robbery was believed to have been committed by members of the Latin Kings. I also believed that George Dzierzynski was a fugitive, jumping Cook County bond on both cases.

Lieutenant Juliano told me that his team had a confidential source into George Dzierzynski. They had information that he was living in Tampa, Florida, under an alias, and that he would be flying up to Chicago Midway Airport in two days. From there, Dzierzynski would meet Juliano's informant in an apartment in Lisle that the lieutenant's team had obtained for the purpose of conducting a sting on Dzierzynski. Investigator Kirk Hooks was working in an undercover capacity with the informant. The plan was that Dzierynski was going to make and sell several counterfeit driver's licenses at the Lisle apartment. Hooks would pose as one of the many customers. According to the informant, Dzierzynski had a supplier of several thousand driver's license laminations.

I was pumped. First the night watchman's friend had described Dzierzynski as the source of his counterfeit license. Then Russ got a fingerprint from the scene of a burglary of six thousand driver's license laminations. Now Juliano had a snitch into Dzierzynski, and the snitch was setting up a sting for us that potentially might net us several thousand stolen laminations as well as several arrests. All this and the information developed from this arrest had the potential to resolve our burglary.

The next day, Sonneveld and I met with Juliano and his team at the Lisle Police Department. Several Lisle officers were also participating in the operation. The purpose of meeting was to be briefed on the operation. Dzierzynski was supposed to fly in that evening and begin the counterfeiting the next day. Even though the customers for the fake licenses were supposed to be suburban college kids, there was a potential for violence. Dzierzynski had contracted the Latin Kings to commit the armed robbery at the Niles driver's license facility and they had used a gun on the manager to steal the camera. When Dzierzynski was busted in Rosemont, he did not resist, but he was packing a pistol. He was also known to use both heroin and cocaine. Whenever drugs are around, there is an increased chance that the suspect will violently resist.

We all shared what we knew about the case. The plan was to get Investigator Hooks inside the apartment when the most customers were there. Hooks would signal us by telephone when he believed the time was right and we would hit the place. We would treat it like a drug raid, coming into the apartment from all sides, using windows as well as doors. The element of surprise would catch all suspects off guard and minimize the potential for resistance. Russ and I were part of the team assigned to go through the back window.

After the briefing, Lieutenant Juliano and Special Agent Son-neveld seemed to develop a comradeship. They joked and laughed as cops often do when they're filling in the time between the action. After LaGrow's conversation with me, I was glad to see Sonneveld interacting with other officers in the Secretary of State Police. Although Sonneveld was a sworn officer with the Department of Inspector General, he was not considered a Secretary of State Police officer by both the official bureaucracy of the Secretary of State's Office and by the subculture of the Secretary of State Police officers. He was viewed as an outsider, and therefore, by some strange unwritten code, he would be snubbed by some. Mike Juliano was too friendly of a person to do that to a fellow cop. Juliano and Sonneveld hit it off and I was glad.

That evening, we participated in a surveillance of Dzierzynski, following him from Midway Airport to a home in Forest Park. We backed off the surveillance at that point because it appeared Dzierzynski was going to crash there for the night. The informant would keep Investigator Hooks advised of any changes.

The next day, Dzierzynski and the informant set up in the Lisle apartment. Hooks would get a call from the informant when it was time for Hooks to go there. Based on information from the confidential source (C/S) all of Dzierzynski's fake driver's license customers were expected to be underage drinkers, less than twenty-one years old and wanting fake licenses in order to purchase alcohol. Investigator Hooks was in his twenties and could easily pass as a nineteen-year-old college kid. When the apartment was full of customers, Hooks was to go in to purchase a fake license. Once his transaction began, he would call Lieutenant Juliano on his beeper. Standing by in a nearby apartment were Lisle police officers, a DuPage County assistant state's attorney, Lieutenant Juliano, Russ Sonneveld, and me.

Hooks went into the apartment. We were now anxious and ready to take down George Dzierzynski. Just one phone call away. To the best of my recollection, it was about a two-hour wait before Lieutenant Juliano's beeper received the signal from Investigator Hooks. Later we learned that the two-hour delay was due to the fact that Dzierzynski had so many customers.

The Lisle officers went through the front door, first knocking and announcing vociferously with a simple, "Police!" Once we heard that, Sonneveld, Juliano, a couple of Lisle officers, and I went in through the apartment's rear windows. Russ was the first to go in. Like all good cops on these types of raids, he was pumped full of adrenalin, not afraid of the potential consequences on the other side, only interested in securing the scene and apprehending the bad guy. The first one in is always envied by the other good cops.

The window had broken glass with sharp edges and Russ cut his arm as he went through. Despite this, he continued with his job of securing the scene. All the subjects inside were arrested and handcuffed.

The informant was right. All the customers were under twenty-one years of age, intending to purchase fake IDs enabling them to illegally buy alcohol.

One note should be made here. Even though they were under twenty-one, according to Illinois criminal statute, if they are seventeen years old or older, they are adults. When arrested, they are treated as adults. They may be charged with criminal violations that can result in a prison sentence. Possession of a fraudulent driver's license or a driver's license-making implement was a felony and, if convicted, could result in a prison sentence.

As I mentioned earlier, because of the potential for violence, this operation was treated like a drug raid. Dzierzynski, our main target, had gang affiliations. For officer safety reasons, we had to be cautious. Officers' weapons were drawn as we entered the premises. Occupants were ordered to lie facedown on the floor. Each occupant was handcuffed and read his or her rights. Included in the group of customers were the son of a suburban chief of police and the daughter of an FBI agent. Two of the female customers wet their pants. These were good kids who were learning a lesson in the law. Each of Dzierzynski's customers was taken back to the Lisle Police Department, charged, and booked for a misdemeanor violation. Once their fingerprints showed they were clear of any outstanding warrants, they were released on their own recognizance.

Dierzynski was charged on a series of felony violations related to the manufacture, sale, and possession of fraudulent driver's licenses. About two thousand driver's license laminations were recovered in the apartment. They were the laminations taken in the burglary from the Chicago West facility. Dzierzynski would also be charged with a felony for each lamination. Even if he could post bond on these violations, he was also facing two outstanding warrants on the felonies from the two prior arrests by the Secretary of State Police. It was time to put the squeeze on him.

While Dezierzynski was in custody, Sonneveld and I began an interrogation on him. Dzeirzynski was flamboyant and a braggart. Getting information from him was like taking candy from a baby. The main thing we wanted from him was his connection to the Chicago West facility burglary. Dzierzynski had met both the night watchman and his friend the driver at Triton College in Maywood. He knew it would be a great opportunity for him to employ the services of the lone, after-hours security guard at a Secretary of State driver's license facility. With stolen laminations, Dzierzynski could manufacture near-perfect counterfeit driver's licenses. The night watchman could deactivate the alarm and allow his cohorts to gain entry to the building. Once inside, they had to find a way into the room where the laminations were kept because the guard did not have access. Thus, the ladder was used to climb into the ceiling and go over the wall.

Dzierzynski was not present for the burglary, but he did develop the scheme. He identified three cohorts: the night watchman, his driver buddy, and a third suspect. The third subject was the suspect whose fingerprints were eventually matched by the State Police crime lab with the print found on the ceiling support.

Dierzynski agreed to cooperate. He not only admitted to planning the burglary, but he was going to help recover the rest of the laminations. He agreed to make a telephone call to the night watchman and arranged to have one or all of the three other suspects deliver the remainder of the stolen laminations to us in DuPage County. This was advantageous to us for prosecutorial reasons. Possession of the stolen laminations is a felony and therefore an assistant state's attorney needed to approve the charges.

For a nonviolent crime, this was very difficult in Cook County. The assistants assigned to the Cook County State's Attorney felony review unit were green and did not understand the criminal statutes beyond your basic murder, rape, robbery, theft, and battery. Cook County courts are overrun with violent criminals. Part of the attorneys' job seems to be to keep as many nonviolent cases out of the system as possible. DuPage County was much different then. The state's attorney and judges were usually conservative, with pro-law-and-order agendas. Nonviolent offenses like the driver's license counterfeiting and possession of driver's license laminations in DuPage County meant felony approval and jail time. Delivery of the contraband to us in DuPage County would result in a smooth arrest and booking.

First Dierzynski called the night watchman. He was vacationing in California and could not make the delivery. Dzierzynski asked him to call one of the other two suspects and have one of them call Dzierzynski. He told the guard he needed the other laminations that night. The night watchman's driver friend called Dzierzynski back and arranged to meet him about an hour later in the parking lot of a nearby fast-food restaurant. One of the younger-looking Lisle officers posed as Dzierzynski's partner.

Dzierzynski and the undercover Lisle officer, supported by a surveillance team that included Russ and me, went to the restaurant. Dzierzynski and the officer placed themselves in a vehicle in the parking lot so that the surveillance could see them from all four sides. About ten minutes after we set up, the two suspects arrived in their vehicle and parked next to Dzierzynski and the officer. As soon as we saw the suspects hand over a package to Dzierzynski, we swept in to bust them. Now we had proof beyond any doubt that the driver friend and the third suspect were co-conspirators in the burglary of six thousand driver's license laminations from the Chicago West Secretary of State facility. We had them in custody in DuPage County, and we could add Cook County burglary charges at a later date. The package handed to Dzierzynski was short about 1,100 laminations. We needed to get statements from the two newly arrested suspects and information on where the rest of the stolen items were.

Both the driver friend and third subject were read their rights back at the Lisle police station. Both invoked the Fifth Amendment and refused to answer any questions. Many defense attorneys will tell their clients that that is a wise thing to do.

As a police officer, I suggest otherwise, unless one is facing the death penalty. If an arrested subject conscientiously knows he is guilty and cooperates early in the booking process, his good intentions will lessen the punishment. Of course, the unwritten rule among criminals is not to rat on your buddies. Be a stand-up guy. These two idiots were stand-up guys. Both were booked and processed into the DuPage County Jail that evening.

Russ and I went to visit them the next day to see if they were willing to cooperate with us regarding the burglary. The driver friend, the smaller of the two, had had a rough night. He had bruises on his face he did not have when he was processed into the jail. He was a nineteen-year-old that got a cruel lesson in the American criminal justice system, but he was a stand-up guy.

There was a little more work to do on the investigation of the burglary and some report writing. We still had to arrest the night watchman when he returned from his California vacation. According to the earlier telephone conversation Dzierzynski had with the night watchman, he was not returning to Illinois for about another week. Two days prior to his return, Sonneveld and I visited the watchman's mother at their home. She had no idea that her son was a suspect in the burglary. She assured us that he would turn himself in upon his return. We were confident from our conversation with her that her son would not skip out on us.

When he returned home, he did indeed call us. We met him at his home, where we took him into custody and charged him with burglary. Unlike his two accomplices, he gave us a complete statement on the burglary plan and how it was carried out. After he met Dzierzynski, the watchman told us Dzierzynski came up with the idea of stealing the laminations. On the day of the burglary, the night watchman disabled the building's alarm, opened the Chicago West facility's front door, and allowed his two accomplices to enter the building. Once they entered, the alarm was reactivated, making the total time it was off about three minutes. They took the building engineer's ladder stored in a closet on the east side of the building and moved it the entire length of the building to the room where the laminations were stored. The ladder had wheels and was easy to move, but it was tall and barely passed through building areas where the ceiling dipped just under ten feet.

About two-thirds of the way into the Driver Services Department application counter area, the top of the ladder struck a ceiling tile, scratching and displacing it. They continued to roll the ladder to the camera area, which was just outside the lamination storage room. At that point, one of the crew climbed the ladder up to the ceiling, removed a ceiling tile, and climbed up and over the storage room wall. Once on the other side of the wall, he accidentally bent and knocked down a tile support and a tile. Next, he climbed down into the storage room by placing his foot on the top of a metal cabinet and carefully balancing himself. From there he had a five-foot jump to the floor.

After his unauthorized entry was complete, he unlocked the door, allowing his cohorts to enter the room. The three of them looked through the unlocked cabinets for the bounty: driver's license laminates. Finding them in boxes of one thousand per box, they emptied six boxes into a plastic bag and placed the empty boxes back into the locker. They then wiped the walls and cabinets with a rag to remove their fingerprints. Before they all left the room through the unlocked door, they realized they still had to deal with the fallen ceiling tile and its support. They wheeled the ladder into the room, and one of them picked up the bent support and secured it back into place. None of them ever thought about wiping fingerprints from the shiny piece of metal; thus, a print was left behind, putting them not only at the crime scene, but at the scene's point of entry. They replaced the fallen tile and left the room, locking the door behind them. They then returned the engineer's ladder to the closet where it was found, wiping it clean of fingerprints before leaving. The night watchman again disabled the building's alarm, allowed the other burglars to leave, and reactivated the alarm.

Our suspect's story was complete, and the pieces of the puzzle fit. Each suspect pleaded guilty to burglary in front Cook County Circuit Court Judge Bill Prendergast and received a sentence of twenty-four months probation. The best part of the case was that Russ Sonneveld and I developed a partnership working with each other every step of the case. We now trusted each other. The fact that he was appointed to his position in the Department of Inspector General through a personal connection to the George Ryan camp was negated. I wholly respected Special Agent Russ Sonneveld as a police investigator and a man. The new guy brought in under Ryan was a partner I could trust. Ironically, that trust would become a valuable asset in uncovering the Ryan corruption.

CHAPTER 5
The Stinky Pile

Mine honour is my life; both grow in one; Take honour from me, and my life is done.
— *William Shakespeare, King Richard II*

In November 1993, an Oak Lawn patrol officer arrested a drunk driver who possessed a fictitious driver's license. The arrested subject, John Traynor, was charged with driving while intoxicated, driving while revoked, possession of a fictitious driver's license, and various traffic offenses. Traynor, whose license was revoked as a result of a prior driving while intoxicated conviction, faced prison time if convicted. Traynor was also a professional truck driver. A driver's license was the most important tool he had to earn a living. A current revocation of his driver's license meant he could not earn that living, so he sought an easy way out of that dilemma. He obtained a fictitious license to drive in the name of John Trainer. So a man convicted of DUI and using a fake identity could get behind the wheel of an eighty-thousand-pound vehicle and endanger all the other motorists driving the same roads.

One could argue that because he was convicted only once for a DUI does not mean he would get drunk and get behind the wheel of his rig, but statistics of convicted drunk drivers will tell you otherwise. The majority of individuals convicted of driving while intoxicated offenses are generally afflicted with alcoholism or some other substance abuse disease that they bring with them to their work environment. Obtaining a fictitious license is a felony that snowballs into a series of crimes involving corroborators and victims. Traynor knew he was in deep, and his only way out was to cooperate with the authorities.

The arresting Oak Lawn officer contacted the Secretary of State Police, and Investigator Keith Lake was assigned. Lake was an honest cop and tenacious. Investigations, especially those that by their very nature are complex and difficult to complete to fruition, require a tenacious cop to work. Unfortunately for George Ryan and Dean Bauer, the SOS Police assigned the tenacious cop to the Traynor case.

Upon arriving at the Oak Lawn police station, Lake was given a private interview room in order to obtain a statement from Traynor. After reading Traynor his rights, Lake obtained a voluntary statement from Traynor. He admitted that his license was revoked. Often a person will be arrested for driving with a revoked or suspended license, and his defense will be that he did not know it was revoked or suspended. Traynor's admission to that was the first hurdle crossed. Traynor went on to say that he was an owner/operator, and he rented a parking space to keep his tractor stored. He identified the person from whom he rented the space as Tony Luna, who was a male white Hispanic and thirty-five to forty years old. The rental space was located at Expressway Transportation Repair and Park near Thirty-fifth and Iron streets in Chicago.

During questioning with Lake, Traynor said he was helped in getting the fictitious license by Luna. Luna told Traynor that with a passport photo and five hundred dollars cash he could secure a fictitious Social Security card and an Immigration Resident Alien card in any name he wanted. Traynor brought Luna the passport photo with five hundred dollars and told him he wanted the name John Trainer. Two days later, Luna gave Traynor the fictitious Social Security and Alien Registration cards.

Luna now instructed Traynor to contact a Gonzales Mendoza, another white Hispanic male, forty to fifty years old, who had a connection inside the Secretary of State Commercial Driver's License testing facility in McCook, Illinois. That person on the inside would help Traynor pass the commercial driver's license written and road test. For this, Traynor was to pay Mendoza four hundred dollars. On May 27, 1993, Mendoza took Traynor with his fake identification documents to the McCook facility. There Traynor was introduced to a female manager who administered the written test to Traynor. After Traynor completed the test, the female manager corrected the mistakes with the same pen that Traynor had used. She corrected his wrong answers and gave him a passing grade.

Traynor never saw Mendoza give the female four hundred dollars, but he believed she was getting part of it for this service. From there, Traynor took the road test without any difficulty. After completing the application process and passing both tests, John Traynor was issued a new commercial driver's license. Now, however, he was no longer John Traynor, DUI convict with a revoked driver's license. He was John Trainer, with a license to drive an eighty-thousand-pound weapon of destruction.

When asked if he could arrange for an undercover investigator to meet with Luna or Mendoza, he emphatically said no. Traynor told Investigator Lake that Luna was very cautious and categorically told Traynor it was a one-time deal. If Traynor was to survive the recoil of his series of criminal offenses, he would have to do better than this.

Upon completing his case report, Investigator Lake consulted with his supervisor in the SOS Police, Sgt. Dennis Serafini. They agreed the case should be reassigned to the Department of Inspector General due to the statement made by Traynor implicating the female manager at the McCook commercial driver's license facility.

On December 14, 1993, Serafini prepared a memo to Chief Deputy Director Jerry LaGrow requesting that the case be reassigned to the Department of Inspector General. Two weeks later, Department of Inspector General Chief Deputy Director Joe Jech opened a case based on the information sent from the SOS Police. The case was assigned to Special Agent Sonneveld. Protocol was followed. An investigator worked a case and, based on information obtained in that process, requested his immediate supervisor to forward the case to a more appropriate department. Following procedure, the supervisor sent the request up the chain of command, where the paperwork sat for ten to fourteen days. Eventually, through the Secretary of State Office's internal mail network, the appropriate department received the paperwork and the case was assigned to an internal investigator.

Forty-five days had passed since Investigator Lake interviewed John Traynor. Traynor was facing felonies with a great potential for doing serious time in a state prison. The pressure he was feeling at the time of his arrest was maximized. He was a perfect candidate to be a confidential source. Investigators who successfully work confidential sources know that the best time to get cooperation is immediately when the pressure is maximized, and the arrested subject is talking. If time goes by, the pressure drops. Things happen. They talk to associates. They get lawyers. Connections are made. Cases are fixed. Informants go cold.

I once had a confidential source that had information on a SOSPD lieutenant. According to the source, the lieutenant allegedly got high on cocaine and then sexually assaulted women in a tavern near his home. I wrote a report along with a case strategy on how we could nab the lieutenant and sent it up the chain of command. The plan involved getting attractive females from the state drug task force to work the tavern while the lieutenant was there partying. The confidential source would help and introduce the undercover females to the lieutenant. They would get close to him and suggest they would get high with him. Hopefully he would do the gentlemanly thing and supply the cocaine for all of them. We figured his sexual curiosity would be stimulated by the attractive undercover cops and he would make the offer. Once he showed the undercover officers the coke, we would make the bust. The undercover officers would send us an electronic signal on a device that looked like a beeper, signaling the officers on surveillance to move in and bust the lieutenant for possession of cocaine.

Chief Deputy Jerry LaGrow sat on the report and suggested plan for more than two weeks before he gave me the green light to go ahead and proceed with my strategy. It required making arrangements with other police agencies for the undercover officers supported by surveillance and backup officers. It also required the cooperation of the confidential source. Too much time had passed and the source went cold. We attempted to work the undercover contact without the confidential source and the lieutenant would not take the bait. I tell you this story because sometimes I wondered if certain people at the top of my chain of command intentionally delayed certain decisions on sensitive cases to protect those that would be affected by the arrest and subsequent negative publicity. Either they knew that snitches had to be worked immediately and intentionally let the snitch go cold, or they didn't remember how to work the street after being behind a desk for so long.

Now LaGrow had let another confidential source, Traynor, go cold. This time, there was also a delay by IG Deputy Director Jech before assigning the case. It appeared that the delays might have been intentional. Shortly after having the case assigned to him, Special Agent Sonneveld attempted to interview Traynor, who no longer wanted to cooperate. He had retained a prominent Chicago criminal attorney, Michael Ettinger. There were a couple of ironies to Traynor's lawyering up. The first was that Ettinger had a reputation for representing Chicago outfit guys. Common knowledge among students of organized crime is that you can often identify outfit guys by the fact they retain the same group of attorneys. Second was that Ettinger later represented former State Representative and lobbyist Roger "the Hog" Stanley in his George Ryan Operation Safe Road federal case. This irony shows the similarity of George Ryan's organization to organized crime, right up to the attorneys who were hired.

The case was not immediately closed for the lack of Traynor's cooperation. Sonneveld figured that more information could be developed from the leads made from Traynor's statement. Also, Traynor could always have a change of heart as his trial date approached. In the meantime, an anonymous male caller to the Department of Inspector General office in March 1994 stated that a manager at the McCook commercial driver's license facility by the name of Marion Seibel was selling commercial driver's licenses for bribes. CDL customers were being brought to the McCook facility by Gonzalo Mendoza, an employee of Nighthawk Trucking, located at 3551 S. Iron in Chicago.

Then, in April 1994, an anonymous female caller, described as irate by the investigator taking the call, stated that CDLs were being sold at McCook for seven hundred dollars. She said her husband had gotten one from a woman named Marion and a man named Velasco. The pieces of the puzzle were coming together. Marion Seibel and George Velasco were managers at the McCook commercial driver's license facility.

Two additional cases were developed regarding Seibel and the accepting of bribes for CDLs. Those cases were fervently pursued by Special Agent Sonneveld and me over the course of several months while Traynor's case remained on the back burner. Then, in October 1994, Sonneveld and I attempted to interview Traynor again, hoping he would have a change of heart. The stress was too much for him and had affected his health. He was living in a duplex in Hometown, Illinois. When he answered the door, he looked pale and sickly. He told us he did not want to answer our questions about his bribery and false application for a CDL. Traynor proceeded to show us plastic tubes connected to his right shoulder. He was being treated for leukemia, and the prognosis was bad. Sonneveld and I agreed not to involve John Traynor in our pursuit of Marion Seibel. Other leads were discovered. We would work those leads and make our case on Seibel without pressuring a dying man.

Before our final interview with Traynor, a case involving Ryan's neighbor and underage lingerie models came to our attention. Sometime in March 1994, a Kane County Sheriff's Office police officer arrested a young woman who produced a fictitious Illinois driver's license during the booking process. That driver's license was issued to the woman at the Office of the Secretary of State's Driver Services Department facility in Joliet. According to Illinois statutes, a driver's license is fictitious when it issued by the Office of the Secretary of State or another state's official driver's license bureau and the applicant has furnished fictitious or false information on the license application. The driver's license application requires the applicant to sign an oath stating that the information on the application is true. Signing an application after furnishing fictitious information is essentially lying under oath, or a form of perjury. Fictitious information could be a false name, address, Social Security number, or date of birth. This young woman's information on the fictitious driver's license was all that. The intent of the Illinois legislature when passing this law was to prevent identity theft, stop convicted drunk drivers from obtaining a license with an alias, keep drug dealers from laundering money with an alias, and thwart underage drinkers from using fake identification to purchase alcohol. This young woman was under twenty-one and needed the fictitious license to get into bars. She was a lingerie model. To perform her trade, she needed to get inside sleazy gin mills.

There are two possible ways to obtain a fictitious driver's license. The first way would be to submit counterfeit identification documents when applying for a driver's license. The Illinois Secretary of State requires driver's license applicants to submit three forms of identification to prove one's identity, address, birth date, Social Security number, and signature. Any combination of three routine documents—such as an official birth certificate, Social Security card, bank account records, utility records, passport, military identification, public aid card, or alien registration—usually will suffice when applying for a driver's license. Counterfeit versions of all the aforementioned documents are also available through various underground sources.

In certain neighborhoods in Chicago with large immigrant populations, street vendors sell fake Social Security cards manufactured in Mexico and smuggled into the United States like illegal drugs. Some are simply sent through the U.S. mail or private shippers like UPS. Birth certificates are often sold the same way. Sometimes employees at county and state vital statistics bureaus illegally print and sell blank certificates to the fake document vendors. Spies and terrorists were using false identification documents long before the Revolutionary War. Organized crime has been in the false identification trade since before Al Capone became synonymous with Chicago. An establishment with strippers and lingerie models often has an affiliation to organized crime, thereby having a ready source for false identification available to any employee or associate willing to pay the price.

The second way an individual could obtain a fictitious driver's license is to have a connection inside the Secretary of State's Office that would be willing to overlook the acceptable identification requirements for the application. This person could be a mid-level manager, such as an area zone manager or a facility manager. It also could be a top-level executive employee like a department director or deputy director. It is even possible that the constitutionally elected secretary of state would overlook the mandated requirements. Each of these senior officials could simply order a subordinate to issue the fictitious driver's license. Or low-level driver's license examiners could simply decide to issue it on their own. An employee of any level doing so is in violation of state employee policy, which is grounds for termination. It is also a criminal act, official misconduct, for a state official to perform an act he or she knows is forbidden. Likewise, if the employee receives any benefit from issuing the fake license, such as gift or money, the additional crime is accepting a bribe. Finally, all state workers, from elected officials on down, take an oath to uphold state law, the Illinois Constitution, and the U.S. Constitution. A state official or employee that knowingly issues a fictitious driver's license violates his or her state oath and the public trust. He or she also contributes to the series of crimes that follow that driver's license.

The Kane County Sheriff's Office forwarded to the Secretary of State Department of Inspector General a complete copy of the case file on the arrest of the lingerie model. Based on statements made by the model at the time of the arrest, they believed there was an employee of the Secretary of State's Office that worked in collusion with the under-age model in the issuance of the fictitious driver's license showing her as twenty-one years of age. Special Agent Russ Sonneveld was assigned the case by Deputy Director Joe Jech. I assisted Sonneveld with the investigation.

The first step in handling a complaint of employee collusion involving a fictitious license is to obtain a copy of the driver's license application. Information contained on the application is a valuable lead in developing a case and for prosecutorial purposes later. This document in a false application investigation is as significant as a fingerprint in a burglary or DNA in a homicide.

The front side of the application contains the applicant's name, address, birth date, physical description, and Social Security number. All that information is entered into the Secretary of State's Office driver's license database by the SOS Driver Services Department's public service clerk. A hard copy application is generated and then printed out. The front side includes the description of the three required documents used by the applicant to prove his or her identity, birth date, address, Social Security number, and signature. That information is written on the hard copy by the public service clerk. The back side of the application contains the record of the eye test, written test, and road test. Another section includes a short inspection of the vehicle done by the road examiner, also known as a pubic service representative. The examiner checks the vehicle for working lights, horn, brakes, and seat belts. The examiner also writes the vehicle registration number (license plate) in this section. On the back side, the applicant signs his or her name, swearing that all the information provided is true. In addition, the application contains a document control number that is also on the issued driver's license. The purpose of the control number is accountability. The application can be specifically matched to a driver's license for auditing or investigative purposes.

Depending on the size of the Driver Services Department facility, one employee may handle every step of the process. In larger facilities, the applicant moves from station to station to complete each process. For example, in one of the large Chicago facilities, an applicant will have the identification documents checked for completeness and validity at the first station. The applicant will then move to a station where the application is typed up and printed. The applicant is handed the application and moves to a third station, where the fee is paid. The next station is the eye test, followed by the written test. Once the applicant passes both those tests, he or she is directed to have the vehicle driven up to an outside location where the road test is initiated. If the applicant's vehicle passes that test, he or she takes the application in hand and goes back inside for the final stage, a photograph. The applicant signs a computer-generated camera card, and a photograph is taken.

Finally, the last employee examines the driver's license with the applicant's photo and makes sure all items on the final document are correct. The Chicago facilities handle up to three thousand applications a day, and a different employee is assigned to each station in the process. They are made accountable by initialing their part on each application. They also place their employee assigned ID number next to their initials. Rarely will one employee handle more than one stage or every stage.

Occasionally a VIP might be applying for a new license or renewing a license. On those rare instances, the Driver Services Department facility manager may handle the entire process. I recall being in Chicago facilities when Muhammad Ali, the famous heavyweight boxing champion, and Barbara Eden, the star of the 1960s television sitcom *I Dream of Jeannie*, were there to renew their licenses. The public there on those days for the same reason immediately recognized both figures as they entered the building, causing a minor distraction for everyone. The smart manager took the VIPs into his office to return the facility to its routine. For any other reason, if one employee handles the entire application process, it is a red flag that something irregular has occurred and the application needs to be looked over more carefully by auditors and investigators responsible for examining such irregularities. Small downstate facilities may be different. The entire staff at one of those locations may be only three public service representatives. It would not be unusual for one employee to handle the entire driver's license application process.

The lingerie model obtained the fake license from the Joliet facility. This facility's size was somewhere in between Chicago and downstate. Several employees' initials and ID numbers appeared on her application. Our follow-up required interviewing each of those employees, as well as questioning the Joliet facility's manager and any other employee that could recall peculiarities occurring during the young lingerie model's day there. If necessary, we would question other members of the public that were there applying for driver's licenses at the same time. By looking at the chronological order of the application control numbers, we could locate applicants that were in the facility about the same time. You would be surprised what people might remember about a lingerie model.

Upon receiving a copy of the model's fake license application, we first reviewed the document, looking to match employees' initials and ID numbers to a list we maintained at the Department of Inspector General office. The list contained employees' names, their assigned employee identification number, and to which Secretary of State facility each employee was assigned. The list was computerized and sent to us monthly from the Department of Personnel. It was a practice I established under Edgar's inspector general, Jim Redenbo. So far, to my surprise, Ryan's IG, Dean Bauer, had not stopped it. We then checked each employee's name through the Illinois State Police computerized network called LEADS (Law Enforcement Agency Data System). We were looking for arrest records of the employees to see if there was any connection to strip bars, lingerie shows, organized crime, drug possession, or even a driving under the influence. We did learn that one male employee had a DUI arrest, but no conviction. We also learned that the same employee had a gambling arrest, but no conviction. The significance of these arrests may seem debatable to some, but substance abuse and gambling addictions are indicators of employee problems in any industry, not just government.

We were not immediately concerned with the documents the lingerie model used. We figured if there was indeed employee corruption, the recollections of the witnesses came first. Agent Sonneveld and I set out for the Joliet facility to begin interviews. Upon arriving, the first thing we learned was the employee with the arrest record had been transferred to a facility closer to his home. He lived in Kankakee and recently had been moved to the facility in Bourbonnais, the neighboring town. Two of the employees and the manager recalled the former Joliet employee handling the majority of the lingerie model's application. Most notably, he handled the review and approval of the applicant's required documents.

The manager took us aside and cautioned us. He wanted to see this employee investigated and terminated. He believed the employee had a drinking problem, but was afraid to pursue disciplinary action because the employee was believed to be both a neighbor and friend of

Secretary of State Ryan. Sonneveld and I took this caution with a grain of salt. We worked with evidence and facts, not rumors and innuendos.

Upon returning to our office in Hillside, we completed our case investigative reports on the interviews. Inspector General Bauer wanted a briefing on what we had uncovered so far. He also inquired as to what our plans were next. This was routine for a police supervisor to ask during an investigation. Supervisors want to be kept informed of the progress made by investigators. They often offer suggestions based on their expertise and experience. We told him we were going to interview the lingerie model and then gather the physical evidence we needed, such as the original license application and the other documents the model might have used when the fictitious application was made. Bauer grumpily asked if we planned on interviewing the suspect employee. We were not concerned about the attitude Bauer gave us when he asked the questions. He seemed grumpy most of the time.

As a matter of fact, the administrative assistants in the office, JoAnn Robertson and Carolyn Miller, often referred to Bauer as Grumpy, Elwyn Tatro as Lumpy, and Dan Gilman as Dumpy. The three IG pals: Grumpy, Lumpy, and Dumpy. I took delight in this metaphor because it had both physical and personality connotations that were accurate in a comical way.

Nonetheless, Bauer's grumpiness did not bother us that day. Neither did the fact that the question he asked was insulting. Of course we were going to question the suspect employee. Standard operating procedure for an internal corruption investigation was to gather all the evidence and statements before questioning the suspect. This placed the advantage in favor of the investigators because often they know the factual answer before the suspect gives his answer. Presenting hard evidence to the suspect during the interrogation puts a lot of pressure on him. He either then gives a lie that is easily disproved or is compelled to tell the truth.

During most of my tenure in the Secretary of State Department of Inspector General, departmental directors and supervisors wanted investigators to immediately interview a suspect employee. They either felt it would resolve the case quicker, or they were worried that as we continued to investigate we might uncover conspiracies in which they were key players. I always resisted the pressure to interview the suspect immediately. This time was different. There was no pressure to interrogate the suspect. Sonneveld and I actually were relieved that Bauer did not push the issue.

Over the course of the next couple of weeks, Sonneveld attempted to contact the lingerie model and obtain her statement. Also, he learned that our suspect had issued a second fictitious driver's license to another under-twenty-one-year-old lingerie model. After finally locating the young ladies, in brief conversations with Sonneveld, they both refused to cooperate. They could have agreed to cooperate in exchange for leniency on the Kane County arrest. We could have pursued charges against both for their respective false application for a driver's license in Will County. Both would have been felonies and separate from the Kane County Sheriff's Office police officer's case.

The fact that they had obtained fictitious licenses in Joliet was a different case from the possession of the same licenses in Kane County. Putting more pressure on each of them in exchange for cooperation against a corrupt Secretary of State driver's license examiner was our job and duty. Inspector General Bauer disagreed. That would go against his goal as a George Ryan team player. Bauer's goal as inspector general was to protect Ryan's image from public embarrassment. Now, you would think arresting and charging a driver's license examiner feloniously issuing fictitious licenses to underage lingerie models would improve Ryan's image as a pro-law-enforcement Republican. After all, he then would be the secretary of state responsible for cleaning house. The truth is, all the secretaries of state for whom I worked—Alan Dixon, Jim Edgar, George Ryan, and Jesse White—preferred to maintain a low public profile when it came to criminal justice issues.

For example, the SOS Police were responsible for enforcing administrative and criminal violations on licensed automobile dealers. One of the biggest contributors to all of the secretaries of states' political fund-raising campaigns is the automobile dealer lobby. Hence any strong enforcement action against a large car dealership or tough enforcement across the board meant decreased campaign contributions. Secretary of State Office internal investigations resulting in employee disciplinary action, termination, or criminal charges meant the case would be public record. Since most of the employees obtained their position through a patronage connection, the political sponsor and the secretary both would be publicly embarrassed, but the record of the employee's misconduct, not to mention another source of political donations, would cease. George Ryan's and Dean Bauer's concern with the lingerie models was more than the usual concern. The employee that issued them the fictitious licenses was a neighbor of Ryan and friend to both Ryan and Bauer.

Upon learning that the models refused to cooperate, Inspector General Bauer ordered Special Agent Sonneveld to close the case. The basis for closing the case was the witnesses, the lingerie models, were uncooperative. Never mind that there was real physical evidence like the fictitious driver's licenses and the license applications. Never mind that there were potential witnesses that could testify to the actions by the defendant. Never mind that we could arrest co-conspirators and negotiate deals, giving them consideration in exchange for their testimony against the corrupt government official, a bigger fish. What mattered was this was George Ryan's neighbor and friend. What mattered was the public would become aware that a political appointee of George Ryan was arrested and indicted for issuing illegal licenses to underage lingerie models. The story was not only about political corruption, otherwise known as business as usual in Illinois. The story was also about sex, and that had the potential for destroying Ryan's later bid for governor. Dean Bauer, Ryan's inspector general and official guardian of the boss's public image, ordered Special Agent Sonneveld to prepare a memo officially closing the lingerie models' case.

Sonneveld and I discussed Bauer's decision over one of our many lunches together. We felt it was at least bordering on obstruction of justice. With both of us being fathers of young girls, the moral issue that it involved underage girls working in a sleazy occupation in bars with groping drunks was also a concern. We did not know where to turn with this new obstruction, but the pile of them was beginning to stink.

CHAPTER 6
Whose F***ing Team Are You On?

Man is a strange animal. He generally cannot read the handwriting on the wall until his back is up against it.

—Adlai E. Stevenson

The first major case the Chicago office of the IG worked as a team under Bauer's and Jech's supervision involved two employees inside the driver's bureau at the Midlothian facility. Based on information developed through a confidential source, Special Agent Pat Dowdle began investigating an allegation that Illinois drivers whose driver's licenses were revoked as a result of a driving under the influence conviction were obtaining fictitious driver's licenses using new identities to circumvent the statutory, mandatory license revocation. They were able to obtain these licenses through a referral made at an alcohol rehabilitation program to a man that enabled the DUI convict to make a license application at the Midlothian Driver's Bureau. The convict paid the middleman five hundred dollars. The middleman then paid one hundred dollars to either a supervisor or the assistant manager inside the driver's bureau to approve a fictitious application on behalf of the applicant.

Dowdle tracked one hundred of these applicants. By examining each of the suspected applications, Dowdle was able to determine some of the suspects' true identities. After generating the application, the applicants took the driver's road test in vehicles registered under their real names. On the back of the application, the driver's license examiner wrote the applicant's license plate number while completing a pre-test vehicle inspection.

Dowdle took that license plate number and ran it in the Secretary of State's Office database to determine the vehicle owner's name. From there, Dowdle ran the owner's name through the driver's license database and determined that the matching owner's driver's license was revoked for DUI. Dowdle was able to identify fifteen of the suspects via this process. The potential impact of these unlawful acts was not only a violation of the public trust, but a risk of severe injury or death as a result of enabling these DUI drivers back on the street, thereby creating the public safety risk.

Based on the information developed by Dowdle, we began a joint undercover operation with the Cook County State's Attorney's Office Investigation Bureau. Like the Secretary of State's Office, many people do not realize the State's Attorney's Office has sworn professional police officers who conduct criminal investigations. Within this bureau is a highly skilled, specialized unit for electronic surveillance.

The State's Attorney's Office investigators, through an introduction made by the case informant, went in the Midlothian Driver's Bureau undercover. They posed as DUI convicts with the intent of paying off one of the two SOS employees for the purpose of securing a fictitious driver's license. Each time an undercover investigator went into the facility, he was equipped with a recording device and transmitter to record the conversations and transactions between the investigator and the suspected SOS employee. The recording devices were court authorized through a consensual overhear order predicated on a police officer's sworn affidavit of probable cause. The undercover contacts were supported by SOS IG agents on visual surveillance and the State's Attorney's Office electronic surveillance investigators.

This type of an operation required a more complex and sophisticated plan than most police investigations. It was a common practice for high-level drug cases, organized crime investigations, and public corruption cases. Besides, we were entering a public facility to conduct unlawful transactions with two or more targeted state employees. The standard the state's attorney wanted to meet was at least three contacts involving criminal activities on each targeted suspect. In another similar case, thirty-one contacts were made over a three-month period in order to complete three criminal transactions with the suspect. This type of investigation might last several weeks because it involves gathering information, developing informants, briefings, state's attorney's review, preparing complex affidavits, and court appearances before the undercover operation even begins. However, the fruits of this type of investigation are bountiful.

The end result of the Midlothian undercover operation was no exception. The evidence recovered included forged documents, incriminating recorded conversations, and cash. In a one-day sweep, with the assistance of uniformed officers from the SOSPD District 1, fifteen of the applicants were located, arrested, and charged with making a false application for a driver's license, driving while revoked, and forgery. The middleman and the two SOS employees were charged with bribery, official misconduct, and conspiracy. Jack O'Malley, the Cook County State's Attorney at the time, and Ryan held a joint press conference after the bust. The conference was held at the Cook County Criminal Courts building.

MAY-20-1992 07:47 FROM INSPECTOR GENERAL   TO   Chicago   P

OFFICE OF THE STATE'S ATTORNEY
COOK COUNTY, ILLINOIS

JACK O'MALLEY
STATE'S ATTORNEY

CRIMINAL DIVISION
2650 SOUTH CALIFORNIA AVE.
CHICAGO, ILLINOIS 60608

May 11, 1992

George H. Ryan
Secretary of State of Illinois
State of Illinois Center
100 West Randolph
Chicago, Illinois 60601

Dear Mr. Ryan,

We are writing to you to commend several members of the Inspector General's division of your office. Specifically we wish to commend Supervisor Joseph Jech and Special Agents Patrick Dowdle and Edward Hammer. As you know the State's Attorney's Office and your office recently conducted a joint investigation which uncovered a scheme to produce fictitious driver's licenses at the Midlothian Secretary of State facility. Mr. Jech and Agents Dowdle and Hammer cooperated with our office fully in this investigation and offered assistance whenever we requested it. As you know this investigation required a lot of hard work and many long hours. Mr. Jech and Agents Dowdle and Hammer dedicated themselves to the success of this operation and put in the hard work and the long hours that were needed. Agent Dowdle worked especially hard at the arduous task of trying to determine the identity of the drivers who obtained fictitious driver's licenses. As a result of the dedicated professional work of these individuals along with the investigators from our office, two supervisors at the Midlothian facility and several civilians were arrested and a dangerous scheme was uncovered.

As you know much work still remains to be done in order to locate all the drivers who obtained fictitious driver's licenses. We are confident that the dedication and high level of

(Letter to Ryan from Cook County assistant state's attorneys page 1)

130

Page 2.

professionalism which Mr. Jech and Agents Dowdle and Hammer exhibited in this investigation will continue to its successful conclusion. We look forward to working with these fine members of your office and we commend them highly for the excellent work they have done on this important investigation.

Sincerely yours,

Patrick Quinn
Supervisor, Public Integrity Unit
Special Prosecutions Bureau

Rimas F. Cernius
Assistant State's Attorney
Public Integrity Unit

PJQ/kc

TOTAL P.03

(letter, page 2)

On the surface it would appear that Ryan was on the side of law and order after announcing the crackdown on the Midlothian Secretary of State facility. What was it actually? It was one of the first indicators of Ryan's arrogance and hands-off attitude toward public corruption. A news reporter asked Ryan what future plans he had to combat further corruption in the Secretary of State's Office. In Ryan's typical blustery manner, he answered that corruption had always existed and always would. Later, when reporters were not present, Patrick Quinn (not the same as Governor Patrick Quinn), the assistant state's attorney in charge of the public corruption unit and now an Illinois Appellate Court justice, made a statement to Ryan that security precautions could be put in the system to prevent abuses. Ryan turned to O'Malley and said, "Whose fuckin' team is he on?" Justice Patrick Quinn eventually testified to this caustic remark by Ryan at Ryan's federal trial for corruption. The statement pretty much sums up Ryan's mind-set when it came to his role as a public servant.

Our next big case involved the Libertyville driver's license facility. We developed information that two Mexican drug dealers were supplying illegal immigrants with counterfeit INS green cards. They manufactured the documents in an apartment in Waukegan and transported their customers to the Libertyville driver's license facility. They then bribed the facility manager or another employee to get driver's licenses for their customers without a required Social Security number.

In an investigation that lasted several weeks, we used undercover opera-
tives from the Illinois State Police, Chicago Police, Bensenville Police,
and the Lake County State's Attorney's Office that posed as counterfeit
alien registration customers. A Lake County consensual overhear order
was obtained for each undercover contact. The undercover officers had
to look Hispanic and speak fluent Spanish.

The Bensenville officer was of Mexican ancestry. He had no problem meeting with the Mexican suppliers of the fake INS cards. He looked
and spoke the part. After obtaining the fake INS document, the suspects
transported the undercover officer to the Libertyville facility. There our
undercover cop observed our suspects paying one of the Secretary of
State's Office employees money in exchange for securing our undercover
cop a driver's license. No identification or driving test was required.

The Chicago detective working with us was of Cuban ancestry.
This presented a minor challenge. Up to this point, the Mexican suspects
only sold INS cards to Mexican immigrants who entered the United
States without legal documentation. The Cuban officer's accent and
Spanish dialect would not fit the profile of an undocumented alien. We
devised a cover that our CPD detective was a drug dealer from Miami
and needed several fake identifications to hide from law enforcement
officials and to launder his drug profits. It worked. Our Chicago detective made several of the same undercover transactions as the Bensenville officer. In fact, while the Secretary of State's Office employees

prepared the false driver's license applications and tests, the detective overheard them many times making racists remarks in English about their non-English-speaking clients.

During the surveillance of these undercover deals, we observed a Chicago Northwest Side driving school also meeting with our targeted SOS employees. An undercover operative was then sent into the driving school. The Illinois State Police trooper for this phase was recruited from Illinois State Police District 17 in LaSalle, Illinois. He was of Puerto Rican ancestry and grew up in Chicago. We felt his cover would not be compromised by his accent or dialect. The owner and operators of the driving school were a father and son who both had emigrated from Italy. They spoke broken Spanish and could not distinguish between a Mexican, Cuban, Puerto Rican, or Chicago dialect. For a few hundred dollars, the ISP trooper secured a fake birth certificate from the driving school and a fictitious driver's license at the Libertyville facility.

On the return trip from Libertyville in the driving school's vehicle, the trooper was confronted about his dialect by one of the driving school's other clients. The client told the trooper he knew he was not Mexican by the trooper's accent. Thinking quickly, the trooper told the client that he was from the Dominican Republic, which would account for his illegal status in the United States.

After several weeks of undercover buys, meetings, and court appearances, we obtained search warrants for the Mexican suspects'

Waukegan apartment and the Chicago driving school. We conducted simultaneous raids at the driving school, the Mexican suspects' apartment, and the Libertyville driver's license facility. A search warrant was not required for the license facility because SOS employees have no Fourth Amendment protection in or at the state-operated workplace.

I executed the search warrant at the driving school with the assistance of the Chicago Police Intelligence Unit. We recovered several incriminating documents, the most interesting being twenty George Ryan fund-raising tickets wrapped in a bundle around two thousand dollars in cash in an envelope marked with the name Carl Catuara. He was the manager of the Chicago West Secretary of State facility and the son of the deceased Al Capone enforcer Jimmy "the Bomber" Catuara. Catuara was eventually caught up in the FBI's "Operation Silver Shovel" case and lost his state employment. The seized money and tickets were inventoried and the inventory was returned to Cook County Judge Deborah Dooling. Much to George Ryan's embarrassment, the inventory of the money and political tickets were now public record and I was on a path of being my boss's nemesis by simply doing my job.

(6-82) CCMC1-218

IN THE CIRCUIT COURT OF COOK COUNTY, ILLINOIS

WARRANT NO. 93SW4947

SEARCH WARRANT INVENTORY

On March 9 , 19 93 , at 10:20 (A.M.) (P.M.)

I EDWARD HAMMER executed a search
(officer)

warrant signed by DEBORAH DOOLING
(Judge)

On MARCH 8 , 19 93 , at 5:26 (A.M.) (P.M.)

which directed that (the person of PETE PRATO AND MIKE PRATO and)

ROMA DRIVING SCHOOL, 7138 W. GRAND, CHICAGO be searched and the following seized:
(premises)

DRIVING SCHOOL RECORDS, SECRETARY OF STATE APPLICATIONS AND FRAUDULENT IDENTIFICATION
DOCUMENTS OF STUDENTS OF THE ROMA DRIVING SCHOOL.

In executing said warrant I seized the following from the person described above and have returned the

same before D. Dooling on 3/17 , 19 93
(Judge)

A) TWENTY FOUR (24) GEORGE RYAN FUND RAISER TICKETS #941-960, #1339-1341 and #1273

B) ONE THOUSAND TWO HUNDRED DOLLARS ($1,200.00) UNITED STATES CURRENCY

C) 1 RECIEPT BOOK MARKED ROMA DRIVING SCHOOL

D) 1 CHECK BOOK MARKED ROMA DRIVING SCHOOL

E) SEVERAL BLANK CHECKS ON THE ACCOUNT OF DIONISIO BROZAN

F) SEVERAL OFFICIAL SECRETARY OF STATE DRIVERS LICENSE APPLICATION WITH APPLICANTS' NAME

ADDRESS, DATE OF BIRTH, AND SOCIAL SECURITY NUMBER HANDWRITTEN ON APPLICATION.

G) 1 BUNDLE OF BLANK OFFICIAL SECRETARY OF STATE DRIVERS APPLICATIONS

H) SEVERAL HUNDRED OFFFICIAL SECRETARY OF STATE DRIVERS LICENSE TESTS AND/OR COPIES OF THE SA:

I) STUDENT RECORDS

J) MISC. NOTES, BUSINESS CARDS, LOGS, AND TELEPHONE BOOKS.

Edward Hammer
Officer

Signed and sworn to before me on 3/18 , 19 93

Judge 603
Judge's No.

CLERK OF THE CIRCUIT COURT OF COOK COUNTY, ILLINOIS

(Driving school search warrant inventory)

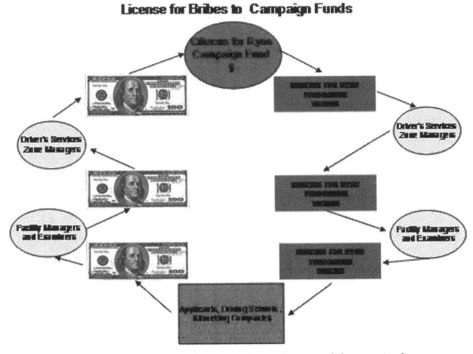

(How the money in the Licenses for Bribes scandal was raised)

Simultaneously as I was recovering the money and political fund-raiser tickets, Mark Lipe, an agent from the Department of Inspector General office in Springfield, recovered two thousand dollars cash and Ryan fund-raiser tickets from an open briefcase sitting on the desk of the regional manager's office at the Secretary of State's Office driver's bureau facility in Libertyville. Mark was our evidence technician and was inventorying the evidence in Libertyville when Dean Bauer ordered Mark to turn over control of the regional manager's briefcase to him. The regional manager, a George Ryan political appointee and Lake County Republican heavy, was never charged with a crime. Bauer was eventually indicted by the federal government for obstruction of justice relating to this Libertyville raid and the manager's lost briefcase.

Around the same time, I was assigned to investigate a manager in the Secretary of State Veterans Affairs Department. I wasn't exactly sure what I was supposed to be investigating, but I knew the manager from a prior sexual harassment case I had worked that had resulted in a ten-day suspension for him.

The sexual harassment case was conducted under the Edgar administration and actually started with the manager filing a complaint against a Secretary of State Police officer. The officer had left a message on the manager's answering machine that said, "I will kick your ass if you don't leave my fiancée alone!" The manager had dated the officer's fiancée at one time. He continued with sexual advances and innuendos after their relationship ended. He was also her boss. The advances continued even after she became engaged to the police officer.

I confronted the officer about the threat. He wholeheartedly admitted to leaving the threat on the manager's answering machine. The officer stated that he would take his punishment like a man. The officer received a five-day suspension without pay. He also told me about the continued sexual harassment the manager directed at his fiancée.

I opened a case, predicated on a description by the officer's fiancée, of the hostile work environment and sexual harassment being conducted by the manager. If one were to search sexual harassment on

Google, the manager's photograph would probably pop up. His conduct was blatant. When I went to interview his co-workers, they described sexually suggestive posters he put up on the walls of his office and conversations at meetings that had sexual overtones. Despite the officer's fiancée demanding that he stop, he sent her cards and letters in the U.S. mail that contained sexual themes. He left messages on her telephone answering machine, telling her that she was missing out on an awesome physical relationship. This was sexual harassment by the classical definition, as well as a violation of the employee policy of the Secretary of State's Office.

When I went to interview the manager, I was especially disturbed by a photograph on his desk of a female child kneeling on a bed, wearing only underwear. She appeared to me to be about eight or nine years old. I was embarrassed by the photo and angered that someone would display it on his desk. The manager told me it was his daughter.

The manager was athletic, handsome, and well dressed. He was also an egomaniac. That is why I believe he could not let go of a former girlfriend. It was too much of a blow to his ego. After I completed the sexual harassment investigation, Jim Edgar gave him a ten-day suspension.

Now I was being assigned a new case under George Ryan's direction. Deputy Director Joe Jech told me that because of my earlier experience investigating this manager, I was being assigned this current investigation. The manager was walking out to the parking lot of his health club after a racquetball game when another club member asked him how he could afford a Mercedes-Benz on the salary of a Secretary of State employee. The manager replied, "You gotta know how to play the game." Apparently the quip angered the fellow club member, resulting in him making a complaint to the Department of Inspector General. My job was to determine what the manager meant by his glib remark. There was no specific violation to investigate, but I figured, knowing what a jerk the guy was from the previous sexual harassment investigation, there could be at least a technical policy violation. After all, what did "play the game" mean? Did it mean he had an illegal source of income from some bribery scam? Was it even possible the Mercedes-Benz he drove was stolen?

I began the investigation with the car. I traced the chain of titles on the vehicle and went to the car dealership where he had purchased it. Everything was legitimate. However, he registered and titled the vehicle with a home address of Springfield, Illinois. Actually, he lived on the South Side of Chicago. I then obtained his state travel records, vouchers, and per diem reports. They all showed he lived in Chicago, and that he was requesting travel reimbursement for mileage, lodging, and meals each time he went to Springfield. That was at least twice a month. Checking with an insurance agent whose office was in the same building as our IG office, the manager was saving about $1,200 per year by reporting Springfield as his home address on his vehicle insurance.

I called him into the office to be interviewed regarding the discrepancies on the addresses. I asked Joe Jech to sit in on the interview with me, because from my prior experiences with this subject, I wanted to conduct a two-on-one interview. On the prior case, he had accused me of falsifying reports. Two IG agents from Springfield retraced all my investigative steps. Of course, there was no wrongdoing on my part. Therefore, his counter-complaint on me was unfounded. Having Jech do the interview with me was meant to prevent any new false accusations being directed toward me.

I told the manager at the beginning of the interview, after being advised of his "play the game" remark, that I first became concerned about the ownership of his Mercedes-Benz. After checking, I determined that his purchase and ownership of the car was legitimate. I did this to humor him, putting him at ease at the beginning of the interview. Then I asked him where he lived. He said that he stayed in Chicago, but Springfield was his legal address. I then asked him from what address he filed his income taxes. He replied Chicago. Next I asked where he was registered to vote. He told me he was not registered to vote. I was shocked! Most employees of the Secretary of State's Office were political animals. They had job sponsors with political clout. Everyone was registered except this guy. So I asked, "How come?"

He said, "I am not registered to vote because Jesse Jackson is my clout."

I asked him to explain what that had to do with him not being registered to vote. He said that since George Ryan was a Republican, it might be embarrassing to him to hire an executive that had Democratic clout, like Jesse Jackson. It was a dumb excuse. He was trying to cover his tracks.

Agent Lipe checked the manager's Springfield address and reported to me that an elderly man now living there had told him that the manager had once dated his daughter. When they dated, he occasionally stayed overnight. The man stated that his daughter did not live with him now and the manager no longer dated his daughter. He also said that the manager had not stayed at his house for over a year. Bottom line, all of the manager's answers to my questions were smoke and mirrors to cover the fact that he was trying to save some nickels and dimes on his auto insurance. The fact is, he either lied on his vehicle registration application, a technical felonious act, or he lied on his travel vouchers, likewise felonious. It didn't matter which one was the lie. The statements on the official documents contradicted each other. That is a technical perjury.

Generally, these types of violations are viewed as minor and are not pursued by prosecutors. I understand and accept this. However, his lying on official state documents and his lack of candor during my interview were indicators of a deceptive personality. As an employer, I would not want an employee in a managerial position that sexually harassed subordinates, created a hostile work environment, and made a habit of lying to the administration.

Tina Prose, director of the Secretary of State Department of Personnel, was a George Ryan appointee. She decided that if he, the manager, paid back his travel voucher money and corrected his vehicle registration application, they would not take disciplinary action against him.

After the case was closed, Ryan was attending a Black History Month event at the DuSable Museum in Chicago. So was this manager. The two were having a very public conversation that was seen and heard by a third party—Eric Robertson, husband to IG secretary JoAnn Robertson. The conversation was loud and clear enough so that anyone standing near could easily hear the topic. The topic was me. The manager was obviously angered by my investigation. He told Ryan that I was an overly zealous cop, jealous of the manager's good looks and stylish clothes. He suggested to Ryan that I be removed from my assignment in the Department of Inspector General.

The next day, JoAnn Robertson reported to me the details of the conversation her husband had heard. Prior to that event, JoAnn and Eric Robertson had never discussed the investigation I had conducted against the manager. It was not JoAnn Robertson's habit to discuss special agent's cases with her spouse. This was the first time Eric Robertson had heard my name connected with the manager.

(Joan and Eric Robertson at Hammer's retirement party

The Secretary of State's Office personnel records showed that, one month after the DuSable Museum event, the manager received a promotion with a 20 percent pay increase. Apparently a combination of sexual harassment and deceit were the criteria for promotion within the George Ryan crony system.

In the spring of 1994, along came a case that became emblematic of Ryan's corruption and cronyism. One of the routine functions of the Secretary of State's Department of Inspector General was to monitor money irregularities in the various facilities around the state. This included SOS Vehicle Services and Driver's License Services facilities that received cash on a daily basis for such things as license renewals.

The amount of money handled at the different facilities could range from a few thousand dollars to amounts close to one million dollars, depending on the number and type of applicants. For example, one of the three major SOS Vehicle Services facilities could handle truck renewal registration. If that facility handled twenty renewals of eighty-thousand-pound rigs with license plates costing as much as $2,400, that facility would take in $48,000 alone on the twenty renewals. Keep in mind that this does not include a whole variety of other license plate and title applications, such as new cars at eighty dollars per application.

Smaller facilities logically managed smaller amounts of money. Most of these types only handled driver's license applications and annual passenger plate renewals. The amounts of cash handled at these facilities were usually in the low four figures.

Auditors monitored all these facilities and their cash flow to ensure that the managers were in compliance with state regulations. Likewise, audits were conducted to prevent employees from skimming cash from taxpayer money.

Occasionally the law enforcement function of the Department of Inspector General would be called in if money was reported lost or stolen. In some rare cases, employees handling cash would succumb to temptation and steal some. The audit trail was easy to follow and the employee was caught with little investigative effort. More frequently, the cash shortages that were reported usually were banking errors.

Special Agent Russ Sonneveld was assigned a case of a $2,500 shortage on a bank deposit with the Naperville driver's license facility. I believe Joe Jech assigned the case to Sonneveld thinking it was a routine banking error and would simply be discovered and fixed. Little did

Jech know that this case would turn out to be a theft of state monies and that George Ryan would get involved later, resulting in an indictment for obstruction of justice.

The reported cash shortage should have been routine. A banking or tabulation error would be discovered and corrected. I went with Sonneveld to Naperville to get a report of facts from Russell Nisavaco, the facility manager. What we got was a variety of stories and excuses. Basically, Nisavaco was supposed to make a deposit drop at the bank of the prior day's receipts. He had been making that drop for four years. Now, suddenly, he could not remember if he left the deposit on the facility's counter and the janitorial service took it. Another scenario he conjured up was that he forgot to go to the bank and the money bag was stolen from his locked car. Or just maybe, after Nisavaco dropped it in the bank's night deposit, somebody came along and took it out of the drop drawer before the bag dropped into the vault.

Those of us who are parents know that when our children lie to us, they often devise two or three different stories to explain a mishap. The same logic applies to police investigating crimes. If a witness voluntarily speculates several different scenarios, the police begin to believe the witness is a suspect. This is especially true if the witness is responsible for missing property or cash.

Based on the manager's blather, Sonneveld and I theorized that he was responsible for the missing $2,500 cash. The question, however, was why Nisavaco would risk a good job for a lousy $2,500 cash. I had a theory. On the ride back to our office, I discussed it with Sonneveld. In about seven days, Ryan was holding a political fund-raiser. This event was to be held at Navy Pier. Historically under secretaries of state Alan Dixon, Jim Edgar, and George Ryan, before this particular type of fund-raising event, all Secretary of State's Office managers were given several fund-raiser tickets and were expected to sell them to their subordinates at one hundred dollars each. This type of event was held annually for a plethora of reasons. It boosted the secretary's political funds by a significant amount. It helped the political powers in charge determine which employees were loyal to the boss and his organization. Finally, the employees responsible for contributing the largest amounts were considered for promotion. Those already in managerial positions might end up demoted if they did not meet a quota.

The Naperville manager was given fifty tickets to sell to the workers at his facility. There had been some recent negative publicity on a local TV station that a Secretary of State field auditor was shaking down licensed vehicle dealerships to pay Ryan fund-raiser tickets. I suggested to Sonneveld that because of the recent bad PR for Ryan, our Naperville manager might have gotten cold feet about shaking down his facility underlings and decided it would be better to steal the cash from the driver's license application revenues. Nisavaco then concocted the lost or stolen money bag story he told us.

Sonneveld later discussed this theory with General Counsel Roger Bickel. He advised Sonneveld to pursue the investigation. Bickel said he would obtain the campaign donation records after the fund-raiser.

Russ and I returned to interview the manager on a later date and this time we turned up the heat. His responses to our questions were inconsistent, so we asked him if he would take a polygraph exam. He asked, "How does the polygraph determine if a person is lying?" This was clearly a sign he was planning to deceive us.

We chose to use Theodore Polygraph Service in Hillside. We knew Steve Theodore, the owner. He was a GOP committee man, so we figured nobody would accuse us of being politically biased against Ryan or other Republicans if we used his services. We briefed Theodore of the circumstances of the missing money. He agreed that our theory of theft of the money for political fund-raising was a likely motive for Nisavaco to steal the facility's money.

Needless to say, Nisavaco failed the lie box exam. After the polygraph, Theodore conducted a post-exam interview. The Naperville manager admitted to the examiner to receiving fifty fund-raiser tickets from his supervisor to sell. He sold twenty-five for one hundred dollars cash each, totaling $2,500. Nisavaco insisted he did not steal any money, but he offered to make restitution because as manager he was ultimately responsible.

94C0045
MDI

THEODORE POLYGRAPH SERVICE

4415 W. HARRISON • HILLSIDE, IL 60162 • 312/449-5020

SUBMITTED TO:

Investigator Russ Sonneveld
Inspector General
Secretary of State
4415 W. Harrison
Hillside, IL 60162

POLYGRAPH LABORATORY

CONFIDENTIAL

CASE NO.	SUBJECT'S NAME	DATE OF TEST	TYPE OF TEST	POSITION
	Russell J. Nisivaco	4-26-94	specific	Manager

DURING THE PRE-TEST INTERVIEW THE EXAMINER EXPLAINED THE PURPOSE OF THE TEST AND THE
POLYGRAPH DETECTION OF DECEPTION TECHNIQUE TO THE SUBJECT.

REPORT

On April 26,1994, Mr Russell J. Nisivaco voluntarily submitted
to a polygraph examination.

The main issue under consideration was whether or not Subject was
telling the truth when he claimed he take or steal the missing
deposit of April 16,1994 from Drivers License Facility in Naperville.

The Miranda warning was given and Subject signed a copy and agreed
to be interviewed and polygraphed. Subject stated that he has been
employed by Secretary of State for approximately 6 years.

During the pre-test interview the Subject stated that he believes
he left the deposit bag on the counter containing about $2,700.

The following questions were then asked:
    1. On or about April 16,1994, did you take the saturday drop
to the Harris Bank?   **Subject answered NO.**
    2. Did you take any part of the missing $2,700?
                                           Subject answered NO.
    3. Are you lying when you stated you did not profit in any way
from the lost deposit?   **Subject answered NO.**
    4. Do you know where any part of the missing $2,700 is now?
                                           Subject answered NO.

Three polygraph tests were then administered.

There were significant emotional disturbances indicative of deception
contained in the Subject's polygra records, when he denied:
    1. Taking any part of the missing $2,700.
    2. Lying when he stated that he did not profit from the
lost deposit.
    3. Knowing where any part of the missing deposit is now.

In the opinion of the Examiner , based solely on the polygraph records,
the Subject **did not tell the truth to the above stated questions.**

    02 cr 310 cfr   23721

(Polygraph report)

Later that same evening, Sonneveld telephoned me at home. He

told me that Dean Bauer had called him at home and had ordered him to

immediately call George Ryan. Sonneveld decided to call me first. I had never spoken directly to the secretary of state since I started working there in 1977. During Edgar's administration, I frequently briefed Inspector General Redenbo or Deputy Director Burke, but had no access to Secretary of State Edgar. Now my partner was being ordered to contact the current secretary of state, George Ryan. I asked Sonneveld to immediately call me back after he spoke with Ryan. Sonneveld said, "I feel like I have to puke!"

About half an hour later, Sonneveld called me back. He told me Ryan had asked for a briefing of the case. Specifically Ryan wanted to know how we developed a theory that the Naperville manager stole the money to pay for the fund-raiser tickets. Sonneveld explained our theory to him. Ryan abruptly ended the conversation with the comment, "Looks like somebody is in trouble."

This telephone call between Sonneveld and Ryan became significant in the federal criminal case against Ryan. In later interviews with the press, Ryan insisted that he did not know either Sonneveld or me and that he had no knowledge of employee corruption connected to his fund-raising. Sonneveld's testimony later proved Ryan to be a liar.

Dean Bauer was waiting for Sonneveld and me in the reception area of our office when we arrived the next day. He ordered us into separate rooms to write memos apart from our routine reports. Those memos were to explain our investigation techniques, including why we had asked questions of the suspect regarding fund-raising. This was a highly unusual demand since we also wrote case reports on our findings.

After we had completing the memos, Bauer took the disk on which they were saved by Carolyn Miller, the office secretary, and placed it in his suit jacket pocket. He then faxed printed copies to Roger Bickel. Bauer ordered the case closed with no further investigation. We were never allowed to follow any leads to determine if the manager's various scenarios were true or false.

Nisavaco would later be given a raise. The disk that Bauer took from us was found by FBI agents a few years later in Bauer's desk drawer. Both Ryan and Bauer were indicted on federal obstruction of justice charges as it related to that incident. I believe that after Nisavaco failed the polygraph, he called his DuPage County clout, possibly State Senate President Pate Philip. It was generally believed that you did not hold a state job within DuPage County unless you had heavy Republican clout, and Philip chaired the county's powerful GOP organization. Nisavaco was also a contributor to Philip's campaign. I believe Nisavaco begged his clout to call off the dogs. The clout called Ryan for the same reason, and Ryan eventually had the aforementioned conversation with Sonneveld. Ultimately the case was ordered closed by Bauer without any attempt to recover stolen taxpayer money. No one received disciplinary action. No one was charged with felony theft. When Ryan told Sonneveld, "Looks like somebody's in trouble," who exactly was he referring to: Sonneveld, me, or both of us? Could it be that Ryan had a premonition he was going to be in trouble?

CHAPTER 7

Not So Routine

Never underestimate the effectiveness of a straight cash bribe.

—*Claude Cockburn, British journalist (1904–1981)*

As special agents with the Secretary of State Department of Inspector General, Sonneveld and I had routine assignments that were not part of any specific cases. Each of us uncovered more corruption performing the routine stuff that was meant to simply keep us busy.

My routine assignment was to visit the driver's license facilities. The purpose was to talk to the managers and determine from them if there was any unusual conduct by any employee. The theory behind these visits was that we would establish a rapport with the managers and assist them in rooting out the bad employees. Theoretically it should have worked. The problem with the Ryan administration was that most of the managers were placed in their positions because they were part of his crony network. They got there because they were able to contribute a significant amount of money to his political campaign, which qualified them for supervisory positions. The managers the special agents met oftentimes could be on the wrong side of the law. More often, reliable sources of information about corruption in the facilities came from the hardworking facility clerks and examiners.

Another problem with the routine assignment was it made us very visible to all employees, especially the corrupt ones, negating any chance we might have had in conducting a covert operation in a facility. Nevertheless, we could get around that issue by using law enforcement agents from other departments. Finally, I believed we were given this assignment because it kept us busy with routine inspections and paperwork, taking us away from the more serious allegations of corruption. Any way you look at it, I believe we were intentionally given these types of assignments by Ryan's people so it appeared that the Department of Inspector General was living up to its responsibilities, when in reality it was meant to camouflage the true malfeasance.

Deputy Director Joe Jech gave me the Charles Chew facility, otherwise known as the Chicago South facility, located at 9901 S. Martin Luther King Drive in Chicago. One of the managers was Mary Ann Dvorak. I had gotten to know Mary Ann several years earlier through my secretary, JoAnn Robertson. JoAnn's brother, James Cacciatolo, was a former Chicago Police officer who worked for former Cook County Sheriff James O'Grady. Mary Ann's husband, Mike Dvorak, was O'Grady's under sheriff. James Cacciatolo and Mike Dvorak were also very good friends. As a result, JoAnn Robertson and Mary Ann Dvorak knew each other fairly well.

The FBI investigated Mike Dvorak for shaking down Cook County Jail corrections officers for contributions to Sheriff O'Grady's reelection campaign. Mike Dvorak was eventually indicted and convicted. At the time of the following visit to the Chicago South facility, Mike Dvorak was serving time in a federal penitentiary for that conviction. Despite her husband's conviction and reputation, I liked Mary Ann Dvorak. As a Secretary of State's Office facility manager, she was friendly and always appeared to do her job conscientiously.

During this particular visit, she was especially conscientious.

I was on the main floor of the Driver Services Department at the Chicago South facility talking with some of the workers when Mary Ann came out of her office and asked to speak with me privately.

We went inside her office and she closed the door behind me. She told me that the state telephone operator had forwarded a call to her that was not intended for her. A man called the general Secretary of State telephone number in Chicago and requested to speak to Marion in Driver Services. The state operator apparently quickly perused the Office of the Secretary of State agency's directory and spotted the name Mary Ann Dvorak in Driver Services. Assuming that this was the person to whom the caller wanted to speak, the operator forwarded the call to Dvorak. When Mary Ann answered, the man told her that he had heard that she could help him obtain a CDL. It was his understanding that she could arrange it so he would not have to take the difficult test, and he was willing to pay for that assistance. The Chicago South facility neither tested nor issued CDLs. Mary Ann Dvorak told the caller he had the wrong person, but she would see to it that the correct person called him back.

As Mary Ann relayed this information to me, I began to devise a plan of operation. Both Mary Ann and I had reckoned the man was looking for more than just help—that he was looking for illegal assistance in helping him obtain the CDL. Through some contact on the street, he had heard that a woman working at the Secretary of State's Office named Marion could assist with this endeavor for the right price.

Up to this point, Sonneveld and I had gathered several leads that Marion Seibel was taking bribes at McCook to assist CDL applicants. It was more than coincidental that the caller wanted to speak with a Marion. As luck would have it, the state operator had connected him with Mary Ann Dvorak and not Marion Seibel.

I believed if an undercover female officer posed as Marion Seibel, the officer could telephone the caller back and arrange a one-on-one meeting. The officer could converse with the caller and verify my hunches, thereby establishing probable cause to obtain a consensual overhear order. The officer could then arrange a second meeting where the bribe would be paid to the undercover cop, and we would bust the caller for attempted bribery. The proof beyond a reasonable doubt would be the recorded conversation, supported by the consensual overhear order. The caller would be facing a serious felony and therefore would make an ideal cooperating witness or snitch. In other words, we would send him into the McCook CDL facility to meet with the real Marion Seibel. I was constantly thinking ahead about undercover operations, recording conversations, and snitches. Those variables almost always added up to a conviction. Rarely was a trial even required. The incriminating conversation was better than a confession and usually meant a plea of guilty. So as Mary Ann Dvorak completed the details of the short, misdirected telephone call, I devised a plan.

On that day, all was falling into place. It just so happened that SOS Police Investigator Mary Beal was assigned to facility patrol at the Chicago South facility on the same day. Beal was a ten-year veteran and had worked a couple of previous undercover assignments. She was smart, trustworthy, and a friend. The few undercover cases she had worked were the result of details of criminal enterprises she cultivated as a uniformed officer and diligently followed up. The district commander rewarded her by allowing her to bring the investigation to fruition by working the undercover part of the cases. The most recent one I had worked with her involved a counterfeit document mill, where an old man manufactured identification documents such as birth certificates and W-2 forms in his South Side home and had been supplying the bogus identification to street gangs for more than twenty years. His first customers were the El Rukns, but since most of them were in federal prison, the Gangster Disciples became his new customers.

Investigator Beal developed a snitch who made an introduction of an undercover officer to the old man. The case was a success, with the old man getting busted and doing time in Stateville. The case was worked as a cooperative effort between the Secretary of State Police, Department of Inspector General, Chicago Police Department, and U.S. Secret Service. It was Beal's efforts that brought the agencies together. Investigator Beal was the right cop for this new assignment.

I approached her at the facility and asked to speak with her confidentially. You never know who could be trying to listen in on your conversation. We were now in the beginning steps of a serious public corruption investigation, and all the facilities were full of cronies looking for ways to protect their political connections. Beal and I went out to her squad car in the parking lot where I passed on the conversation I had with Mary Ann Dvorak. I also laid out my undercover idea. The immediate effect of that conversation on Investigator Beal was enthusiasm. Most cops never get the opportunity to work an undercover assignment their entire career. This was a thrilling adventure for Investigator Beal that would take her away from the daily humdrum assignments. We then had two hurdles to clear. One was her district commander. The other was my boss.

(Ron Swanson, Jr. and Mary Beal at police department party)

I was concerned that the SOS Police district commander would want to know the details of Investigator Beal's role in my request for her assistance with a Department of Inspector General case. Her commander was Maj. Arthur Hartmann. He was well liked by most of the rank-and-file investigators under his command because he always defended and protected his officers from bureaucratic and political nonsense that was part of the history of the Secretary of State's Office. He, however, was very much a political animal. He obtained his job and made his rank through political connections and favors.

I was one of those people who liked Major Hartmann. He was my boss immediately after graduating from the police academy and was good to me. I hadn't worked directly under him for years, but I remained loyal to him. He sat on the promotion board that got me sergeant stripes, which ultimately landed me in the Department of Inspector General. He never asked me for favors or information the whole time I was assigned there. I knew, however, that I had to be cautious in sharing investigative information with him, not knowing for sure where his loyalties ultimately lay. To my surprise and relief, Major Hartmann approved Investigator Beal's temporary assignment with the Department of Inspector General without asking the who, the what, or the where.

The next hurdle was Chief Deputy Director Jech. The proper procedure for most police investigative agencies when opening a case was to write an initiation report and obtain a case number. Then, of course, the report would go up the chain of command for the supervisors to read and approve. Jech was the next person in my chain of command. The procedure was the way an organization with integrity should and must operate. Jech believed that it was his job to keep the facility and departmental managers advised of investigations we conducted on their subordinates. Jech's belief, whether righteous or sinister, could be disastrous to public corruption investigations.

Advising a CDL facility supervisor that one of his or her underlings was being investigated by the Department of Inspector General was like posting an announcement on the bulletin board in the employee lunchroom. They were being shaken down by their supervisors to buy Citizens for Ryan fund-raiser tickets. Where were they supposed to get the money? Jech never contemplated these questions. He believed the supervisors should be allowed the courtesy of being informed of cases in their facilities. I opened the case and prepared the case initiation report. We would proceed with our undercover contact.

The caller's name was Charles Shirkey. He had an arrest record in both Illinois and Florida that included possession of narcotics. That record could make it difficult for him to get a CDL. If he found an illegal way to obtain the CDL, once it was issued, it might have been more difficult to cancel or revoke it. Investigator Mary Beal placed a telephone call to Shirkey and identified herself as Marion Seibel. Shirkey told her he had learned through a mutual friend that she could assist him in obtaining a CDL. He did not wish to discuss any more over the telephone. Beal agreed to call him in a week and arrange a one-on-one meeting.

The last week of October 1994, Investigator Beal posed as Marion Seibel and met Charles Shirkey at the Beef and Brandy Restaurant in Countryside, Illinois. Special Agent Sonneveld and I sat at the booth next to the meeting. Shirkey told Beal that he had heard that she and he had a mutual friend whose name was Chuck. It was Chuck who told Shirkey to call Seibel. Shirkey said that Chuck told him Seibel could ease him through the CDL test and facilitate his obtaining a CDL. Shirkey told Beal that he felt he could pass the written and road test, but he would give her two hundred dollars to grease the way for him. He knew it was illegal to offer her money, but he worried about the road test and wanted to be certain he passed. Beal told Shirkey she would get back to him and advise him how they would proceed. This ruse would allow us to equip Beal with a court ordered recording device to enable us to record incriminating conversation by Shirkey.

When Investigator Beal contacted Shirkey by phone at his place of employment, he seemed to have had a change of heart. He stated he did not want help obtaining a CDL and did not require Seibel's assistance with the tests and application for a CDL. He did not want any further contact with Seibel, our undercover investigator Mary Beal. On November 21, 1994, Deputy Director Joe Jech officially closed the Shirkey case on a case-action report with the remark "successful conclusion questionable."

Why did Shirkey go cold? Was he tipped off by someone in the Secretary of State's Office? Did the fact that Jech informed a supervisor at the McCook CDL facility that we were targeting an employee, Marion Seibel, somehow cause Shirkey to be tipped off? Did Shirkey feel Mary Beal did not fit the image of Seibel based on the information he obtained from his alleged mutual acquaintance, Chuck? We did not know. What we did know was that there seemed to be a repeated pattern of cases getting closed under questionable circumstances.

Sonneveld's routine assignment was more technical than mine. It also served a purpose deeply coveted by the corrupt organization headed by Ryan.

Ryan's organization was paranoid, much like the Richard Nixon presidency. Nixon's White House was filled with paranoia. Some members of his White House staff were afraid of their own boss. The thought that he might have them wiretapped or might have maintained files on them that would expose their not-so-perfect lives left them with the fear that it would cost them their prestigious careers. Others on the same staff were afraid that people out to get Nixon might be wiretapping them to get information on illegal or unethical conduct. Political enemies likewise might attempt to gain information to get a political advantage. If such wiretaps were being conducted on Nixon and his staff, the only ones being legally conducted would have been by the FBI, through authorization from the Justice Department based on probable cause. Bottom line was, Nixon and some members of his staff were committing crimes and covering them up, which gave them good reason to be paranoid.

George Ryan and his associates also were paranoid. During his tenure as Illinois secretary of state, he routinely had his executive offices electronically swept to determine if he and his staff were being bugged. In order to make these sweeps, Ryan relied on specially trained investigators from the Department of Inspector General. Although operating the electronic tools necessary to make the sweep requires only a small amount of training, the legal issues involved, including both criminal and civil, require officers carrying out such sweeps to have the advanced training and certification. Special Agent Mark Lipe was hired by Jim Redenbo, Secretary of State Jim Edgar's inspector general, because he was one of these specialists. Special Agent Sonneveld, hired under Ryan's reign, also had the training. If Ryan knew that this would add to his demise, both agents probably would never have gotten the job.

Under my command, agents routinely used body wires to make cases of bribery and official misconduct on corrupt SOS employees. Obtaining the court-ordered body wires and carrying out the electronic surveillance required us to have some officers with this training. All the special agents in the Department of Inspector General were elated when Redenbo hired Lipe and Ryan hired Sonneveld. Their employment gave the department two resources that improved on the investigative process. Ryan decided to use their specialties to protect him from the long arm of the law.

Ryan routinely used Lipe or Sonneveld to conduct the electronic sweeps of his offices. Another special agent, Elwyn Tatro, often accompanied them. Tatro was a former truck driver with some prior law enforcement experience with the Kankakee Sheriff's Office. He was Dean Bauer's buddy and had been hired to keep an eye on what were perceived as our renegade investigations. If any of the sweeps they performed uncovered planted bugs, Tatro would have immediately reported the information to Bauer, Chief of Staff Scott Fawell, General Counsel Roger Bickel, or possibly even Secretary George Ryan directly. I am not certain what would have happened next. By Illinois law, if a wiretap is uncovered, the officers performing the sweep are required to report it to the Illinois State Police. To the best of my knowledge, no bugs were discovered, so there was no need to advise the ISP. Both Lipe and Sonneveld told me they never located any bugs in the offices they swept. This does not mean that Tatro, acting on his own, might have found some type of electronic eavesdropping device in one of Ryan's offices and neither Lipe nor Sonneveld were ever told.

Why was Ryan looking for bugs? Who would be spying on him? Could it be Illinois Democrats? If they were conducting electronic eavesdropping on Ryan in his state facilities, they were breaking the law and could be both criminally charged and civilly sued. Likewise, the publicity fallout from discovering them placing bugs in the opponents offices would be damaging to their party for years. Ryan had to realize this.

Ryan was well aware of the unlawful actions in which his cronies were engaging. He encouraged it because it fattened his campaign fund. It also made him paranoid. It was not possible for the Illinois State Police to place the bugs. Illinois law does not allow for this type of evidence gathering. Besides, no local, county, or state law enforcement agency historically ever investigated a constitutionally elected government executive. If anybody would tap Ryan's conversations, it would be the FBI. Ryan was paranoid that the Feds were listening in on his conversations.

This presented an ethical dilemma for Lipe and Sonneveld. It was not illegal for them to sweep the offices for bugs. However, if they located a device, they would be inhibiting the FBI from conducting an official investigation. Reporting the eavesdropping device to Ryan or one of his cronies also might have been construed as obstruction of justice. By obeying orders, Tatro, Lipe, and Sonneveld potentially could have been charged with a federal crime. In order for the FBI to wiretap a conversation, they had to have probable cause and establish that a conversation was going to take place that involved a discussion of criminal conduct. They also had to show that they had exhausted all other means of gathering evidence.

Ryan made another big mistake. He had the agents carry out sweeps beyond his official state offices. Ryan used the agents of the Department of Inspector General to make a sweep of one of his political campaign offices. In the fall of 1994, Scott Fawell directed Bauer to have Tatro and Sonneveld conduct a sweep of Ryan's Rosemont campaign headquarters. Sonneveld had swept Secretary of State offices before, but this was the first time he was ordered to do a political office. Illinois law clearly prohibited using state workers or state time for political campaigns. All through Ryan's time as secretary of state, there were rumors of state employees making campaign-related calls from state telephones and on state time. This time, highly trained criminal investigators were being used to protect Ryan from a federal criminal investigation.

The sweep lasted approximately half a day, and no evidence of bugging devices was located. Sonneveld did all the work while Tatro stood by and watched. Susan Twiss, a close friend of Fawell, was also present. She was in charge of the office. Sonneveld felt she was arrogant because she refused to engage in friendly conversation. In retrospect, he believed her attitude might have been due to the fact she did not approve of the sweep or was afraid of being part of an illegal operation. Fawell eventually would testify that Twiss was an associate to whom he once gave a job at McPier, the regulatory agency for Navy Pier and McCormick Place. The job required no actual work.

Sonneveld told me that if he had discovered evidence of a wire in the Rosemont campaign office, he would not have reported it to any of Ryan's staff. He would have reported it to our friend at the U.S. Attorney's Office, Don Norton, or to the FBI. But Sonneveld never felt anyone would take all the criminal and civil risks to politically spy on Ryan. He always felt that it was an insurance policy if he appeared to be an eager-beaver employee, easily manipulated by Bauer and the others. At the same time, Sonneveld was taking copious mental notes in a Columbo fashion, thereby setting the trap for these fools.

The FBI's investigation into Ryan's campaign could not find evidence that the campaign paid the state back for Tatro's and Sonneveld's time and services. Sonneveld felt that he had been placed in an awful position by Bauer. He eventually would testify about the event.

Ryan was well aware that trained law enforcement officers were being used to search for bugging devices in both his official state offices and his campaign offices. He even conceded the sweeps were being conducted by saying it's "not unusual" and playing down their significance. However, when probed further by news reporters, he would never furnish specifics for his reasons in using the special agents to conduct the sweeps.

Sonneveld eventually told me that he thought Ryan's people were a bunch of Nixonian characters. He said, "They were so paranoid, stupid, and thought the spy stuff was for real." He described them as, "Amateurs at best, riding on the instant success power train."

Sonneveld told me that he approached the sweeps with "the team player attitude; the 'isn't this wonderful' attitude." He continued, "Doing all the technical stuff, and putting on a show until they left the room; isn't this great? Sometimes it was like being invisible, especially in Ryan's Chicago office. They'd let me in and they'd duck out. It was like, 'what's he doing there?' and 'I don't want to know' at the same time. I did Ryan's office in Chicago along with his conference room. I did it one time while he was there and with a civilian who I think now may have been Larry Warner (Ryan's co-defendant). Again I was there, but invisible."

The routine assignments we worked eventually became more obstruction of justice charges for Ryan. Now the abuse of state time and funds would be added to the growing heap.

CHAPTER 8

Death in Milwaukee, Obstruction in Illinois

Power does not corrupt. Fear corrupts...perhaps the fear of a loss of power.

—*John Steinbeck*

Between the time Ryan was sworn in as secretary of state and the spring of 1994, he asked for a sexual harassment investigation to go away, called off an interrogation subsequent to a fake license arrest, interfered in an investigation of theft of state monies, and used internal investigators to look for federal wiretaps in his campaign office. None of these were as serious as the obstruction of justice that occurred in November 1994.

I found it very difficult to sit down at my computer to begin to type the thoughts I had regarding the Rev. Scott Willis, Janet Willis, and their family. Every time I read the story of the Willis children and the tragic accident that occurred in Milwaukee in November 1994, I got a gut-wrenching pain. Whenever the Chicago TV news channels had a story about the George Ryan corruption case and showed a photograph of the deceased Willis children, I'd break down and cry.

Then I thought of Scott and Janet Willis and wondered what their pain was like. I'd ask myself, how is it possible that a parent can physically, emotionally, and spiritually survive an ordeal of this nature?

Any adult who has raised children must experience the same feeling I had. In the circle of life, children are not supposed to die before their parents. They are not supposed to die in an unjust and violent instant.

I was present at the birth of all three of my children. The experience of each birth is a distinct and unique image in my brain that I can recall at will. These bring me an overwhelming feeling of love. Throughout each of my kid's lives, there are similar experiences I recall that give me the same feelings. To no longer be able to hear their voices, not to be able to watch them grow into complete, magnificent human beings, and not to be able to keep those images in my thoughts are things I cannot fathom. Little League, first Holy Communions, proms, graduations, and Christmas mornings are part of the parent experience that most continue to have after a child's birth. On that awful day in Milwaukee, for Scott and Janet that ability with six of their children—Ben, Joe, Sam, Hank, Elizabeth, and Pete—ended. Despite what any other parents or I might feel about this tragic event, we could never feel what Scott and Janet Willis felt the day God took their children from them. Nor can we feel what they feel now.

Tears began to swell in my eyes. Images of the children flashed through my mind. I would get past this. Knowing the strength that Scott and Janet Willis possess would get me through this chapter. When one meets them, one sees that strength is the most obvious characteristic they possess. If you ask them, their strength comes from their faith in

God. I did not write this chapter to convert readers to believe what the Willises do or to promote the religion that they practice. I am writing the story about George Ryan's corruption because it is a story of human costs. Ryan was convicted of the crimes of mail fraud, tax evasion, and obstruction of justice. These are abstract concepts to many, especially the cynics. He denied knowledge of bribery and cover-ups. His defense lawyers called it business as usual, but the untimely deaths of children were the ultimate cost and what the George Ryan story of corruption is really about. This is something with which we can all identify. Scott and Janet Willis's family is the symbol of the human cost of the Ryan corruption.

Special Agents Dowdle, Sonneveld, and I investigated allegations of malfeasance within the Office of the Illinois Secretary of State under the reign of Ryan, beginning in 1991. Those malfeasances included theft, bribery, and official misconduct. During that time period, we began to notice there was a pattern of crime and corruption connected to the politics of the office. The pattern was that money taken or exchanged through those repeated acts of corruption was being directed to George Ryan's political campaign, known as Citizens for Ryan (CFR). Employees contributing to the campaign were rewarded with choice job assignments or promotions. This pattern of corruption was not new in the historical Illinois style of politics and patronage, but it appeared to be more blatant under Ryan.

Beginning in 1993, we began to investigate repeated allegations of specific employees taking bribes in exchange for commercial driver's licenses (CDLs). Individuals accepting those CDLs had the authority to drive complex tractor-trailer combinations weighing up to eighty thousand pounds and often carrying hazardous material across state highways.

The reason a majority of these illegal CDL applicants had to bribe a driver's license examiner was because they could neither read nor write English. On October 26, 1986, the United States Congress passed the Commercial Motor Vehicle Safety Act. This law requires each state to meet the same minimum standards for commercial driver licensing. The standards require truck drivers to get a CDL. The United States Department of Transportation's regulations require that commercial licensed drivers have a working knowledge of English. As a result, the CDL test was in the English language. The truck drivers behind the wheel of these vehicles of potential destruction must make decisions related to operating their rigs based on the ability to read and understand regulatory and warning signs in English. They must know how to operate the vehicle's air brakes and other safety features. They must understand double- and triple-trailer combinations and demonstrate that ability in a practical way. Hazardous materials are a special concern, and applicants have to explain what precautions they must take when transporting them. CDL applicants are required to conduct pre-trip inspections that include checking brakes, fluids, gauges, suspensions, tires, rims, lines, steering, lighting, and emergency equipment.

Unskilled workers with little or no knowledge of English sought out the occupation of truck driver. They had the false impression that a commercial driver was a low-skilled profession. On the contrary, the 1986 law required truck drivers to be highly skilled, with the ability to communicate those skills in English. The unskilled and non-English-speaking CDL applicants turned to bribery. The political savvy and greed of the Citizens for Ryan welcomed the bribery as an opportunity to fatten the war chest of its leader.

Marion Seibel was an assistant manager at the Office of the Secretary of State Commercial Driver's License testing facility located in McCook, Illinois. While Special Agents Sonneveld, Dowdle, and I investigated Secretary of State's Office employees' malfeasances, Marion Seibel became a suspect in several allegations. Sources alleged she accepted bribes in exchange for issuing CDLs to unqualified applicants. Simultaneously, while we conducted these investigations, Ricardo Guzman, unable to speak or read English, obtained a driver's license at the McCook location with Seibel's help.

Then, in November 1994, on Interstate 94 just outside of Milwaukee, Guzman was driving a tractor-trailer combination. In the pocket of his nylon jacket was a worn brown wallet containing the CDL he paid for with a bribe at the McCook facility. Earlier that evening, a devout Baptist minister from the Mount Greenwood neighborhood on Chicago's South Side said a prayer with his family. The prayer was said by the Willis family every time they set out on a trip in their van. They asked God to keep them safe.

That day, they were traveling to Wisconsin to visit relatives. Guzman's rig was equipped with a citizen's band radio, but he didn't understand the truckers speaking the truck-driving jargon coming through his speaker, or if he did, he chose to ignore it. It is a form of English unique to truck driving. However, when an emergency occurs the language becomes clearer and more precise. Hanging from the rig Guzman was driving was a loose metal mud flap-taillight assembly. The hanging assembly was seen by other truckers on the same route. Realizing it was a dangerous situation, they got on the CB to warn the unaware driver.

The metal assembly fell from the rig, and within seconds, a Plymouth Voyager van driven by the Rev. Scott Willis passed over it. The fallen metal object pierced the van's gas tank, resulting in it immediately bursting into flames. Sleeping in the back seats were Ben, Joe, Sam, Hank, Elizabeth, and Pete Willis. They were six of Scott and Janet Willis's nine children, ranging in age from six months to thirteen years. Instantly they became engulfed in flames.

Ben, the thirteen-year-old, escaped the inferno, running from the van with his clothes on fire. A passing motorist stopped and ran to Ben.

The motorist heroically placed his coat around the boy and got him to drop and roll.

Janet Willis was blown out of the vehicle and onto the asphalt. Scott Willis, fearing the worst, struggled to get free from his seat belt. Once free, he escaped the hellhole and turned back to see the flames that swallowed up his children. Despite the fact that he believed any attempt to save them was now futile, his paternal instincts kicked in. His arms were severely burned, rendering them useless, but he beat on the van's windows with his elbows, hoping that God would somehow intervene and end this nightmare.

His attempts were in vain. A Wisconsin trooper later told Mrs. Willis that the five children remaining in the van died instantly. What might have been an instant to the trooper would be an eternal memory for a mother. A medevac helicopter arrived on the scene. Ben was placed on a stretcher and carried to the chopper. Janet Willis walked beside the stretcher and looked into the eyes of the charred teenager she loved and barely recognized him. "I will bless the Lord at all times. His praise shall continually be in my mouth. Many are the afflictions of the righteous," she recited as her son was placed in the helicopter. It was the Thirty-fourth Psalm. Ben died a few hours later in the hospital. He reportedly was calm and without pain.

(The Willis Children, Christmas, 1993)

The next day, the Chicago news was filled with reports of the horrific accident. Coincidently, all the investigations we had up to that point went south. Informants no longer cooperated. Bosses closed cases prematurely. We were looking at three separate Secretary of State Commercial Driver's License testing facilities for allegations of selling licenses for bribes. I had boxes filled with CDL applications from the Chicago South facility stacked to the ceiling. Based on information from a variety of sources that unknown employees were selling the CDLs from that facility, I ordered the applications from the records in Springfield. When I had downtime between working regular cases, I reviewed the CDL applications to see if there was a commonality to the applications that appeared suspicious. Suspicious applications were those that might have had a driving school or other similar entity connected to the applicant. Commonality would be the same employees handling applicants from those entities. The inspector general, Dean Bauer, frequently complained about the mess the boxes of applications made in my office and demanded I get them out of there as soon as possible.

Sonneveld began to put a case together on Guzman. He contacted Yvonne Yard, our contact person for the SOS Driver Services Department in Springfield, to have Guzman's CDL application faxed to the Chicago office. Marion Seibel's initials were on the application authorizing Guzman's CDL. Sonneveld specifically had cases on Seibel at the McCook CDL facility that were closed by Bauer prematurely. Now the media was reporting on this tragic accident in Milwaukee and that Ricardo Guzman, the driver of the rig that caused the accident, might have obtained a CDL in Illinois illegally. I gave Sonneveld an article from the *Chicago Sun-Times* about the accident and allegations of bribery. No longer were our investigations about simple bribery and official misconduct. Our main suspect in the licenses for bribes investigation was up to her neck in a controversy that revolved around the deaths of six children.

Next, Sonneveld contacted the police in Milwaukee. He asked them if he could go up there and speak with Guzman. Sonneveld was told that Guzman did not speak English. He told them he could bring an officer from Illinois with him who would translate. Sonneveld was thinking of me, remembering that I knew some Spanish. He was told that they would welcome us to come speak with Guzman. The Milwaukee police faxed Sonneveld the accident report.

We needed to move on this fast before there were roadblocks and detours intentionally placed in our path. Special Agent Sonneveld immediately opened a case on Marion Seibel predicated on the issuance of Ricardo Guzman's commercial driver's license. Sonneveld then sat down with Bauer in Sonneveld's office. He presented Bauer with his case initiation report, Guzman's CDL application, the computer driver's license record, the *Sun-Times* article, and Milwaukee's accident report. Sonneveld explained to Bauer the necessity to open a case. Bauer abruptly grabbed the paperwork and left Sonneveld's office. Looking back, Sonneveld told me he believed Bauer left to make a telephone call. Bauer was indecisive and always checked with a higher-up like Roger Bickel, Scott Fawell, or Ryan himself before making a critical decision.

A short time later, Bauer returned to Sonneveld's office. Bauer always seemed grumpy to us. Sonneveld remembered that you could not reason with Bauer. If he disagreed with you, he would get frustrated. If you presented him with a series of logical facts, he would stop you and then base his decision on the fact that he was in charge and without offering an explanation. This time, Sonneveld described Bauer as more obstinate than usual. Dean Bauer reacted to Sonneveld's new case by stating, "Close the case and let the Milwaukee authorities handle it."

In April 1994, Chief Deputy Director Joe Jech had composed a memo directed to all the SOS IG agents. That memo mandated that agents not discuss any cases with outside agencies or interview witnesses without prior notification and permission from Jech or Bauer. Ryan's inspector general refused to allow Sonneveld to investigate all the allegations surrounding the issuance of Ricardo Guzman's illegal license. Based on

Jech's standing orders, both Bauer and Sonneveld knew that the Wisconsin authorities knew nothing of the corruption investigations because Sonneveld was not authorized to share that information with them. Furthermore, the Wisconsin authorities had no jurisdiction for the false driver's license application, bribery, official misconduct, and other related charges when those acts occurred in Illinois. All criminal cases on Guzman and Seibel connected to the bribes for CDLs and the horrific accident came to a halt as a result of Bauer's order. That order was made to protect his boss and friend, George Ryan. Bauer had to protect Ryan. Ryan wanted to be governor.

OFFICE OF THE SECRETARY OF STATE   DEPARTMENT OF THE INSPECTOR GENERAL
_____

4415 HARRISON ROAD, SUITE 230
Hillside, ILLINOIS 60162
(708) 449-2330

GEORGE H. RYAN
SECRETARY OF STATE

M E M O R A N D U M

TO   : All Special Agents
            Hillside

FROM   : Joseph Jech
            Chief Deputy

SUBJECT: Investigative Interviews and Referrals

DATE   : April 18, 1994

Until further notice:

1) Notify me before you interview any employee who is the subject of, or a witness in, any investigation;

2) Notify me before discussing the facts in a case with, or referring any case to, a States Attorney to obtain a prosecutive decision.

This procedure will reduce mis-communication and/or misunderstanding among all persons interested in the status of our investigations.

(Jech memo to IG staff)

OFFIC   E SECRETAR F STATE   DEPARTMENT OF POLICE

MEMORANDUM   OPERATIONS DIVISION

:   Director Giacomo A. Pecoraro   DATE: November 16, 1994

OM :   Chief Deputy Director Willie H. Thompson

SUBJECT: Ricardo Guzman   **CONFIDENTIAL**
            3224 W. Wabansia
            Chicago, IL
            DL# G255-7366-5213
            DOB 07/27/65
            SSN 549-65-4319

Director Dean Bauer, of the Inspector General's Office, called yesterday to advise that he is actively pursuing a case on the above individual. Guzman, while driving a tractor trailer truck in the State of Wisconsin sometime during last week, lost a portion or object of his load. The object struck a van, puncturing the gasoline tank, creating a fire and at such time, several individuals died. Director Bauer advises that there is a strong possibility that this individual obtained his CDL illegally.

Director Bauer requests that any information or inquiries regarding this individual, be forwarded to him immediately. At this time, Director Bauer also believes that the above individual obtained his CDL at the McCook Driver Facility, of which there is also an on-going internal investigation.

The above subject matter should be kept as confidential as possible.

WHT/da
cc: Dean Bauer
      Deputy Director Jerry LaGrow

(Police memo furhter identifying the Secretary of State's
office covering up an investigation)

After Bauer's intervention, Sonneveld, Dowdle, and I were con-

fused and angry. I knew before this, that in the case of the theft of money

from the Naperville driver's license facility, both Ryan and Bauer had committed an obstruction of justice. Proving it beyond a reasonable doubt was difficult. I did not know who to turn to without it affecting my job and my family. I discussed this with Sonneveld and Dowdle. We went into my office and closed the door. My office was the farthest away from Bauer's office and there was less of a chance that Ryan's buddy could hear what we were discussing. I was angry, and when I am angry, my voice gets indiscreetly louder. Dowdle didn't get louder but would talk more, and it didn't matter to whom he talked. Sonneveld was the soft-spoken one of our group. You could see the anxiety on his face and hear the frustration in his voice, but he remained soft-spoken. It was our duty to resolve this atrocity.

All three of us agreed that an obstruction of justice had been committed by Bauer and that there was a connection to Ryan. The kaffeeklatsches that were our bonding sessions in the past were now our daily brainstorming sessions. Was the obstruction intentional? Who could we trust? Could we do the investigation? If we did, were we insubordinate? How could this happen? Our bosses were not killers. They weren't mobsters or drug dealers.

The weeks, months, and years that followed helped us to better understand. Some people might say that there was no connection between George Ryan and the deaths of the Willis children. Some might say that the fact Guzman bribed an employee of the Illinois Secretary of State to obtain a commercial driver's license was not connected to the accident. Others might even think that Guzman was not responsible for the vehicular explosion that caused the tragedy. The really hard-hearted would say that Scott and Janet Willis needed to blame someone to ease their pain and make sense of all that occurred. The investigation was obstructed because of a lust for power. Power was Ryan's drug. Sonneveld, Dowdle, and I decided to go to the U.S. attorney. We knew that Scott and Janet Willis were entitled to a good faith investigation. Bauer and Ryan obstructed that process.

CHAPTER 9

Talking to the Feds

*There are no easy answers but there are simple answers.
We must have the courage to do what we know is morally
right.*

—Ronald Reagan

In November 1994, Russ Sonneveld and I made a decision to
report the cover-ups and obstructions to a prosecutor. We were unsure
of where to turn. There were several choices, but we were hesitant to
jump in blindly, risking that the information might leak and our careers
would be in jeopardy.

Normally, state, county, and local law enforcement report to the
county state's attorney based on the county where the crime occurred.
For example, a crime that is committed in Chicago is prosecuted in
Cook County criminal courts. This is what is referred to as jurisdiction,
the court that has the authority to try the case. The other legal term that
is often confused with jurisdiction is venue. That term refers to the court
that actually holds the trial. That is why you sometimes hear defense
lawyers asking for a change of venue. Usually that is based on an issue
like jury pool bias. It might be difficult to try the case in the jurisdiction
where the crime occurred because the extensive media coverage might
affect the defense's ability to find unbiased jurors from the jury pool.

There was talk at one time of changing the federal venue of George Ryan's case for this very reason.

One detail Sonneveld and I had to consider was the jurisdiction of where the corruption or multiple acts of corruption occurred. We had a theft of state funds from a Naperville facility in DuPage County. We had Bauer unlawfully hiding evidence from a case in Lake County and moving the tainted evidence to Cook and then Will counties. We had Bauer obstructing justice in Cook and Will counties, closing cases before they were properly investigated. We had Bauer and Ryan obstructing justice from both Sangamon and Kankakee counties via telephone in conversations with us in our Cook County homes. The state's attorney's offices in all the counties each had jurisdiction on some of the cases. Each of the state's attorneys in their respective counties was a Republican. State's attorneys are elected officials with loyalty to the political party they belong to.

Up to this point, most of the felonies Sonneveld and I investigated while assigned to the Department of Inspector General were prosecuted in Cook County. Even the Cook County State's Attorney, normally a Democrat, was Jack O'Malley, a Republican. In my opinion, O'Malley was a great prosecutor and we had several successful prosecutions by his Public Integrity Bureau. The bureau was led by a no-nonsense prosecutor named Patrick Quinn. Quinn was a former police officer who eventually became an assistant state's attorney and loved cops. In time, he was promoted and oversaw the special prosecution unit charged with trying cases against public employees. Quinn is a Democrat and currently an appellate court justice. He is not to be confused with the Democratic Lieutenant Governor Patrick Quinn, although they sat next to each other when taking the Illinois Bar exam many years ago. I liked Assistant State's Attorney Quinn a lot and trusted him as well, but Sonneveld and I did not trust everybody in the highly politicized Office of the Cook County State's Attorney. Quinn's boss, O'Malley, was not only a loyal Republican, it was rumored that he had his eye on the governor's office. We did not distrust O'Malley per se, but we did not want to take a chance with his and his allies' political loyalty. He certainly would not dare accuse Ryan or anyone in Ryan's camp of official misconduct. Besides, the Office of the Cook County State's Attorney almost never took on high-profile political corruption cases. The cases we took to the Public Integrity Bureau up to this point were low-level government employees, with no loyalty to George Ryan or his political organization. So we ruled out the Cook County State's Attorney's Office.

Since there were multiple county jurisdictions involved, another possibility was the Federal Bureau of Investigation. They had a public corruption unit and had a history of taking on powerful, big-shot public officials in cases like Operation Greylord. Sonneveld and I had recently worked with them on a couple of cases. One of those cases eventually became public and was known as Operation Silver Shovel. I, however, had a concern with the FBI's possible lack of interest based on a brief encounter I had with the Chicago special agent in charge, Bill Brennan, and his assistant special agent in charge, Ed Krause.

In January 1995, I was attending the Northern Illinois Chapter of the FBI National Academy Associates' monthly meeting. Since graduating from the National Academy in March 1991, I made it part of my routine to attend the monthly meetings. All the meetings were a combination of social gatherings and training. The meetings were also an opportunity to interface with other law enforcement officers in the area. They usually revolved around a meal and an hour-and-a-half training seminar on a contemporary criminal justice topic. The FBI referred to them as "monthly retrainers."

The January 1995 meeting was held at the once famous German Chicago restaurant and bierstube, Zum Deutschen Eck, located on Southport Avenue on the North Side. It was popular for its seven-course authentic German meals that included sauerbraten and spaetzle; beef tenderloin à la Deutsch with fresh mushrooms, green peppers, onions, shallots, and tomatoes; roast duckling with red cabbage; and my preference, wiener schnitzel. All that food was washed down with imported German beer. It was one of my favorite National Academy meetings, and a chance to eat some of the best food served in Chicagoland combined with cops telling war stories.

After the meeting and dinner, several members of the association, including me, would linger at the bierstube to drink more beer and socialize. I was stuffed from the rich Teutonic feast, but wanted one more beer to finish off the meal. As I walked over to the bar, I saw Brennan, the SAC, and Krause, the ASAC, leaning against it. I had never met Bill Brennan, but I knew Ed Krause. I met Krause at a 10K race in Springfield sponsored by the Illinois chapter of the FBI National Academy Associates. The race was one part of an annual state two-day conference. I was a runner then and ran four miles five times week. I never felt I was much of an athlete, and I have had a slight gut for many years despite the running, but I always did well with long-distance runs. Gary Kissinger, the FBI agent responsible for training in the Chicago office, finished first. I passed Ed Krause about two-thirds of the way into the race. I finished second and he finished third. On at least two other occasions since that race, Kissinger introduced me to Krause, stating I was the guy that beat him in the 10K race. Krause always acted as if he did not know me and never admitted that I had passed him. He had an athletic build and I think his big FBI ego would not allow him to recall that he had been beaten by a cop with a big gut.

Now standing at the Zum Deutschen Eck bar, ASAC Ed Krause did not remember me again. I ordered a beer and introduced myself to Krause and his boss, William Brennan. Brennan was a round-faced Irishman from Ohio. His looks and mannerisms fit in quite well with the

Chicago cop culture. Brennan asked me who I worked for and I told him the Secretary of State Department of Inspector General. He immediately responded with what I felt was a political rejoinder that put me on the defensive, "So you work for George Ryan!"

I tensed up. My heart began to race. My meal wanted to make its way back up to my throat. I replied, "No, I work for the people of the State of Illinois. George Ryan is a criminal." I launched into a diatribe that had been building up in me for months. I had no outlet until now, and it was my chance to tell a person who could do something about the corruption and obstruction that was going on. I told Brennan about the allegations of licenses for sale, theft of money for campaign donations, the premature closing of cases, and the deaths of the Willis children.

After regurgitating all I could remember that my brain would allow while trying to digest the huge meal and beer, Brennan's riposte to my diatribe was, "Well, good luck with that, then." He slapped me on the back as he and Krause walked away. I felt abandoned. The world's greatest law enforcement agency had just let me down.

Several months earlier, Sal Murcerino, a suspected associate of the Chicago Mob, came to the Department of Inspector General office in Hillside. He wanted to lodge a complaint against Secretary of State's Office employee Carl Catuara, the son of Jimmy "the Bomber" Catuara, an Al Capone associate and reputed hitman. Carl Catuara was the SOS Driver Services Department manager at the Chicago West Secretary of

State facility. Murcerino considered Carl Catuara an old friend. While visiting Catuara at the driver's license facility, Catuara introduced Murcerino to another associate, John Devito. Devito told Murcerino that he was starting a business and needed a loan. He asked if Murcerino would loan him the money. I don't remember the amount, but I know it was a five-figure number. Catuara agreed to cosign the loan on behalf of Devito. The paperwork was drawn up right then and there in the Secretary of State facility and all the parties signed.

Devito later defaulted on the loan and now Murcerino was suing Devito and Catuara. I know this isn't how mobsters usually work. You'd think that Murcerino would sick a couple of tough guys on Devito to collect gargantuan amounts of interest or break his legs. For some reason unknown to me, Murcerino was using Cook County chancery court. He was now advising us that Carl Catuara, an SOS employee, was a defendant in a lawsuit.

Although I was very familiar with Catuara and his reputation, the only wrongdoing I could see based on this complaint was the loan transaction occurred at a Secretary of State facility on state time, a violation of the employee policy. I personally worked a prior internal investigation on Catuara while Jim Edgar was the secretary of state. At that time, Catuara cosigned several loans at some Chicago area banks on behalf of John "Quarters" Boyle. Boyle bought Public Armor Car and had contracts with the Illinois State Toll Highway Authority and the Chicago West Secretary of State facility to pick up and transport cash revenues and then take them to the bank. Catuara was then Chicago West Vehicle Services manager. He drove to work in a brand-new Lincoln Continental equipped with a car phone, a true luxury item in the 1980s. The telephone and car both belonged to Public Armor Car. Catuara was also listed as a principal and employee of Public Armor Car, Inc. Since he was the facility manager and Public Armor Car held a state contract with the facility he managed, it was a conflict of interest and in violation of the state statute requiring state employees to report on an annual statement of economic interest any source of income from state contractors. He failed to report these and many other interests, including a large capital gain and a job with the Cook County Sheriff's Office as a weekend deputy under Republican Sheriff James O'Grady.

Violation of the state statute was a business offense punishable with a fine only. I worked the case for a year and a half getting Catuara to agree to give me five years of his federal income tax returns. The returns showed he failed to report all sorts of economic interests for those five years. I felt the series of violations was a felony, official misconduct. The Cook County State's Attorney and the Sangamon County State's Attorney both declined the felony. While all this was going on, the FBI and the FDIC were investigating John "Quarters" Boyle for losing three million dollars of federally insured money. Eventually, $1.5 million was recovered and Boyle was charged with federal crimes. I always believed the missing money was a juice payoff to Catuara for cosigning the banks loans. The banks would get their legal interest and Boyle would steal money to pay Catuara's juice. That was beyond my ability and resources to investigate. That was a job for the G-men.

I closed the case in June 1990 and Catuara did not receive Secretary of State's Office employee disciplinary action until October 1990. Edgar was running for governor and WGN-TV had a story of a minor scandal about Edgar. The story criticized Edgar for not taking action on Catuara for the conflict of interest. I did not tip the TV station, but my reports were quoted verbatim on the evening news. I figured somebody inside the Cook County State's Attorney's Office leaked it to WGN-TV. Edgar gave Catuara a ten-day suspension based on my year-and-a-half investigation after the scandal broke on the news.

Catuara always claimed that I forced him to declare bankruptcy. He also would jump against the wall and spread-eagle whenever he saw me walk into his facility on official business, which I did often. It was a big joke for everyone. I am sure they also knew that I would have taken great pleasure in arresting, searching, and cuffing Catuara.

Murcerino's complaint looked like another policy violation on the surface. Then I did what all experienced investigators do when initiating a new case: I ran the name of all the subjects involved through the National Crime Information Center (NCIC), a database of criminal arrests and convictions nationwide. It turned out John Devito was an alias used by John Christopher. Christopher had been convicted in a federal case involving fraud at the Cosmopolitan Bank in Chicago. Jerry Cosentino, a Democrat and George Ryan's first opponent for secretary of state, was also convicted in the same scandal. Now Christopher was apparently involved in another scam. Christopher obtained a first-time driver's license under the name John Devito at the Chicago West facility the same day he signed for the loan from Murcerino. Applying for the license using a fictitious name was a felony and Carl Catuara's name was all over the application, officially approving it. The initial complaint jumped from a violation of employee policy to a felony.

I next devised a plan. I would get an arrest warrant for Christopher, get his cooperation as an informant, have him introduce an undercover agent to Catuara, and have the undercover agent buy a fictitious license from Catuara while the agent was equipped with a recording device. Before I could follow through with this plan, there was a small hurdle to overcome. Inspector General Bauer frowned upon us arresting people who were not employees of the Secretary of State's Office. I figured since Christopher was a convicted felon and was facing another conviction with possible time in the slammer, I could flip him and use him as a snitch on Catuara. Before I did this, I decided to call the FBI agent that was the case agent on the Cosmopolitan Bank fraud case. I asked him if Christopher could be flipped, and if so, if he could be reliable.

He said he couldn't talk about Christopher, but he'd have another FBI agent get back to me.

About three weeks later, I received a call from FBI Special Agent Jim Davis of the public corruption squad. He said he understood I had a case on John Christopher and that I wanted to obtain a felony warrant for his arrest. Davis went on to say that he would like to meet with me and further discuss my investigation. He stated the FBI had a renewed interest in Christopher and discussion was pertinent to this interest. I sensed that whatever was going on with the FBI and John Christopher had to be big. The Chicago FBI office did not go after small fish in little ponds, especially the public corruption squad. Whatever it was, it had to be tied in with some big-time public officials, and somehow I stepped into it with Murcerino's complaint. I told Davis that I was concerned with him coming to the IG office. Dean Bauer and Joe Jech both could be present in the office, and anything Davis might discuss with me had a chance of being overheard and then leaked. He concurred, and we agreed to meet at a west suburban Burger King restaurant.

After the telephone conversation, I asked Russ Sonneveld to join me at the meeting. I wanted a witness. I believed most FBI agents' intentions were noble. I also believed that the FBI bureaucracy or a zealous agent could wreak havoc with my life. If they were working a big case, and if to make the case meant that my career or family got in the way, their priority would be their big case. I could lose my job or become financially wounded. An FBI agent once confirmed this concern. If Sonneveld was present at this meeting with Davis, then at least I would have a witness to all that was said.

Sonneveld and I arrived at the Burger King first and sat down at a table away from other patrons. Special Agent Davis arrived alone shortly after. He was tall, in good physical condition, and, like most G-men, was wearing a business suit. I introduced myself to Davis and then told him that I felt more comfortable having a partner with me than meeting alone. I then introduced Sonneveld. Davis without hesitation agreed to Sonneveld's presence. I was surprised by what happened next. I expected Davis to start grilling us for information. He was different from many federal agents. When you meet them, they are often aloof and only want to take information. They don't want to share. Sometimes their aloofness goes so far it makes you feel as though you are a suspect.

Davis was open and friendly. He told us he was working a case that involved some important public officials in the Cook County area. He then asked if I would wait to arrest John Christopher. Sonneveld and I both laughed. I told Davis that I probably would retire before the FBI completed their big Cook County public official case. I explained to him that Carl Catuara had long been a sought-after target of many law enforcement officers. He was believed to be organized crime's inside man at the Secretary of State's Office. He had clout with every elected secretary of state I had worked for, including the current one, George Ryan. Mary Catuara, Carl's wife, was a contributor to the Ryan campaign. Many in law enforcement believed that Carl Catuara supplied members of organized crime with driver's license and vehicle registration data to further their criminal enterprises. However, no one had ever put a criminal case on him until now. I had the case of a fictitious driver's license issued to John Christopher in the name of John Devito, and that license was issued by Catuara. Furthermore, if I worked Christopher as an undercover informant, I could get Catuara in a hand-to-hand buy of a fake license with an undercover cop.

Special Agent Davis laughed with us, then got serious and became sympathetic to our cause. He told us his father was a retired Detroit police officer who, like us, had graduated from the FBI National Academy. I don't remember if we told Davis we were FBI NA grads earlier in our conversation or if he had researched this before we met. Nevertheless, we were becoming simpatico during the course of the conversation. Davis, unlike many other FBI agents, held a special place in his heart for street cops like his dad, especially FBI NA grads. He told us he trusted us and he would tell us why he did not want us to immediately pursue the arrest of John Christopher, but we had to assure him we would not repeat it to anyone.

Sonneveld spoke up and told Davis we would agree only if we were protected by the U.S. Attorney's Office with a letter stating we were federal grand jury witnesses. Sonneveld said the letter must indicate we were officially allowed access to information on the investigation, but would prohibit us from discussing the Christopher case with anybody, including our own supervisors. This would later prove to be invaluable.

Davis agreed. He then stuck his neck way out. He told us that John Christopher was a federal informant on a case that involved several local politicians. If we arrested Christopher, it could blow the FBI's case. Davis said he did not know that Christopher had obtained the John Devito driver's license from Carl Catuara. Christopher was acting on his own without FBI authorization when he obtained his license. Davis promised that he would use Christopher as a snitch to get him to introduce an undercover FBI agent to buy a fictitious driver's license from Carl Catuara.

I was satisfied with this plan. Catuara would eventually be taken down, Sonneveld and I would be protected by the U.S. Attorney's Office, and the FBI would be able to snatch up more corrupt politicians. The FBI would take all the glory, but that was not an issue with either Sonneveld or me.

The big case in which John Christopher was the snitch hit the news a couple of years later and was called Operation Silver Shovel. Christopher was called the FBI's secret mole by the media. He arranged through bribes with City of Chicago aldermen illegal dumping in their respective wards. He also arranged an FBI's undercover purchase of a fake driver's license from Carl Catuara. Catuara was fired from the Secretary of State's Office when Operation Silver Shovel hit the news. However, he died of a heart attack before he could be prosecuted. Sonneveld and I met with Special Agent Jim Davis at the Chicago U.S. Attorney's Office, where we received a 6E letter, a document allowing us access to information on a federal grand jury investigation as well as prohibiting us from discussing the case.

We now had a new friend inside the public corruption squad of the FBI. We needed their assistance on a lead we had on Marion Seibel and the McCook commercial driver's license facility. Sonneveld developed a lead from a confidential source that Advance Driving School, located in the Chinatown section of Chicago, was bringing non-English-speaking commercial driver's license applicants to Marion Seibel in McCook. The informant alleged that Seibel was passing the applicants on the CDL exam in exchange for bribes. Advance Driving School was owned by Waitung "Tony" Chan and catered to Asian customers, mostly Chinese. Chan had a prior federal felony conviction. Several years earlier, IG Special Agent Pat Dowdle worked with investigators from the State Department on Chan. He had helped an illegal Chinese immigrant enter the United States through Miami, and then helped her obtain an Illinois driver's license. Dowdle testified in Miami on the case and Chan received probation.

We now needed an undercover cop that was Chinese and spoke Chinese. Sonneveld and I went to the Chicago FBI office to meet with Jim Davis and the public corruption squad supervisor. We told them we wanted to send an undercover cop into Advance Driving School to see if Chan would take the cop to McCook for an illegal commercial driver's license. It just so happened that the Chicago FBI had a rookie agent that was Asian and spoke the Cantonese dialect. The FBI, however, had a policy against rookie agents working undercover. They preferred their agents to have a few years of experience under their belts before sending them off to a covert assignment. Davis's supervisor was going to contact FBI headquarters to see if the agency's brass would make an exception for this situation. Several weeks passed, and they did make the exception. The covert agent made contact with Chan at the Chinatown school, but we were told that Chan refused to help him. We don't know if Chan was tipped off by one of our supervisors, Bauer or Jech. Both were aware of the Chan case because we opened a file based on the informant's information.

The undercover agent did not look like an immigrant, most of whom look tired and worn-out from their struggle in their homeland followed by their struggle in the United States. The Asian FBI agent looked like an FBI agent. It was obvious he worked out daily; he had a thick, muscular neck and an athletic build that showed through the FBI standard mode of dress, a dark suit with a tight-fitting jacket. It was possible that Chan did not buy the fact that the agent was an immigrant. The FBI agent's lack of experience and athletic looks might have raised Chan's suspicions.

Something concerned Sonneveld and me when we met with Davis in the squad room of the public integrity unit of the FBI. While Davis was introducing us to other members of the squad, one agent stuck out. I do not recall his real name, but the other agents in the squad room nicknamed him "Poindexter," an allusion to the nerdy kid in the television cartoon series *Felix the Cat*. The agent was short and wore thick horn-rims and a crew cut. When Davis introduced us to him, he popped out of his chair and announced that he had an excellent source in the Secretary of State's Office named Roger Bickel—who, of course, was George Ryan's legal counsel and confidante. Rumors among Secretary of State's Office employees were that Ryan and Bickel were so close that Bickel was actually Ryan's illegitimate son. That was never substantiated, although I thought Bickel and Ryan had some similar physical attributes. After meeting Agent Poindexter and his spontaneous announcement of his relationship with Bickel, I was leery of discussing any IG case with the FBI.

FICE OF THE SECRETARY OF STATE

MEMORANDUM

TO: Dean R. Bauer   DATE: March 16, 1994
             Inspector General

FROM: Russell B. Sonneveld

SUBJECT: Information

This is to inform you of an ongoing investigation of a case assigned to me and the involvement of the FBI in the investigation. The case subject is MARION V. SEIBEL, Manager, McCook CDL Facility.

At present, there are two open cases on Seibel. One involves the Advanced Driving School owned and operated by a Chinese man named Waitung Chan aka Tony Chan. The other involves an individual named John Traynor, a truck driver whose driving rights were suspended.

Both cases involve allegations of bribe payments to Seibel for the issuance of CDL's for unqualified person(s) or with new identities.

Attempts were made to interview Traynor, however, he is represented by counsel and refused to make a statement.

When initially arrested Traynor said he obtained his new CDL through a third party, Gonzolo Mendoza. Mendoza is alleged to have paid Seibel several hundred dollars for Traynor's CDL.

Mendoza has been subsequently identified as working for Nighthawk Trucking, 3900 W. 41st St., Chicago, IL, (312)523-9038.

The case involving Chan alleges Chan is making bribe payments to Seibel for issuing CDL's to unqualified Chinese citizens and non citizens. This case appears to be the best route to conduct an undercover investigation. The reason being all applicants are Oriental and speak little or no English. Chan and Seibel administer an oral exam with one or both providing the answers. Business can be safely transacted in front of the applicant.

I have requested the assistance of the FBI's Asian Task Force to pursue contacting Chan. Myself and Ed Hammer have met with the FBI several times since mid-December, 1993 to formulate a plan of action and proceed accordingly.

(Memo from Sonneveld to Bauer regarding licenses for bribes)

Russ Sonneveld and I had an old and trusted friend in the U.S. Attorney's Office. Don Norton was a retired Illinois State Police captain, a retired U.S. Army Reserve colonel, and was now an investigator with the U.S. Attorney's Office. He had the reputation for being a hard-nosed straight shooter. Weeks after the tragic accident in Milwaukee, we discussed our options. We had to go to someone and report the obstructions. Norton was the only option. We trusted him. He was a man who would help us do the right thing.

In January 1995, Norton met with Russ and me at the Marquette Inn, a downtown Chicago restaurant near the Dirksen Building. We discussed the cover-ups, bribes, and cronyism. Norton prepared a one-page memo summarizing what we knew and what we suspected. He arranged for me to meet with the then U.S. Attorney Jim Burns's first assistant in charge of public corruption, Scott Mendeloff. I considered myself a professional law enforcement officer that was bringing evidence of a crime to a prosecutor, but Mendeloff treated me like some street snitch and did nothing with the information I provided.

(Norton honoring Hammer at his retirement)

The meeting started off friendly enough. Mendeloff had some music compact discs stacked on his desk. One was by 10,000 Maniacs, a musical group that I appreciated. I mentioned to Mendeloff our common taste in music. He responded with a halfhearted smile and a grunt. I then mentioned to him that I was concerned about my career and afraid that someone in power might retaliate against me for talking to a prosecutor about the corruption, I didn't want to be fired and lose my means of support for my family. My two oldest kids were in grade school and my youngest was a toddler. Being a cop was the only thing I had done for the last seventeen years. At that time, I didn't care whether someone was prosecuted or not. I was not going to get caught up in these cover-ups and allow some federal agent or prosecutor to question why I did not take any action.

However, I did not want the information to leak out for political reasons and have the exposure come back to haunt me. Jim Burns was the Chicago U.S. Attorney then, and he had his eye on the governor's office. With his hands on this information, he could generate a scandal against Ryan and boost his chances of a Democrat retaking the governor's office. If Burns used this information for political gain, I would be hurt by the wrath of Ryan.

Mendeloff became angry. He showed no concern for me. He made me feel like a snitch, not a cop that was living by his oath. He snarled at me, "Look, you came to me with this shit. You don't want to tell me, then leave and live with the consequences. Or tell me what you know and deal with it."

I felt nervous and sick to my stomach. Who could I turn to? This was the last place I felt I could go. It was the right thing to do to expose George Ryan and his organization of corruption, but how was this going to impact me? More importantly, what would it do to my family? I had to talk. It was the end of the line.

I told Mendeloff everything I knew and some stuff I suspected. I talked about the theft of state funds from the Naperville Driver Services facility and how the money was earmarked for a George Ryan fund-raiser. I told him how I believed James "Pate" Philip, the top DuPage Republican who was the state senate president, called Ryan about the theft and how Ryan then spoke to Sonneveld on the telephone. I told him about the underage lingerie models getting driver's licenses from a Ryan crony. I told him how every time we got close on a bribe for a commercial driver's license case, somehow the case always went cold. I told him how Dean Bauer ordered all these cases closed before we were able to follow up on all the leads. I told him how I suspected that Ryan broke property leases because the landlord refused to donate to Ryan's campaign fund, and how his buddies got leases that returned big profits, some of which went to Ryan or his campaign. I told him that I had a case of drug dealers locked up in the Federal Metropolitan Correctional Center that could identify a Secretary of State's Office employee that sold them vehicle registration information. I described how I had a case of a Secretary of State's Office employee that was selling personal driver's license abstracts to an insurance company with a West Side organized crime boss who was acting as the broker. I explained how all these cases were ordered closed prematurely by the bosses of Ryan's Department of Inspector General.

We concluded the meeting cordially, but without any guarantee of a follow-up. The ball was now in the U.S. attorney's court.

Nothing was done for three years. In that three-year time period, despite all the corruption, George Ryan got himself elected governor.

About a year after the gubernatorial election and after the Feds finally started an investigation, a *Chicago Tribune* article written by Gary Marx quoted Mendeloff on why he never acted on my information. Mendeloff said, "I thought it was piddly..." Of course, the ellipses at the end of the *Tribune* quote probably meant he said "piddly shit." I wanted to ask Mendeloff if "piddly shit" was a legal term he learned at Georgetown University Law Center, where he earned his juris doctor.

I did call Gary Marx that evening and asked him if he ever spoke to any of the other prosecutors I had dealt with in the past. I assured him that if he had, they never would have said I brought them piddly shit cases.

Mendeloff allegedly never reported the information to Jim Burns, his boss. State campaign records, however, show that Mendeloff financially backed Burns's Democrat primary bid for governor. I thought this was odd; you'd think that in the dog-eat-dog political environment of Illinois, Jim Burns would have wanted to take advantage of the information on Ryan's corruption. The corruption story was more valuable than a campaign contribution of cash. Besides, to investigate my tips was simply the right thing to do. The fact that they did not shows either extreme neglect or outright incompetence. It demonstrates how a prosecutor that wanted to be governor dropped the ball in addressing perhaps Illinois' biggest political scandal.

The irony is that Jim Burns is currently Secretary of State Jesse White's number-one corruption buster, the inspector general. Mendeloff is currently with the politically connected law firm of Sidley and Austin. The firm's Web site lists his areas of specialty as internal investigations, government contracts civil and criminal, and RICO and fraud practice. He is also an executive board member of the Chicago Crime Commission. Their mission statement is: "The Chicago Crime Commission is a non-partisan, not-for-profit organization of civic leaders committed to improving the quality of public safety and justice." Mr. Mendeloff fumbled the ball in 1995. The federal investigation into Ryan called Operation Safe Road began in 1998. He left the U.S. Attorney's Office in 1997.

CHAPTER 10

Politics, a Favor, and More Obstruction

*The accomplice to the crime of corruption is frequently
our own indifference.*

—Bess Myerson, former Miss America

Sometime around December 1994, there was rumor going around
the Hillside, Illinois, office (the Chicago area office) of the Department
of Inspector General that the office was being moved. The Hillside office was the northern Illinois headquarters for the Department of Inspector General staff and the Springfield office was the headquarters for the
southern Illinois staff. Dean Bauer and Joe Jech maintained space at
both headquarters. Both of them preferred working in Hillside. Bauer
lived in Kankakee. Jech lived in Naperville. The commute to Springfield would have been at least three hours for either one. The commute
to Hillside was no more than an hour and a half.

In December 1987, when I first started with the Department of
Inspector General, our northern Illinois office was located in the Hillside Shopping Mall. It was accessed from a loading dock and did not
look very professional. I often joked that it reminded me of the 1960s
TV comedy series *Get Smart*, where the secret agents' access to their
headquarters was made clandestinely though a dry cleaner's storefront.

In 1990, Jim Redenbo asked me to look for a new office. I looked at four locations: LaGrange, Countryside, Bridgeview, and Hillside. I showed all four locations to Jim Redenbo and Jim Burke, and both liked the new Hillside location. It was roughly one-eighth of a mile from the mall office, but was in a professional office building that housed doctors, lawyers, brokers, and a variety of other professional businesses.

With input from all the staff, we designed the office layout, including separate offices for each agent, a conference room, an employee kitchen, and a reception area. Now we looked like respectable professionals. At the previous office, we had only four telephone lines. Two were for telephone calls, one was a dedicated fax line, and one was a computer telephone line to access the Law Enforcement Aid Data System and the National Crime Information Computer networks, the databases police officers use to run driver's licenses, license plates, and criminal histories. In the new location, each agent had his own telephone line that included voice mail, and there were two additional office lines. I arranged for the mover, and with the help of my secretary, the relocation went very smoothly. I was personally proud of our new workplace.

When George Ryan appointed Ron Gibbs as his first inspector general, Gibbs only maintained an office in Springfield. When Spencer Leak, the deputy director, was appointed, he immediately took over the conference room in Hillside and made it his oversized personal office. When Bauer and Jech took over, Jech moved into Leak's space and Bauer took a smaller office that was vacant. I think Bauer took the smaller room because his main office was supposed to be Springfield, and Hillside was only a satellite workplace for him.

Then, in the fall of 1994, the rumors started. Ronnie Swanson, the son of former state senator Ron Swanson Sr., a lobbyist and one of Ryan's closest friends, worked in the Office of the Secretary of State Physical Services Department. Physical Services was responsible for managing and maintaining property, both owned and leased. Ron came to the Hillside IG office with an unknown person. Together they walked around and the unknown wrote down information. Ronnie told me that he was getting estimates to paint the office. To me, something did not seem right. Later I realized that the unknown person was not making notes about painting estimates; he was making notes about moving costs.

When a state agency signs a lease, there is always an escape clause that allows the lease to be broken. That clause basically states that if the government runs out of funds to pay for leased property, it can break the contract and vacate the premises. I had a gut feeling that what was really going on in the fall of 1994 was representatives from the Physical Services Department went to the property owners of the Hillside office with their hands out for a donation to the George Ryan campaign. When the property owners refused to contribute, the lease was broken. Later, in 1995, I passed on this concern to the U.S. Attorney's Office.

Dean Bauer abruptly asked Russ Sonneveld and me if we had seen the new Joliet office. There were no memos. There were no meetings. There were no instructions. Bauer, at that time, did not even tell us the address. Later in the week, we were conducting an investigation in the Joliet area. With a limited amount of information, we deduced the new office location at 605 Maple Road. Having the new address, I contacted Jack Townsend, an Illinois State Police master sergeant and commander of a Will County organized crime task force. I asked Townsend if he could determine who owned the property in Joliet that the Secretary of State's Office was about to lease. Townsend got back to me with a photocopy of a title held by a trust for which Larry Warner was the trustee. Warner was a Chicago businessman and friend of Ryan. Warner would also eventually be named as George Ryan's co-defendant in a federal indictment.

We moved in early 1995 into the Joliet facility, an old office building once owned by the EJ&E Railroad and now linked to Warner. The facility was two floors. The Department of Inspector General staff occupied half the top floor. The other half was occupied by the Secretary of State Police Auto Theft Investigation Unit. The bottom floor was occupied by the Department of Administrative Hearings and included an employee lunchroom.

The building was remodeled for our use, but it was old and still lacked many modern necessities. One was handicapped access. I brought that to Bauer's attention, and he barked back at me that there was no need because we would not have any handicapped visitors. In other words, Bauer was saying we would not have handicapped suspects, witnesses, attorneys, or employees. The Hearing Department held hearings for drivers charged with driving while intoxicated, and apparently Bauer believed none of them or their lawyers would be handicapped. I pointed out to him that the likelihood of a DUI driver being handicapped might be rare, but was still possible, and that it was very likely that an attorney representing a driver could be handicapped. Besides, handicapped access was federal law. Two weeks later, handicapped parking spaces were placed in the parking lot and there was a wheelchair route that required a person to travel halfway around the building before he could enter it. The entrance was into the employee lunchroom and appeared quite cumbersome to me.

Another concern was the building's water. It smelled like rotten eggs and always had a brown tint when the faucets were first turned on. The building had been built in the 1930s, and I was concerned about lead and asbestos. I believe one of the Auto Theft investigators complained to Deputy Police Chief Jerry LaGrow. He arranged for a bottled water vendor and Bauer was livid about it. We had no building manager, but I guess Bauer felt all building decisions had to go through him.

You'd think he would have been more concerned with the fact that his employees needed healthy drinking water.

I do not recall ever meeting our building's landlord, Warner. The twenty-two-count federal indictment against him contended that Warner concealed the ownership of our Joliet office. His profit from its lease from 1995 to 1999, while Ryan was secretary of state, was $387,500. In total, Warner made approximately three million dollars from contracts and leases acquired through Ryan.

All in all the purpose of the new office was to profit one of George Ryan's biggest contributors and eventually filter some of that money into Ryan's twenty-million-dollar campaign fund for governor. There was little concern for employees or citizens that used the facility.

In March 1995, Deputy Director Joe Jech resigned. All the staff was aware that he met with Scott Fawell the day he resigned. He later returned to the Joliet office and met with some of the Department of Inspector General agents individually. Jech called me into his office and told me he had just resigned. Then, in what may have been a rare moment of morality, he cautioned me. He told me to be careful because the politicians that ran the office were looking for a reason to get rid of the Department of Inspector General. I never trusted Jech before and I took his caution lightly. I felt he was up to something and had an ulterior motive for warning me. All the same, I continued my responsibilities, the principal one being rooting out corruption.

On a Sunday afternoon in the spring of 1995, I received a call from an Orland Park police detective. He had two females in custody. They were attempting to pass stolen checks at the Orland Square Mall Marshall Field's. They had fictitious driver's licenses matching the names on the stolen checks. The detective asked if I would be interested in coming over to the station to interview the defendants and specifically to question them on how they obtained the fake licenses. I was more than anxious. Based on preliminary information furnished by the detective, I was certain the driver's licenses were obtained at the Chicago Charles Chew facility at Ninety-ninth and King Drive. Special Agent Dowdle had previously developed information on a new employee at that facility and the detective's case fit the modus operandi.

There were two black females in custody: a middle-aged, heavy-set woman and a nineteen-year-old kid. I interviewed the older woman first. She was a hard woman and streetwise. She would not give an inch and refused to discuss the source of the fake driver's licenses with me. The teenage girl was much different. Despite the crime for which she was being accused, she had a naivety about her. She agreed that in exchange for her cooperation I would discuss with the state's attorney leniency for her. She said her partner set her up through an associate with a worker at the Charles Chew facility whom she paid one hundred dollars for the fictitious license. Her partner's associate was fencing the merchandise purchased with the stolen checks.

I asked her if she could go back to the Charles Chew facility and buy another license without going through her partner or her partner's associate. She said she thought she could. I then asked if she could introduce a companion when she went back, with the intent that the companion would also buy a fake license. She said she thought she could do that too, but the companion had to be black.

Since Orland Park Police had started the case, I inquired if they would be interested in continuing with it by assisting in the undercover operation I was planning. Orland Park is a village in the southwest suburbs of Chicago; its population is more than 90 percent Caucasian. I was delighted to hear they recently had hired Nathaniel Motton, an African American patrol officer. I was also delighted to hear that Chief McCarthy had temporarily assigned him to assist the SOS IG in an undercover investigation to purchase a fictitious driver's license for a bribe. We planned to go in on the undercover deal by Tuesday.

That Sunday evening, after some serious contemplation, I fulfilled my next job requirement. I called Inspector General Dean Bauer at home and briefed him on the case. He seemed concerned that the undercover operation was already planned out. He asked if I had contacted anyone within the Cook County State's Attorney's Office and briefed them. I told him no. Actually, I recalled Joe Jech's memo one year earlier ordering us not to contact the state's attorney's office without clearing it with him or Bauer first. Doing so would have been violating a direct order. Jech had told me the order was so the secretary would not be embarrassed by our actions. I found the order insulting and the Secretary of State's Office embarrassing. I, however, was definitely walking on thin ice at this point and was not going to get fired over this issue. Bauer then ordered me not to tell anyone at the Cook County State's Attorney's Office and to go ahead and complete our undercover deal.

On that Tuesday, Orland Park Officer Motton—supported by four detectives, Dowdle, and myself—set out for the Charles Chew facility with our informant. Motton was to go inside the driver's license facility with the informant. Once inside, the informant would introduce Motton to the Secretary of State's Office employee and request a fictitious identification card for both Motton and herself. The price for each card was one hundred dollars. The employee would have to get both the officer and the informant through all the stages of the application process, including the photograph and actual issuance. This was to be done under the watchful eyes of other SOS employees and their various supervisors.

That Tuesday afternoon, the nineteen-year-old female and the Orland Park patrol officer each purchased a fictitious Illinois Identification Card for one hundred dollars from a black male Secretary of State Driver Services Department employee at the Chicago Charles Chew facility. The felonies of accepting a bribe, conspiracy to make false application for a state ID card, and official misconduct were consummated.

The standard operating procedure for this type of undercover case would then be to contact the state's attorney having jurisdiction to approve obtaining a consensual overhear order, which we would use for one or two more deals. The purpose of the order was to negate all chances of reasonable doubt on the part of our target by engaging him in incriminating conversation while making the undercover transaction. After the undercover buy, I again briefed Bauer and he again ordered me to hold off contacting the Cook County State's Attorney's Office.

Early the next Thursday morning, Pat Dowdle and I were told that the black male employee at the Charles Chew facility had been fired. He was a probationary employee and they did not need a reason to let him go. Dowdle and I were livid. First and foremost, by their thoughtless action, they now had exposed the nineteen-year-old female as an informant. Her life was in danger. I later called her. She was in tears and afraid that she was going to be killed. Second, after an undercover case of the one employee was completed it possibly could lead to the exposure of other corrupt employees. Third, the arrest of the one employee and possibly others also could lead to a major stolen check and fencing operation. Inevitably, these types of operations when worked through to fruition net massive results, with multiple arrests and the recovery of thousands of dollars' worth of merchandise.

Dowdle and I both decided to let Bauer have it. I went first. After entering his office, I told him how the decision to terminate the

216

employee might lead to the death of our source. He didn't seem to care. Then I told him how the chief of police of Orland Park, Tim McCarthy, was a national hero as the U.S. Secret Service Agent shot while protecting former President Ronald Reagan. I told Bauer that Ryan missed an opportunity to have a joint press release on television with Tim McCarthy by not allowing us to follow through with the case. Certainly if we had been allowed to continue, the stolen check and fencing operation would have been exposed by the Orland Park detectives, and both the OPPD and the SOS IG could have shared the glory. Of course, it would have been Chief McCarthy and Secretary Ryan in front of the TV cameras. Ryan wanted to be governor and this would have been an awesome public relations opportunity. To Bauer, Ryan's buddy, it didn't seem to matter.

I left and Dowdle entered. He told Bauer he still wanted to arrest the Charles Chew employee. Bauer told Dowdle no. Dowdle asked Ryan's inspector general why not. Bauer answered that Cook County State's Attorney Jack O'Malley had his eye on the Illinois governor's mansion and they did not want to give any positive press to O'Malley, a possible primary opponent to Ryan. Bauer's lack of interest in the Orland Park case now made sense. In summary, it was politics before justice.

CHAPTER 11

The Biggest Obstruction of Justice

Rather than love, than money, than fame, give me truth.

—Henry David Thoreau

Deputy Director Joe Jech had hinted that the Department of the Inspector General might disband. By April 1995, there were other clues that this was going to happen. Elwyn Tatro, Dean Bauer's confidant, stopped coming to work in April. In the typical Bauer fashion, there was no announcement about Tatro leaving. There wasn't even any office rumor. He just wasn't there anymore. It always baffled me that Bauer believed he could keep things like office relocation and employee re-assignments a secret from us, and that somehow that protected Ryan. To determine Tatro's employment status meant checking the personnel records on the Secretary of State Office's computer, standard operating procedure for IG agents. Sonneveld and I checked together. The record not only indicated he was transferred to the Driver Services Department, but he had received a pay raise. He was no longer a special agent. His new job title was executive. I suspected he was transferred to protect him from what was about to occur.

On May 31, 1995, the entire Joliet staff of the Department of Inspector General attended a seminar at the Hillside Holiday Inn across the street from the old IG headquarters prior to our Joliet move. I don't recall specifically what the seminar was about, but I believe it was about driver's license security features. I also seem to recall there were people from other agencies and businesses attending. We occasionally received training on the job and infrequently we were sent to outside seminars. On this particular day, it seemed different. There were some Springfield staff members at this, but not all. Mark Lipe was there, and he seemed particularly nervous. He told us at the break he heard that some people were being fired from the Department of Inspector General. Those in the IG allocated from the SOS Police would be reassigned to the SOS Police. All others, sworn agents and support, were to be terminated. Lipe told me that he believed I was going to be placed in charge of the SOS Police Northern Illinois Auto Theft Investigation Section. It actually sounded like an assignment I would like. However, I was very suspicious of Ryan's administration.

On June 1, 1995, the next morning, I learned that George Ryan had dissolved the Department of Inspector General, effective immediately. No official reason was given. He kept his longtime, loyal buddy Dean Bauer on as the inspector general. All the agents that were not SOS Police officers, like Russ Sonneveld and Mark Lipe, were fired. All the agents like me, who were SOS Police, were sent back to the SOS Police Department at our last rank there. I was going back as a sergeant. That was a demotion.

My suspicions from the night before proved to be right. While we were all attending the Hillside workshop, several SOS Police supervisors were being briefed on a coup that was about to take place. They were instructed that the IG's office was being dissolved and several people were being fired. This was to take place the next day, June 1, and they were to be at the Joliet office for security purposes. I guess that because IG agents were sworn police officers and carried 9 mm semi-automatics, they figured that these honest career cops would go postal. Also, some regime-trusted individuals were assigned to rifle through individual desks to determine if IG agents were keeping any files that would incriminate Bauer, Ryan, Fawell, Bickel, or other Ryan cronies in any crimes against the public trust.

As expected, employees of the Department of Inspector General were greeted by Inspector General Dean Bauer, SOS Police Chief Deputy Director Jerry LaGrow, Assistant General Counsel Rob Powers, and an assortment of sergeants and lieutenants from the SOS Police. Each of the IG employees was ordered in the IG's conference room one by one. About seven people went before me. The one I remember the most was JoAnn Robertson. She was in tears. They told her she was fired with thirty days compensation pay. The same news was conveyed to Carolyn Miller. There was no explanation of why their jobs were being cut. The agents who were assigned to the IG from the Department of Police were terminated from their special agent positions and reassigned to their previous rank with the SOS Police. Some agents were actually making less in the IG and returning to their old rank. That meant under the FOP union contract they would get raises. Those affected by this were Murphy, Gilman, and Richter, all the agents that remained silent while the obstructions and corruption were occurring right under their noses.

Pat Dowdle would move up a rank. When he was assigned to the IG under the Jim Edgar administration, he was a sergeant with the SOS Police. At that time, he was home on a job-related disability when he was ordered to return to work. The on-the-job injury he had incurred made it impossible for him to pass the mandatory SOS Police physical fitness test. As a compromise, they assigned him to the IG as a Special Agent I, a payroll equivalent to an SOS Police investigator, a demotion. Now, with this Department of Inspector General purge, they were reassigning him to the SOS Police as a sergeant. I believe they were anticipating that when it was his turn to take the annual fitness test, he would fail, thus beginning the disciplinary steps that would eventually lead to Dowdle's termination. Fortunately for Dowdle, this never happened, and he was able to retire sometime later, combining his Cook County Sheriff and SOS Police retirement plans.

Those special agents who were never employed by the SOS Police were let go. The equivalent purge was occurring simultaneously in the Springfield office of the IG. Mark Lipe was able to transfer to the SOS Police in a non-sworn administrative position answering to Jack

Pecoraro, the chief. Lipe knew we were on a sinking ship and was able to make arrangements before the purge. Robert Vasconcelles was able to secure a job the next day with the Illinois Department of Central Management Services. The way I interpret Vasconcelles's incredible ability to get a new politically connected state job immediately after being let go from another state job was that he was part of the behind-the-scenes conspiracy to purge the IG and was better able to land on his feet. After all, he was like a cat silently stalking its prey in the dark of night.

Likewise, the members of the Springfield support staff were able to land on their feet by immediately obtaining new state jobs. Barb Shultz, Dean Bauer's Springfield administrative assistant, was married to a man that had strong ties with Jim Edgar. Nobody in Springfield, other than Mark Lipe, was considered unfriendly or disloyal to the George Ryan administration. Therefore, if they were advised in advance of the dissolution of the IG's office, Barb Shultz could help them and herself prepare for it.

I was not so well prepared. My only advance notice was Mark Lipe's rumor the day before. I was called into the conference room to be told by Jerry LaGrow that he had both good news and bads news. He said that Ryan was no longer in need of my services as a Special Agent III. That alone actually could have been both the bad and good news. LaGrow went on to say that the good news was the SOS Police would take me back as a sergeant if I would agree to sign off on a demotion.

It would not be a loss in pay or benefits, but my pay range for future increases would drop. I was to be assigned as the junior sergeant to the Northern Illinois Auto Theft Squad, answering to the senior sergeant and a longtime nemesis, Dennis Serafini. My thoughts as I signed the demotion form were, *Thank you, God, I still have a job*. I could support my family and do what I love doing, being a cop. Mark Lipe was only half right about the rumor.

OFFICE OF THE SECRETARY OF STATE

DEPARTMENT OF POLICE
BUDGET & RESOURCE
MANAGEMENT DIVISION

MEMORANDUM

DATE: June 14, 1995

TO   :   Sgt. Edward Hammer

FROM   :   Mary Kuruc, Administrator

SUBJECT: Voluntary Reduction

Per your request, this memorandum is to clarify that effective June 1, 1995, you accepted a voluntary reduction position with the Department of Police as an Investigator-Sergeant. This reduction was accepted in lieu of receiving a layoff as a result of the abolishment of the Department of Inspector General.

_____ _____
Signature   Date

MK:td

cc: Personnel File

(Hammer's demotion memo)

The person most hurt by this purge was Russ Sonneveld. He was on vacation at the time and would not get the bad news until he returned.

I called him that evening and told him what was happening. We were both pretty certain he would be fired. Later in the George Ryan federal trial for corruption, evidence would be introduced by the prosecution that Scott Fawell, Ryan's chief of staff, prepared a memo planning the dissolution of the Department of Inspector General. In the memo, Fawell told Ryan that they needed to get rid of certain investigators. Fawell's memo said, "we need...someone in there who won't screw our friends, won't ask about fund-raising tickets."

When Sonneveld returned from his vacation, he was fired from his position of special agent. Sonneveld was the number-one investigator they wanted to dump. Mark Lipe, Pat Dowdle, and I were close seconds. Sonneveld had had incriminating conversations with both Bauer and Ryan. Sonneveld, Dowdle, and I had routinely asked questions about fund-raising while conducting investigations. We did it because, historically, it was the most common denominator in bribery cases within the Office of the Secretary of State. What Ryan did on June 1 was the biggest obstruction of justice he had done so far. It was clear to me then that he was going down eventually. The Department of Justice would eventually charge him for this obstruction.

Later that same day, an assistant general counsel for Ryan, Rob Powers, had me sign an affidavit stating that I did not hold any property belonging to the Secretary of State Department of Inspector General, including any official reports or files. I signed the affidavit but told

Powers that when the U.S. Attorney's Office went after this office that he, Powers, could wipe his ass with that affidavit. I later learned Sonneveld said the exact same words to Bauer when told he was fired. Eventually George Ryan's own chief of staff and campaign manager testified against Ryan about this obstruction. I wonder now if Rob Powers has had a chance to use that affidavit yet.

Shortly after I signed the affidavit, Sgt. Dennis Serafini, supervisor of the Auto Theft Squad, entered my office. I was packing up my personal property to move down the hall. He had a snotty look on his face, like he had a bad case of colitis and it was my fault. He asked me if I understood the game plan. Game plan is a cliché that pushes my buttons.

I replied in a sarcastic tone that I did not understand and asked if he could explain it to me. He said he would be in charge and I would answer to him. Serafini then asked if there was a problem with that. I answered, "Yes, there is a problem with that. I am smarter than you, I am better educated than you, I am better trained than you, and I am a better supervisor than you." I wanted to say I was also better looking, but felt that was carrying it too far. I thought the sergeant was going to cry. He ran out of the office and practically dragged Deputy Chief LaGrow back. LaGrow angrily asked me if I had said all those things. I proudly told him that I had. He asked why I thought I could talk to Serafini that way. I told him because it was true, and asked why Serafini thought he could come into my office with such a piss-poor attitude. In his mind,

I'll bet LaGrow was laughing but frustrated. Nevertheless, he told me that I was to answer to Serafini.

Despite the fact that George Ryan, Dean Bauer, and Scott Fawell obstructed justice on June 1, 1995, by disbanding the law enforcement arm that was responsible for investigating crimes committed by Secretary of State's Office employees, Ryan still needed the function of internal investigation. He only wanted to get rid of Russ Sonneveld, Pat Dowdle, and me because we attempted to complete our investigations. Doing so uncovered crimes committed by people loyal to the Ryan political organization. Loyalty meant they gave Ryan or his campaign organization money and gifts. What Ryan and the others did not realize was misconduct allegations against employees did not go away simply because they sent us away.

People who care about right and wrong get involved. Good citizens, other law enforcement agencies, honest employees, and even police informants continued to contact the Office of the Secretary of State with information about employee misconduct. Likewise, there was a record of the previous cases worked by the dismissed staff. What Ryan needed was a new staff that would do a dog and pony show. They could go through the motions of investigating the complaints, then shut down the case for a lack of evidence. Not aggressively pursuing leads would be the unwritten policy they would operate under.

By July 1995, the secretaries who were fired were brought back. First JoAnn Robertson was reassigned as Dean Bauer's secretary at the

Joliet office. If there still was an inspector general responsible for internal investigations, he should have a secretary. Carolyn Miller wasn't brought back at the same time. As I mentioned in an earlier chapter, I believe Bauer is a racist. Carolyn Miller is African American, and Bauer barely acknowledged she even existed. Once Robertson was brought back, someone had to realize that Ryan and the Office of the Secretary of State could be facing a complaint to the U.S. Equal Employment Opportunity Commission or a lawsuit for race discrimination.

Ryan didn't want that kind of publicity. Miller was rehired and assigned to be the Auto Theft Investigation Unit's secretary in Joliet. Both women were honest, loyal employees. It was unfair to let them go in the first place. Neither was investigating misconduct by Ryan's cronies. They were responsible for typing reports, filing, and answering telephones. They did not openly discuss any concerns with outsiders. They did their jobs. Their unfortunate firing on June 1 was peripheral damage as a result of cages being rattled by Sonneveld, Dowdle, and me.

One of the first attempts to fix the dilemma of the pending cases was to review the cases that remained opened. I was now assigned to the Auto Theft squad headquartered in the same Joliet building in which the dissolved Department of Inspector General office was located. On the other side of the same floor was where my new assignment was located. The Department of Inspector General agents' offices were empty. Dean Bauer, however, remained in his office. Even though the Department

228

of Inspector General was dissolved, the position of inspector general remained intact, and Bauer was still that person. The change moved the position and job title of inspector general to the Secretary of State Police under the police department's chief, Jack Pecoraro. Apparently Fawell, Ryan's chief of staff, felt that Bauer was not capable on his own to watch over Ryan's reputation. Pecoraro was needed to carefully watch Bauer. This was made evident by the ensuing review by the police department's chief deputy.

In midsummer of 1995, I was contacted by telephone by the SOS Deputy Police Chief Jerry LaGrow. He was coming up from Springfield to discuss some issues with me. I was not told what the issues were, which made me apprehensive about the meeting, but this was typical of LaGrow's style. He wanted 100 percent control of all meetings with his subordinates. Allowing me to know what the meeting was about beforehand would give some control to me.

The day we met, he ordered me to come to the conference room on the Department of Inspector General side of the building. When I entered the room, LaGrow was sitting at the conference table writing on a yellow legal pad. Stacked to the right of him on the table was a pile of russet file folders. They were the IG cases that remained opened on and after June 1, 1995. LaGrow was a touch friendlier than when I saw him last, the day I was demoted. It put me at ease, but I suspected he needed something. He told me to sit down right in front of him. He then reached for the first case on top of the pile. It was a case assigned to Special Agent Frank Murphy. I do not recall what the case was about, but I do remember LaGrow asked me to tell him what I knew about Murphy's case.

I knew nothing about it. When I was in charge of the IG's Chicago office under former Secretary of State Jim Edgar, I knew details of all the cases the agents under my command were working. I prepared a monthly summary for Jim Redenbo, my boss and Edgar's inspector general. The summary on each case included a synopsis, what progress had been made over the last thirty days, and if we were encountering any difficulties on the case. Even if I could not recall specific details on a particular case if questioned by Redenbo, I could always refer to any of the monthly summaries, all of which I kept in one spiral notebook. This was a practice I learned when I was assigned to the auto theft task force with the State Police. I brought it with me when I was promoted and assigned to the SOS Department of Inspector General. Redenbo always seemed impressed with it. Preparing and saving the monthly summaries was the first supervisory routine ordered stopped and taken away from me when Ryan's people took over in early 1991. By 1995, I was no longer supervising and I had no idea what Special Agent Murphy had been working—nor, for that matter, what any of the IG agents had been working, other than Sonneveld and Dowdle.

I told LaGrow I did not know about Murphy's case. He continued, acting surprised that I did not know about other agents' cases.

I wondered if he was under the assumption that I was still supervising them. Did he not know that the inspector general and his chief deputy stopped that several years earlier? The next file was Special Agent Richter's case and the one after that was Special Agent Gilman's. The entire pile was cases worked by other agents. LaGrow asked me about each one. I was confused. He didn't realize that although I was a Special Agent III, the highest-ranking agent in the IG, I had not supervised any agents since 1991. Dean Bauer and Joe Jech took all that away from me.

I told him the only cases I knew any details on were those assigned to me. Nevertheless, he asked about all of them and my answer was always the same. I now believe LaGrow was part of this corrupt regime and he was only pumping me to see how much I knew about the whole operation that would be damaging to Ryan so he could report back to Pecoraro or Fawell. Then, if necessary, they could take action to protect George Ryan. Besides, Bauer was in charge of the cases. He should have known all the details LaGrow was asking for.

The very last case in the pile was the only case that was opened in my name. It was the Carl Catuara and John Christopher case, also known as the federal Operation Silver Shovel case. I could not discuss it with LaGrow or I'd be held in contempt of a federal grand jury. I had to dance around LaGrow. What I told him was true; I did not lie. I said, "It is an FBI case and they've got something big going on. I don't know much more. You know how it is. The FBI doesn't tell you much. They asked me to back off. So I stopped working it and was waiting for them to give me the green light to start up again."

I purposely left out an extremely important detail. I did not tell LaGrow that John Christopher was the FBI's snitch. He nodded and agreed with what I had just told him. I was relieved. I wanted the FBI to make their big case. FBI Agent Jim Davis promised they would get Catuara. Also, other corrupt public officials were going down. I was hoping George Ryan was one. The meeting with LaGrow was finished. He did thank me and shook my hand. I left the conference room with even less respect for the man than I might have had before.

The oddest thing was that he only asked me about that one case assigned to me. There were several others. One in particular involved a man convicted of drunk driving. He had been arrested by the Oakbrook Terrace Police Department for another DUI, but this time he had a whole new driver's license. I tracked the application back to discover that Russell Nisavaco was the SOS Driver Services Department employee responsible for issuing the new fictitious driver's license. Nisavaco was the manager at the Naperville facility whom Sonneveld and I had investigated for the theft of money from that facility. That is the case Sonneveld had the telephone conversation about with George Ryan. I was just beginning to gather information on this new fictitious license case when the Department of

Inspector General was officially dissolved by George Ryan and Scott Fawell. This new case, along with many others, was not being worked.

I believe that Scott Fawell and George Ryan would have preferred to fire Pat Dowdle and me like they did Sonneveld. It would have been the Machiavellian thing to do. I also believe they had their legal eagles and political advisors research this idea before the June 1, 1995, IG purge and decided it was too risky. They probably believed that they would be facing very public lawsuits, since I had an eighteen-year untarnished record as a Secretary of State Police officer and Dowdle had twenty-four years. Lawsuits would lead to further exposure in the press of their fund-raising schemes and thereby cost Ryan his ultimate prize, the governor's office. And they were right. I always knew that I was doing my job as an internal investigator both lawfully and ethically. I did not want to have to go through costly litigation to regain my job. But if I was fired, I would have to sue to get my job and pay back. This would not only be costly, it would also take a long time. If I was fired and had to sue, I knew that a jury would be sympathetic. Nevertheless, the impact to my family would have been devastating. I was ever so thankful to God for not allowing that to happen.

So Ryan and his co-conspirators went to Plan B. They placed Pat Dowdle and me in positions where we were closely watched by paranoid supervisors. That meant to the administration that we would not be investigating any case that involved Secretary of State's Office employee misconduct.

Despite Fawell and Ryan's attempt to rid the Department of Inspector General of agents that would "screw our friends," the corruption continued for another three years, and so did the investigations.

CHAPTER 12

Internal Investigations after the Big Obstruction

*Is this (corruption) systemic, or is it an anomaly? I don't
really know the answer.*
—Patrick Collins, former Assistant U.S. Attorney

After the June 1, 1995, Department of Inspector General dissolution, I was assigned as the junior sergeant in a SOSPD Auto Theft
Investigation Unit. Under Sgt. Dennis Serafini, I was instructed that I
was not to do any supervisory work over the investigators in the unit.
Like the rank-and-file investigators, I was given a caseload. Basically,
we were handling two types of cases. Our historical priority was auto
theft investigations. Those cases were predicated upon leads generated
in discrepancies discovered in the vehicle titling and registering application process. For example, an individual would apply for an Illinois
vehicle title using counterfeit or altered documents. Another example
might be that the vehicle registration database contained duplicate vehicle identification numbers (VIN), meaning one person owned the car
while another possessed a car with a false VIN or serial number.

A new type of case we were working involved underage drinkers
caught with fake IDs. SOS employees trained licensed liquor establishments to spot fake IDs, collect them, and turn the fakes over to the SOS
Police. Investigators were assigned cases to locate the underage drinkers

and interview them to obtain an admission or proof that they had used the seized fake document to purchase alcoholic beverages. Sometimes the fake license contained the true names of the underage drinkers. We had to go to their homes and talk to them. Some of the cases included notes from a bar employee or a short report that included a signed statement from the violator. The statement might include an admission, as well as the source of the fake identification. The source could be an older brother, sister, or a school friend. We would then verify the information in the statement.

On a few occasions, we would get a fake license that did not match a real person's name. An employee at a liquor establishment might have seized the fake but failed to get details from the violator. We would then go through the computer driver's license records for common denominators on the fake identification to match with a real person, such as name, address, date of birth, and Social Security number. If we found a close match, we then checked with the local police department and looked in high school yearbooks to see if the face on the fake identification matched a yearbook photograph. If the completed investigation established the proof, the underage drinker's Illinois driver's license was suspended for one year.

An interesting part of these assignments was the parent reaction. About half of the parents were angered with their teenagers for violating a serious law. Under the State of Illinois Dram Shop Act, an underage person using fake identification is subject to a one-year suspension of his or her driver's license. The Illinois Vehicle Code made possessing another person's license or a fictitious license punishable by up to a year in jail. Possessing a counterfeit or homemade license could mean more than one year in a state penitentiary. The SOSPD was not in the business of sending teenagers trying to buy a six-pack of beer to prison, but the violation of any of these statutes was most certainly worthy of an administrative sanction like suspending one's driving privileges.

The other half of the parents reacted with anger toward the police. They often made excuses for their kids. I remember one mother in Wilmette. I drove up the driveway to a home that was worth almost one million dollars. The driveway was a semicircle and at least one hundred fifty feet long. The girl I was there to question was seventeen years old. Her fake identification was seized by an employee at the famous Chicago hangout the Crow Bar. The mother answered the door. I identified myself to her, simultaneously showing her my police credentials. I then stated my purpose and asked for her daughter. She said her daughter was only seventeen. I explained to her that, under Illinois law, her daughter was an adult and I could arrest and charge her with a crime, but all I wanted to do was confirm some information.

The mother became flustered and began to ridicule me. First, she stated that of course her daughter had a fake ID; most of her daughter's friends were twenty-one and older. Having the fake ID was the only way her daughter could hang out with those friends. Second, she began to dress me down for coming to her house on a very holy day. She told me it was Rosh Hashanah and they were having guests, and she pointed to the dining room. The room was obviously set for a dinner party of at least sixteen people. I had no idea that it was a Jewish holiday and apologized. The seventeen-year-old came down a staircase and identified herself to me. With some discourse from the mother, the teenager agreed to go out to the driveway and discuss the matter of the fake license with me without her mother's involvement.

I confronted her with the physical evidence, a fake ID with her photo. She admitted to purchasing the fake ID from a friend and using it at the Crow Bar. I advised her that I was submitting a report that would result in a twelve-month suspension of her driving privileges. She and I went back in the house, where she told her mother of the driving sanctions with tears in her eyes. Again her mother began to dress me down for bringing this horrific news to her on a holy day, finishing with the fact that her husband was an attorney and would look into the matter. I told her that was her daughter's right if she chose and left the premises.

Although I was trained by the FBI National Academy, the best law enforcement executive school, at the expense of the U.S. taxpayer, I was being used for the routine work of a rank-and-file SOS cop. Don't get me wrong, I enjoyed the assignments and accepted the fact that I was doing a police service, but all the years of leadership training and experience were going to waste.

The main purpose of keeping me busy and happy with these types of assignments was to keep me away from the continuous corruption taking place. What they couldn't stop were the contacts I had with other agencies' investigators and confidential sources. Investigators from other law enforcement agencies still called me from time to time, advising me on information that might develop into a lead on a bribery case. Confidential sources likewise remained in contact with me. They had a variety of reasons to give me information on corrupt employees. Money, revenge, and competition were among them. When the source's information was reliable, it usually meant a successful apprehension.

I was contacted by a reliable source who had given me information on a Secretary of State's Office employee in the Ford City driver's license facility accepting bribes. The source was motivated by competition. The source owned and operated a driving school. The employee he was describing was getting unlawful identification cards for customers of a competitor driving school. If the SOS employee was to be busted, so would the source's competitor. Without advising the senior sergeant, Serafini, I obtained the details from the informant at his place of business. Later the same day, I wrote up a report identifying the informant only as an undocumented confidential source. I sent my report up the chain of command to Sergeant Serafini.

The next day Sergeant Serafini called me into his office. He was the type of supervisor who only called you into his office to chew you out. He never complimented his people for a good job and always focused on the negative. Our conversation began with negativity. He immediately wanted to know who the source was. The source was not a paid informant, so I was not required to write a report containing his identifiers. The SOS Police policy only required us to open a confidential source file if the source was paid from state funds. I also felt there was no need to reveal the name of the source in an investigative report because the information he furnished was not crucial enough to result in probable cause to make an arrest or obtain a search warrant. The information was simply intelligence, or at best, a lead, meaning it directed the police to conduct an investigation of alleged illegal activity. It did not establish a reason to believe that a crime had been committed or was about to be committed. Nor did it establish a reason to believe that specific evidence of a crime existed at a specific location. Once the information was obtained, it was up to me or some other investigator to gather more information through routine, overt, or covert investigative procedures then establish probable cause to make an arrest. If the source was able to establish probable cause coming out of the gate, then I would have had to identify him in a report or affidavit.

I was apprehensive about telling Serafini the source's name. I never believed Serafini was a dishonest cop. He did, however, have a side job as a cashier at one of the Illinois racetracks. Rumor around the office was that it takes a Chicago Mob connection to get that job. I never witnessed or had knowledge of Serafini committing malfeasance. Nor did I believe he would have wittingly participated in criminal activity. I did, however, believe he would do whatever he was ordered to do by his supervisors, without question. He could always rationalize that there was no illegal activity involved because the order came from above him in the chain of command, and none of our bosses were criminals. Unlike Serafini, I did not trust some of the bosses, especially in light of what was occurring under the boss of bosses, George Ryan. I did not want to tell Serafini the source's name.

There is an unwritten code that you protect your sources from retaliation by those that are impacted by the source's revelations. You do this by not identifying them. If, perchance, that source is revealed in a court procedure, then he might become a protected witness. The only law enforcement agency that truly protects witnesses is the U. S. Marshals Service. Those usually are big, organized-crime federal cases, not something as inconsequential as a snitch ratting on a driver's license clerk for taking fifty-dollar bribes. However, retaliation in the form of threats related to the source's license or business could be the least of the types of retaliation on my source. Not revealing the source's identity to co-workers, supervisors, or prosecutors would be a way to prevent retaliation. Since it is an unwritten code, it is not binding. It is viewed by some as a matter of ethics. To reveal the name of a confidential source to your supervisor meant you blindly trusted him. In this situation, there was a multitude of factors I had to consider.

I was certain Serafini was instructed to report back to Deputy Chief Jerry LaGrow any activity on my part that might indicate I was conducting a corruption investigation. Information supplied by a confidential source of a driver's license examiner accepting bribes would definitely fit into that category. A corrupt administration would most definitely have needed to identify the confidential source and quash the investigation before it reached higher levels, especially if the bribe money was flowing to the top. Another consideration was that Sergeant Serafini was my immediate supervisor. That meant he could order me to reveal the source's name. If I refused, he could charge me with insubordination and I would be fired.

I had to decide if this informant and the information he had furnished was that important. The source owned and operated a Hispanic driving school. There were several in the Chicago area, and they were highly competitive with each other. It was also well documented that these schools often resorted to bribing the Secretary of State's Office employees to get the schools' clients their driver's licenses. The school owners would tell authorities that the competing schools were involved in these bribery schemes. More often than not, the school owner doing the snitching was engaged in a similar bribery scheme and was attempting to eliminate the competition. The practice of ratting on one's competition has been around as long as the world's oldest profession, and it neither meant the information was reliable or unreliable. It was the cops' job to find out. Finally, did the confidential source care if I used his name in a report or identified him to my supervisor? The source unquestionably did not want me to discuss the matter with people outside my law enforcement network, but reporting to my supervisor was standard operating procedure.

After searching my conscience and ego, I came to the conclusion that the main reason I might not want to reveal the confidential source's identity was to challenge Sergeant Serafini's self-perceived authority. He would get angry, probably call Deputy Chief LaGrow on the telephone, and whine that I would not do what I was being told. LaGrow then would direct Serafini to write me up for insubordination. I did not have a plan on how far I would take this battle, so I decided it was not worth it. If I was going to get fired, it had to be over something much more substantial. I hated playing into Serafini's little power trip, but what followed was more revealing.

What happened after I identified to Serafini the driving school owner as the confidential source with information on a driver's examiner accepting bribes is that he promptly attempted to assign the case to another investigator. Investigator Ross Finnelly was a ten-year veteran of the SOS Police. At that time, he had worked in plainclothes under

Serafini's direction for about six years. He came from a family of cops. His father and brother were both police officers. Finnelly was unable to obtain a job as a police officer with some of the departments for which he applied because his left arm was slightly deformed. However, it did not interfere with his passing the state required physical fitness test; likewise, it did not interfere with his job performance. Therefore, the SOS Police hired him despite the deformity.

I admired him for not letting this minor handicap prevent him from being a cop. He was brash, with a hard-ass attitude, always saying something to bust someone's balls. Serafini liked that in him because he, too, often tried to bust balls. They were two peas in a pod. They had a love-hate relationship, but Finnelly was ten times the cop Serafini was. Finnelly liked short-term cases. He wanted nothing to do with cases that took too much time to investigate and resolve. Gather some conclusive information in three days or less and make an arrest was his style. He avoided any investigations that involved long periods of time or complex concepts.

Finnelly immediately spoke with resistance upon getting the employee bribery investigation. He did not want to do it and began arguing with Serafini. He told the sergeant that the case should be worked by me since it was my confidential source, and he should be responsible for following his own leads. "You catch, you clean 'em," Finnelly said, using the metaphor often used by police referring to catching smelly fish.

Serafini and Finnelly bantered back and forth for the next ten minutes. Finnelly had sound arguments. He said he had no rapport with the snitch but I did. He stated that he would have to re-interview the source and duplicate the work I had already done. Serafini had no comebacks, other than he was the boss and he was ordering it.

I finally stopped the exchange. I said to Serafini, "I know why you want to take this case away from me and give it to Finnelly. You have been ordered by Deputy Chief Jerry LaGrow to keep me away from all Secretary of State internal investigations."

Serafini looked like a deer caught in headlights. Then his expression relaxed and he smirked. Along with the smirk came an affirmative nod. The Ryan administration wanted to keep me away from all investigations that in any way connected them to corruption or could publicly embarrass them. They dissolved the arm responsible for investigating corruption, thereby summarily ending the attempt by honest cops to root out corruption. Internal investigations were still handled, but none was being self-generated by any rank-and-file investigators or special agents. Instead, they were being carefully screened by SOS Police Chief Jack Pecoraro, Deputy Chief Jerry LaGrow, or the remaining inspector general, Dean Bauer. From there, the cases were assigned to a carefully selected investigator whom they hoped would not dig into the deep, underlying reasons for bribery. Of course, those reasons were that the monies were going to the Ryan campaign. Most investigators did not have the wherewithal to follow through with that deep of an investigation. It could cost them a career. Ryan already proved that with the firing of Special Agent Sonneveld.

I told Serafini it didn't matter to me that Finnelly was getting the case. I knew that enough incidents of corruption already had occurred and been documented, and Ryan's house of cards would eventually fall. I also knew Ryan and his cronies were greedy SOBs. They wanted money and power. If I worked one more case, it would not make a difference. Their greed would blind them to their vulnerability, and they would get caught. Finnelly took the case without further argument. He probably figured he would close the case as unsubstantiated in three days or less.

Now, internal investigation cases were opened and assigned to SOS Police investigators. The investigators answered to Dean Bauer when working the cases. My friend Keith Lake was one of those investigators. In particular, employees from the McCook facility were complaining about the open and blatant bribery occurring at their facility. Tammy Raynor and Tony Berlin were two of the whistle-blowers. Over the next several years, several Office of the Secretary of State employees were described by the media as whistle-blowers. I too was described as one. The term does not fit me. I was a police investigator whose job was to gather evidence of a crime and take that evidence to a prosecutor. In particular, my responsibility was to investigate public corruption inside the Office of the Secretary of State. I did not blow the whistle on anyone in particular. I took evidence of corruption to the United States attorney. Reporting corruption to the authorities was neither Raynor's nor Berlin's responsibility. By Illinois statute, a state employee is technically obligated to report bribery to a prosecutor if he or she is aware of it, but it rarely happens. Raynor and Berlin were taking risks by reporting the briberies they observed internally to investigators that reported to Dean Bauer. They were doing the right thing, but they were facing retaliation from their bosses and the Ryan political organization.

Investigator Keith Lake was assigned the cases generated by Raynor and Berlin. They both took notes and maintained diaries of dates, times, and applicant names of those who bribed McCook facility employees for commercial driver's licenses. All this continued to occur after the 1994 election that got Ryan his second term as secretary of state. All these briberies continued despite the news and adverse publicity for Ryan that followed the Milwaukee accident that resulted in the deaths of the six Willis children. All this corruption continued despite the Chicago news media identifying Ricardo Guzman as the truck driver that caused the accident, the truck driver who obtained his CDL from McCook.

As a matter of fact, Raynor and Berlin named Marion Seibel, their supervisor, as one of the people taking the bribes. Sonneveld and I worked cases on her that were closed by Dean Bauer. Sonneveld identified Seibel as the person issuing Guzman the CDL, and Bauer stopped that investigation. Yet she continued to take bribes with all that heat around her. The whistle-blowers also identified George Velasco, the McCook facility manager, as another participant in the licenses for bribes scheme. They reported the bribery to Bauer. Nothing got done. They eventually went to their political sponsors, the Internal Revenue Service, and the FBI. Raynor and Berlin would not let it go.

Berlin first saw bribes for licenses in 1985, six years before Ryan became secretary of state. Berlin worked at the Niles Driver Services Department facility then. He saw applicants put money in magazines and leave them on the front seat of their vehicles when they took the driver's road test. Or they left money in the ashtray or in a cigarette pack. Berlin also reported that he was pressured to buy campaign fund-raiser tickets. The culture of corruption was ingrained into the Office of the Secretary of State's system.

By 1990, Berlin was working at the new McCook CDL facility. It was the same scam, but now it was more serious. The licenses being sold were going to unqualified truck drivers who would get behind the wheels of eighty-thousand-pound rigs, some carrying hazardous materials. Money was passed to a middleman, usually an employee of a trucking company or a driving school. Berlin reported that McCook's manager once told the facility workers at a meeting that there was "nothing wrong with taking a couple bucks here and there."

Berlin, a Vietnam veteran, tried to follow the chain of command. He reported the corruption to the Office of the Secretary of State's inspector general. The corruption continued. In 1996, he went to the IRS and the FBI. He told them that Illinois Department of Transportation workers were receiving bribes in exchange for illegally providing IDOT vehicles to be used for CDL road tests at McCook. He also reported that despite the fact that CDL applicants were failing tests, they were getting their CDLs. Berlin even speculated that Ricardo Guzman, the truck driver responsible for the Wisconsin fatal crash, received his CDL at McCook through bribery.

Tammy Raynor, Berlin's co-worker, was simultaneously complaining to the McCook facility bosses about bribery. In 1996, she alleged that a customer asked her to whom he should give the money in order to pass his CDL test. Raynor called for Marion Seibel, the assistant manager. Seibel only badgered Raynor for complaining. That same night, George Velasco, the McCook manager, called Raynor at home. Later Mark Sniegowski, Velasco's boss, also called. Sniegowski reported the allegation to the inspector general. The problem with this was that it was Sniegowski's political job as zone manager to distribute George Ryan fund-raiser tickets to the facilities' managers, like Velasco. How those tickets were paid for was not a concern to zone managers. They only had to get them distributed to the next person down the chain of the political hierarchy.

It became routine for Investigator Lake to interview Raynor and Berlin. They became frustrated because nothing was being done. Lake uncovered a fictitious license that Seibel issued herself using an alias. He believed he finally had a felony for which she could be criminally charged: false application for a driver's license. I remember how excited Lake was. He showed me the evidence he had, including the application Seibel signed to get her fake license. I warned Lake then that Bauer or another Ryan crony would stop the investigation. By now, George Ryan had replaced Roger Bickel, his longtime confidant and general counsel, with a new general counsel, Diane Ford. Both Ford and the assistant general counsel, Rob Powers, ordered Investigator Lake not to present the felony case to the Cook County State's Attorney's Office for prosecution. Despite a new general counsel, the pattern was being repeated.

Raynor eventually met with Bauer. Nothing was done. She was even physically attacked by Seibel on her lunch break at a restaurant near the facility. Raynor did not report the fight to the police, but Seibel did, resulting in Raynor's arrest for assault. Raynor's mother was a staunch Republican. She personally, on her daughter's behalf, submitted a letter about the continued corruption to Lura Lynn Ryan, George Ryan's wife. Raynor was transferred so she would not cause any more trouble. The Ryan people—Dean Bauer, Diane Ford, and Lura Lynn Ryan—let the corruption continue.

SOS Police Investigator Debbie Thompson was from the Springfield office and was assigned to work the internal complaints for the inspector general. She eventually was brought to McCook CDL facility to work undercover. She was brought in as a newly hired employee and worked under the supervision of the two biggest bribery suspects, Marion Seibel and Velasco. Her cover was quickly blown. One day George Velasco approached Thompson and told her he had heard from the downtown office that she had been placed in the facility as an undercover cop to spy. I don't know what member of the Ryan teamed warned Velasco and compromised Investigator Thompson's undercover assignment, but it seemed that the honest people inside the office needed help from the outside to fight off the pervasive culture of corruption nurtured by the Ryan people.

By late 1995 or early 1996, I do not remember exactly when, certain former agents were being brought back to the Department of Inspector General. Elwyn Tatro was assigned to the Driver Services Department to do facility inspections about two months prior to the June dissolution of the Department of Inspector General. Now, around a year later, he was brought back. Dan Gilman, who worked as Tatro's partner prior to Tatro's spring 1994 reassignment to the SOS Driver Services Department, returned to the Department of Inspector General as a special agent. Former Special Agent Frank Murphy was also brought back, but now he was made a deputy director, Joe Jech's old position.

Deputy director positions are given only to those with powerful political clout. I can only assume, since he was a loyal DuPage County Republican, that someone from the DuPage Republican organization pulled some strings with Ryan to get Murphy the position. I believe the reason that these people were brought back to the IG office a year after the IG purge was because it was an attempt to disguise the fact that they did not want to get rid of the internal affairs function. They only wanted to rid the IG of specific people that were hurting the Ryan campaign. The agents they brought back were viewed as loyal employees who followed all the mandates of Bauer to the letter. On the other hand, Sonneveld, Dowdle, and I were uncovering accusations of bribery and theft that led directly to the Citizens for Ryan campaign fund. Specifically targeting us would have possibly brought adverse public action and negative publicity. It was wiser for Ryan and Fawell to quietly dissolve the department and then several months later to quietly bring the Ryan loyalists back.

New contractual employees also were hired as special agents. One was John Johnson, a former one-term Republican Sheriff of Will County. He was beaten out the next term by the Democratic candidate, Thomas P. Fitzgerald, which was unusual for the Republican stronghold of Will County. Typical of local politics, there were accusations of patronage, political cronyism, and incompetence in the 1990 sheriff's election.

By January 1997, Operation Silver Shovel hit the news. Chicago city officials were charged with accepting bribes from John Christopher in exchange for allowing him to illegally dump old concrete in their wards. It was announced that Carl Catuara, a Secretary of State's Office employee, was also a subject of the probe. Catuara did sell campaign fund-raiser tickets for the Ryan campaign. His name was on the envelope of tickets, and cash was found in the desk at the driving school I searched in 1994. According to state campaign records, his wife contributed to the Ryan fund. However, to my knowledge there was no attempt to cover up any investigation on Catuara. The FBI stepped in and requested I back off on Catuara. The only thing that might have occurred was LaGrow's attempt to get details from me on the FBI's case, but the Ryan people had no control of what the FBI already knew about bribery for licenses at that point. It was even possible that Catuara was cooperating with "the G." Even though he was questioned by FBI agents, he had not yet been charged. Ryan made a move to terminate Catuara's employment. Sergeant Serafini received the honors of serving Catuara's termination papers on him. That should have been my job, but I was purposely kept from that assignment.

Then, in September 1998, the U.S. Postal Inspection Service executed a search warrant at the Melrose Park driver's license station and busted two employees for receiving bribes in exchange for CDLs. The employees were said to be giving their bribe money to the Ryan campaign for governor. All of a sudden, whistle-blowers were coming out of the woodwork. Despite all the bad publicity, Ryan was elected governor in 1998. Now the federal investigation was in full force, with FBI agents, USPIS inspectors, IRS agents, and assistant U.S. attorneys leaving no stone unturned.

It was a long haul. Jim Burns was no longer the U.S. attorney. The federal investigation began under U.S. Attorney Scott Lassar. He even announced just before the 1998 election that Ryan was not a target of the investigation. His reasoning might have been that he did not want the Department of Justice to have influence over an election. As I watched the investigation publicly unfold, I was frustrated with Ryan moving into the governor's mansion and the length of time it was taking to get him indicted. When I reflect back on it now, it was a very methodical choice by the prosecutors. They went after the little fish one by one until the whole house of cards tumbled down.

CHAPTER 13

From Secretary to Governor

A fool and his money are soon elected.

—*Will Rogers*

In April 1998, Chuck Goudie, a WLS-TV newsman, reported that an investigation revealed a link between CDLs being sold for bribes and the Willis crash in Milwaukee. Ryan's public response to that was, "Nobody has given us anything solid." That was a contention Ryan made again and again in 1998, the gubernatorial election year.

The standing governor, Jim Edgar, had served two terms, the maximum allowed by the Illinois Constitution. It was now George Ryan's chance to go after the position he had been lusting for since 1990. It is estimated he had up to twenty million dollars in his campaign war chest. Sonneveld, Dowdle, and I knew that the source of a large portion of that campaign money was bribery and theft, without any concern for the public's safety on the highway. Other law enforcement officials were aware of this too.

Sometime in 1998, the U.S. Postal Inspection Service began an investigation on Secretary of State's Office employees selling commercial driver's licenses to unqualified truck drivers in exchange for bribes. Their investigation zeroed in on the Melrose Park driver's license facility, two employees working there, and one former employee. The postal inspectors developed information that unqualified truck drivers were obtaining commercial driver's licenses in the state of Florida. The inspectors sent an undercover operative into a Florida driver's license facility to obtain a Florida CDL. From that investigative step, they developed information on the Melrose Park location. By the summer of 1998, they were conducting surveillances on the facility.

Located in a shopping mall on Mannheim Road just north of North Avenue, the Office of the Secretary of State driver's license facility in Melrose Park would probably go unnoticed by most motorists passing from any direction, except for the fact there were long lines of cars. Many of those cars were equipped with large wooden signs on the top with names like Triple A Driving School, Chicago Driving School, and Caribe Driving School. These were businesses that catered to immigrants, primarily Eastern European and Hispanic. Traditionally, based on my years of observation as a Secretary of State Police investigator, the driving schools had a cozy relationship with the SOS Driver Services Department employees, especially the managers. The school owners bought campaign fund-raiser tickets from the managers. This gave the appearance that the path for the schools' clients to obtain their Illinois driver's license was somehow greased. Among their clients were individuals that did not have the proper identification to obtain an Illinois license, including proof of residency and a Social Security number. Some clients could not pass the required written or road test. It was the driving schools that were supposed to teach their clients the rules of the road and driving, but often this was not the case.

The most dangerous of these aspects were the non-English-speaking CDL applicants. The federal law required them to understand English before a state could issue them a license to drive eighty-thousand-pound rigs. The postal inspectors watched carefully to see which schools had the coziest relationship with the Secretary of State's Office employees. One day while the postal inspectors were on surveillance, they watched as a driving school owner parked next to their surveillance van and passed money to a Secretary of State's Office worker. Neither of the two persons involved in the illegal transaction suspected that they were being observed by a federal law enforcement agency.

The Secretary of State Police district headquarters where I was assigned as the district lieutenant was located in Bellwood, about two miles south of the Melrose Park facility. I often drove by. On occasion I stopped and watched the driving school cars going in and out. I felt frustration. I was no longer able to do anything. I was no longer conducting internal investigations. I had my hands full with commanding a district with thirty-five officers. I had to manage shift schedules, patrol assignments, and over four thousand complaints on car dealers and vehicle titles per month.

I watched as the driving schools lined up their cars for the road test. Although I drove an unmarked squad car, it was a dark blue 1991 Chevrolet Caprice that most of the driving school owners and SOS employees were familiar with. I also was dressed in the blue SOS Police uniform. It was futile for me to attempt to gather information during those occasional stops. I did not know the postal inspectors, my brother cops, were there doing just that, watching the corruption.

By September 1998, two months before the election, they had enough probable cause to obtain a federal search warrant for the facility. The postal inspectors executed the warrant on September 3, 1998, seizing documents, records, and computers, all evidence to be used against individuals engaged in acts of bribery and official misconduct. They also had arrest warrants for Mary Ann Mastrodomenico, the facility's manager; Phyllis Volpe, the assistant manager; and Carmen Fajdich, a retired SOS employee. Volpe and Fajdich were new names to me. Mastrodomenico was formerly the assistant manager at the Ninety-ninth and Martin Luther King Drive facility. She was one of the suspect employees there whom I was collecting driver's license applications on when Bauer complained to me about the mess the boxes of applications were making in the office. Later she was manager at the Midlothian facility on which Special Agent Sonneveld had over one hundred suspect applications before he was fired. The Ryan cronies stopped us in 1995, but the federal investigation that would take down their house of cards was just now getting started.

Also arrested on September 3, 1998, were Janusz Krzyzak, an instructor for Mega Driving School, and Miodrag Dobrosavljevich, owner of Brookfield Truck Repair. Beginning in 1998 and eventually ending in 2006, seventy-nine defendants were netted by the federal investigation. Seventy-five were convicted. Thirty were Office of the Secretary of State employees, including Dean Bauer, the inspector general; Scott Fawell, the chief of staff; and George Ryan, the secretary of state.

Before the November election, Ryan responded to the potentially damaging fallout from the postal inspectors' bust. He exclaimed that he was angry with the employees but "proud of the fact that we brought it to the forefront." Later, new reports hinted the Feds were attempting to ascertain if the bribe money taken in the CDL scandal was being routed to the Ryan campaign fund. Ryan quickly dismissed the reports as "speculative stuff."

By October, the U.S. Attorney's Office alleged that employees at the McCook CDL testing facility channeled bribe money into Ryan's campaign fund. George Ryan vowed cooperation with the federal authorities and alluded to his truck safety record, claiming, "I'm not going to allow a few bad employees to tear that down."

Just eight weeks before the elecion, U.S. Attorney Scott Lassar gave Ryan a clean bill of health by saying he was not a target of the federal investigation. I can only speculate now that had Lassar publicly announced that Ryan was either a subject or target of an investigation, Democrat Glenn Poshard would have been elected governor.

Eventually for damage control, Ryan hired Jeremy Margolis, a former assistant United States attorney and former director of the Illinois State Police. Margolis, now an attorney in private practice, was paid from Ryan's campaign fund. The American criminal justice system entitles all defendants to an attorney. Those who can afford to pay for the best get the best. Margolis dismissed the allegations, saying they were blown out of proportion just before the gubernatorial election for publicity reasons. Ryan paying for Margolis with campaign funds reminds me of indicted drug dealers paying for high-priced attorneys from their illegal drug profits.

The extortion of Secretary of State's Office employees and license applicants continued past the dissolution of the Department of Inspector General. Ryan's act of obstruction only sent a message to his cronies and think-alikes that they now had a green light to pursue this unethical and illegal form of fund-raising. Dean Bauer remained in the position of inspector general, but now he was under the control of SOS Police Director Jack Pecoraro. Investigators in the SOS Police were being assigned internal investigation, but they were very carefully watched and assigned. The problem for Ryan would be that no matter how much he trusted those in charge, those types of investigations would always be initiated internally. One problem might be if a case was brought to Bauer or Pecoraro from an outside law enforcement agency and there were issues of fund-raising in the case. They had to find ways to bury it. For a short time, they were able to call off the dogs, or at least keep them on a choke chain.

Ryan needed the support of certain interest groups to get elected governor, especially those groups that did not traditionally support a Republican. Liberals, moderates, African Americans, and unions were all sought after. When he was first elected secretary of state in 1991, he initially ignored one of those groups, the Fraternal Order of Police. The FOP was the bargaining unit for the Secretary of State Police. The rank-and-file police officers had maintained a contract with the Office of the Secretary of State since the mid-1980s. The FOP was largely responsible for the professionalism of the SOS Police.

Historically, the various secretary of state administrations resisted change and had very little concern for law enforcement issues, including officer safety. The FOP, through negotiations and enforcement of assorted contract clauses, did more for the improvement of the SOS Police than any elected secretary or his respective appointee. Lodge 95 of the Fraternal Order of Police represented approximately 140 of the officers. A total of 170 manned the department.

Due to the fact there was a union contract, the FOP members were not under any patronage control. Police officers could not be forced into donating to any campaign or into working a political campaign. In the Ryan mind-set, this meant the SOS Police were useless to him, possibly even a liability. Ryan's answer to that was simply not to hire new officers as others quit or retired. He also never allowed for updating or replacing officer equipment. The officers' safety and their ability to serve were deeply compromised by the lack of personnel and personal concern.

Sometime near the end of Ryan's second term as secretary of state, he realized he needed the endorsement of the FOP to help him get elected governor. The SOS Police bargaining unit belonged to a larger state organization. The four-thousand-man Illinois State Police's bargaining unit was the FOP, as was the Chicago Police's thirteen thousand police officers. Not counting the smaller police departments in Illinois represented by the FOP, if each member of the respective lodges of SOS, ISP, and CPD could influence the vote of one person—a spouse, a brother, a parent, or a friend—that meant the potential of more than thirty-two thousand votes. These were numbers Ryan understood.

(Press release photo of George Ryan)

Lodge 95 of the FOP approached Ryan in 1997and made an offer. The FOP would endorse Ryan for governor if he agreed to remove Jack Pecoraro as its police chief and hire new police officers to beef up the low numbers. Ryan asked the FOP for a suggestion of a replacement for Pecoraro.

Robert (Bob) Howlett, son of former Secretary of State Michael Howlett, was the FOP's suggestion. Bob Howlett became a Secretary of State Police officer during the time his father was the secretary of state.

It was rumored in the SOS Police that Bob's father was opposed to Bob joining the SOS Police. The rumor was that the old man even ordered to stop the hiring process of his son. Rumor had it that Bob Howlett's mother allegedly stepped in and demanded that the old man hire the kid.

Bob Howlett was a very likeable guy. He made friends with everyone. I certainly had a fondness for him. My first encounter with Howlett was when I went through basic training at the Illinois State Police Academy. The Secretary of State Police had its own training staff and program certified by the Illinois Law Enforcement Training Board. Bob Howlett was the deputy director of training and, as a result, was assigned the rank of lieutenant. He often coordinated daily academy activity and sometimes taught classes. Basic law enforcement academy training is very similar to military boot camp. There is daily intense physical training, defensive tactics, and classes in law and policy. The academy rules were rigid, and failure in any activity meant discharge from employment. Howlett was respected and fair. He frequently participated with the recruits in most of the activities. He was not the brightest instructor and was viewed by some members of the SOS Police as slow on the uptake. In my opinion, he was not a book-smart person, but smart enough to win friends and influence people. I am convinced that this latter trait was something Howlett learned from the political environment in which he was raised.

The respect my fellow recruits and I had for Bob Howlett was carried forward throughout his career with the SOS Police. He became the commander of the statewide auto theft investigation unit. During my assignment with that squad, Commander Howlett was open to innovative and creative ideas. He always listened to his underlings and rarely resorted to a purely militaristic command style of leadership common in law enforcment. He eventually became the SOS Police district commander for the Central Illinois District. This district was responsible for the policing on the State Capitol Complex, including the capitol building, the Illinois Supreme Court, the State Library, and the Secretary of State records facility, now called the Michael J. Howlett Building. It officially was so named by George Ryan during his administration.

While Bob Howlett was district commander, he formed the bomb squad and SWAT team for the protection of the State Capitol Complex. From a police officer's perspective, these specialties were necessary for the protection of the government officials and properties housed at the complex. Most Secretary of State's Office administrators and their fellow hacks would scoff at these innovations, seeing no personal political benefit. Bob Howlett appeared to be a police officer's police commander.

Based on Bob Howlett's respect, political savvy, and professional experience, it seemed obvious that he would emerge out of Ryan's negotiations with the FOP to become the director of the SOS Police. Pecoraro was removed, Howlett was made chief, and Ryan received the endorsement for governor he coveted from FOP Lodge 95.

What most of the rank-and-file did not know, nor did I, was the extent of the close relationship Bob Howlett and his family had with George Ryan. I personally felt that Michael J. Howlett and George Ryan were two peas in a pod. Both had a public persona of grumpy and arrogant old men. Secretary of State Michael Howlett was not a very popular secretary with the employees. Ryan also was not popular. He was more feared because of the power he wielded and only popular to those that benefited from his abuses. By contrast, Secretary of State Jim Edgar was popular with employees, whether Republican, Democrat, or independent. I believe that the pressure to contribute time, money, or both to the Michael Howlett campaign was as great as it was under Ryan's reign. Although Howlett was a Democrat and Ryan a Republican, they were very analogous as well as being close friends. Their respective families were close too.

Sometime in January 1999, I was contacted by Patrick Collins, an assistant United States attorney. He said that he understood I had information he might be interested in regarding corruption within the Illinois Secretary of State's Office. I replied that I had already told what I knew to an AUSA in 1995, and nothing was done. Collins said there was a new U.S. attorney and now something was being done. In September 1998, after completing an undercover operation, the U.S. postal inspectors busted two Secretary of State's Office employees for selling commercial driver's licenses for bribes. There were implications that Ryan was aware of and even benefited from the corruption. In the fall 1998 gubernatorial election, Glenn Poshard, a conservative downstate Democrat, was Ryan's opponent. Poshard used the implications of corruption and even the untimely deaths of the Willis children as campaign issues. Despite an abundance of negative press, Ryan won the 1998 election for governor. The investigation into corruption within the Secretary of State's Office and the George Ryan campaign was just beginning. Collins's reaching out to me was an extension of that investigation.

I told Collins I would welcome telling him everything I had already told Scott Mendeloff, but I asked if he would send me a subpoena. I did not want it to overtly appear that I was initiating conversations with the federal government about internal gripes I had with the Secretary of State's Office. I wanted to wave the subpoena in the face of the upper echelon because I have a little bit of ball buster in me. Collins agreed to send me a subpoena.

SOS Police policy required that we report the receipt of subpoenas up the chain of command. I could hardly wait and did that just as soon as I received the government order. Howlett ordered me into his office to discuss the matter. I was prepared. Howlett asked me what the U.S. attorney was going to ask me. I told him I did not know. After all, they did not give me a list of questions they were going to ask. Howlett told me I did not have to worry about repercussions because the Ryan people were all gone. Ryan had been inaugurated governor, and Jesse White was the newly elected secretary of state.

Despite not knowing at the time how close the Howletts were to the Ryans, I still was being elusive to Howlett about the circumstances regarding the subpoena. I was elusive because I did not trust anybody in my agency. Howlett may not have gone to Ryan directly with information, but he might have passed it unwittingly to a messenger for Ryan. Besides, there were still Ryan people in the Secretary of State's Office. Moreover, Ryan was governor and held more power in Illinois politics than ever before. He could destroy my career, my pension, and my ability to support my family. Howlett asked me again. This time, not only did I tell him I didn't know, I also told him I could have a gag order placed on me when I met with the federal prosecutor. If I told anyone what I discussed with the AUSA, I told Howlett, I could be held in contempt of a federal grand jury. I also told him he might be looked at for obstruction of justice for pressuring me for answers.

(Director Bob Howlett with Lt. Hammer)

Howlett never asked me again about my several meetings with Collins and later my testimony to the federal grand jury. I was right not to trust him. State campaign records show that members of the Howlett family, Democrats, officially contributed one thousand dollars to the Citizens for Ryan campaign fund. Secretary of State Police Deputy Director Stephen Rutledge contributed $775 to Citizens for Ryan. Rutledge was originally appointed to the deputy director job by Ryan, and he stayed on after Jesse White took office. As a matter of fact, campaign records show he contributed to White's campaign the day after White was sworn into office. I guess the purpose of that contribution was to make White more aware of Rutledge's job qualifications. Jesse White contributed to George Ryan's campaign fund too. No, the Ryan people were not all gone. They were above, below, and right next to me.

(Police Deputy Director Rutledge, unknown SOS official, and police Director Howlett)

I later met with Collins and Postal Inspector Basil Demczak. I told them about all the incidents that occurred in as much detail as I could remember. I was motivated by my own anger and was filled with it. I was angry at the system for taking four years to even consider my testimony. I was a good cop and very successful in all my investigations, whether they were auto theft, driver's license fraud, or public corruption. I was not some conspiracy wacko that should be shunned by the system. All one had to do was to ask the other state and federal prosecutors who tried my cases. I was a cop who brought incriminating details to the criminal justice process. I was also an articulate witness for the good guys. Mendeloff and his superior, former U.S. Attorney Jim Burns, eschewed the evidence of corruption I gave them four years earlier. Not only did that cause me a demotion, my friends were fired. Worse yet, the corruption continued with even more momentum. Collins and his boss, U.S. Attorney Scott Lassar, were now giving the evidence a second chance.

I retired from the SOS Police on September 30, 2002. Bob Howlett retired one month before me. I attended an extravagant retirement dinner on his behalf at the Springfield Crown Plaza. Often officers attended these types of social functions to gain career brownie points. Those points could help them advance their career. I was a captain and retiring in less than thirty days. I did not need any points. Despite his family connection to Ryan and occasional differences we had, Howlett supported me throughout most of my career, including my promotion to captain. Howlett deserved my respect. It was the right thing to do. I attended the retirement dinner to show Howlett my respect.

During the course of the dinner, Howlett family members and friends spoke to honor the retiring chief. While paying their respects, they also announced their admiration for George Ryan. They mentioned what a great friend Ryan was to the Howlett family. At one point, the room was so thick with Ryan praises that it seemed more like the George Ryan award banquet than a dinner honoring a retiring police chief. My friend Don Norton, retired state police captain and U.S. Attorney's Office investigator, got up and left the room in the midst of the Ryan accolades. Making Bob Howlett director of the Secretary of State Police had not been a difficult decision to make. It was a patronage decision and politics as usual.

CHAPTER 14
Mr. Hammer, This Is a Political Office

If an injury has to be done to a man it should be so severe
that his vengeance need not be feared.

—Machiavelli

"Let the Milwaukee authorities handle it." The words spoken by Dean Bauer, Ryan's close friend and inspector general, were the driving force behind Russ Sonneveld and me going to the U.S. Attorney's Office in 1995. Three years had passed since I met with Assistant U.S. Attorney Scott Mendeloff. Then, shortly after the USPIS postal inspectors arrested the employees at the Melrose Park Driver Services facility, Sonneveld and I both were contacted by Assistant U.S. Attorney Patrick Collins. Our subsequent meetings were followed by grand jury testimony and Bauer's indictment on federal crimes.

Ryan appointed Bauer to investigate allegations of SOS employee corruption. I cynically can say now that Bauer may have been so incompetent that he misread the employee policy manual and thought it said he was supposed to instigate corruption instead of investigate it. Actually, he knew exactly what he was doing. Special Agent Mark Lipe testified at Ryan's trial that Bauer stated at an SOSPD staff meeting that his job was "to protect George Ryan." Ultimately he did protect Ryan. Bauer never testified against his boss and went to prison. He never flipped on his friend and political mentor from Kankakee.

On February 1, 2000, Dean Bauer was indicted by a grand jury on five counts. Many of the charges were based on my grand jury testimony and that of Sonneveld. According to the indictment, Bauer concealed employee misconduct to avoid personal and political embarrassment to Ryan. It describes Bauer's conduct as racketeering. He specifically did this by purposely closing investigations prematurely and failing to pursue credible allegations of employee misconduct. As a sworn police officer, Bauer took an oath to uphold the laws of Illinois, the Illinois Constitution, and the U.S. Constitution. He did the opposite.

On January 17, 2001, almost one year after the indictment, I met with Assistant U.S. Attorneys Patrick Collins and Zack Fardon, along with Postal Inspector Basil Demczak, at the Dirksen Federal Building in downtown Chicago. Bauer's trial was to begin in a few days and they wanted to prepare me for it. I was not nervous about the trial because I had testified at several trials during my twenty-four years as a cop. I had even testified at several federal trials during that time. I was excited about getting my version of the story made public.

Despite the fact that reporters from all the Chicago TV news shows and the two major newspapers were calling me, I never told any of them the full story because Collins asked me not to speak to the media. It was the prosecutors' mind-set that any discussion I would have with the media might jeopardize the case. We disagreed about this point, and I often wrote letters to the editors when the local newspapers ran editorials or columns that showed George Ryan in a favorable light. I wanted to set the public straight. I know this made Collins uneasy, fearing that it appeared I had a grudge to bear. A public grudge would be a point on which a defense attorney could attack me. I had no more of a grudge to bear for Dean Bauer or George Ryan than I did for any other criminal I investigated.

When I walked in the conference room at the Chicago branch of the U.S. Attorney's Office, sitting on the table was a copy of my personnel file from the Secretary of State's Office. In all the previous trials where I testified, my employment record was never an issue. Now the prosecution team was preparing for just that. It was about two inches thick. It contained forms announcing promotions, raises, and transfers. It also included evaluations and commendations. What it did not contain was disciplinary action. In twenty-four years, my record was free of written reprimands and suspensions, until one week prior to this meeting.

I received a written reprimand for the first time based on an internal investigation done by Sgt. Dave Poeshell, from the SOS Police command center in Springfield. The previous November, Investigator Cardell Dobbins, an officer under my command, arrested his brother-in-law for some Class C misdemeanors related to a vehicle rebuilding business the brother-in-law was not licensed to operate. The business was located in Dobbins's beat assignment, and regulating the vehicle industry was part of the Secretary of State Police's mission statement. Dobbins asked me before going to the business if he was clear to make an arrest based on any violations he might find. I told him to take another officer with him in case there were any false accusations made. I was confident that Dobbins would follow the procedures specifically outlined by the SOS Police's policy. He was a by-the-book kind of cop. He took two fellow officers and a civilian audit team with him. He cited his brother-in-law for several violations and the brother-in-law's attorney cried foul.

That afternoon, after Dobbins issued the citations, Chief Bob Howlett called me from Springfield and ordered me to pull the citations so they would not reach the court. I went to the district SOS Police court officer's file and they were not there. I immediately contacted Dobbins, who told me that he had submitted the citations to the court officer. The fact that they were gone this late in the day meant the SOS court officer had already submitted the paperwork to the clerk of the court. He routinely submitted the district's citations every afternoon before three o'clock.

I next called John Feeley, a Cook County Assistant State's Attorney. I asked Feeley if it was unlawful to have citations pulled from the court files once they were officially logged into the record. He told me it was highly irregular and unethical. He advised me against doing it because it could be construed as official misconduct. I called Howlett back and told him the citations were already in the hands of the court. I anticipated his next order: pull them from the court record. I told him what ASA Feeley advised me. I could not be compelled to obey an unlawful order.

Jesse White, a Democrat, was now the secretary of state. He was elected to the office at the same time his predecessor, Ryan, was elected governor. A popular Democrat from the North Side of Chicago, White was elected after receiving Republican Ryan's endorsement in the 1998 election. White's newly appointed general counsel, Donna Leonard, called me a couple of days after Dobbins's visit to his brother-in-law's unlicensed business. Leonard told me that the brother-in-law's attorney had filed a complaint against Dobbins based on a conflict of interest. I defended Dobbins's action and Leonard became agitated. I told her that if she felt Dobbins's action had violated any policy, she should turn the complaint over to Burns, White's new inspector general. She asked with an obvious tone of indignation, "Is that how you feel?"

I told her that was what I felt was the right thing to do, and she hung up. I did not understand her tone. It seemed to me it was standard operating procedure to have the Department of Inspector General investigate citizens' complaints of employee impropriety. I was also very secure with the fact that neither Dobbins nor I had done anything wrong. The new IG or any of his agents did not do the internal investigation. Chief Bob Howlett assigned Sgt. Dave Poeshell to do it.

About a week later, Poeshell came to the Chicago district headquarters. He was dressed in a tweed sport jacket, blue jeans, and cowboy boots. We were friendly because we had worked auto theft investigations in the past and always seemed to bond. He used that bond and played me for a fool. Walking into my office, he sat down and put his cowboy boots up on my desk. I was comfortable with his country boy mannerisms and did not feel an interrogation was coming. He asked what happened with the Dobbins case. I confidently told Poeshell I had given Dobbins the green light to do what he did.

In early January, Lt. Dennis DiGiore from the SOS Police district immediately to the west of my district was promoted to the regional captain's position. DiGiore and I were the only two lieutenants who submitted for the promotion. Chief Howlett came up to Chicago to announce the promotion. After telling DiGiore that he got it, Howlett had a private meeting with me. He told me I did not get the promotion because of the "Dobbins thing." I was angry. I had an overall better resume and better district statistics than DiGiore. He got the promotion over me because I did the ethical and lawful thing, and now it was being used against me. One week later, to back up Howlett's decision, I received the letter of reprimand. I also received the written reprimand one week before Dean Bauer's trial was to begin. Was it now going to somehow be used against me in his defense? Did it muddy the waters of what was a pretty clear-cut case against Bauer?

(Jesse White)

 U. S. Department of Justice

United States Attorney

Northern District of Illinois

Patrick M. Collins *Assistant United States Attorney*	*Dirksen Federal Building* *219 South Dearborn Street, Fifth Floor* *Chicago, Illinois 60604*	*Direct Line: (312) 886-7625* *Fax: (312) 353-8298*

January 23, 2001

Secretary Jesse White
Secretary of State
100 W. Randolph, 5-400
Chicago, Illinois 60601

Dear Secretary White:

On behalf of the United States Attorney's Office and the prosecutors involved in Operation Safe Road, we are writing to commend Lieutenant Ed Hammer for his persistence, courage and dedication to duty during his detail to the Secretary of State Inspector General's Office through June 1995, as well as his professionalism during his recent cooperation leading up to the prosecution of Dean Bauer. As you undoubtedly know, Lt. Hammer played a significant part in exposing the improper conduct engaged in by defendant Bauer during his tenure as Inspector General. It was his (and other agents') refusal to allow justice to be compromised by politics that exposed this criminal interference with the law enforcement function.

During the course of our trial preparation, our investigators interviewed many law enforcement personnel. Lt. Hammer was routinely described as a hardworking and aggressive investigator. Most importantly, he was also described as a person of integrity, even by those who were no friends to this investigation.

Lt. Hammer is a credit to his profession. We are proud to share the law enforcement profession with him. Please express our gratitude to Ed for a job well done.

Sincerely,

Scott R. Lassar
United States Attorney

Patrick M. Collins
Assistant United States Attorney

(Letter to Jesse White from US Attorney Lassar and assistant US Attorney Collins recognizing Hammer for his professionalism)

Bauer's attorney was Edward Genson. Early in my career, Genson represented several organized crime chop shop operators I was investigating. He was now more notorious for representing defendants in the federal courts on drug and corruption cases. Earlier in the year, a couple of private investigators working for Genson on the Bauer case attempted to interview me at my home. In my entire career, I had never been approached by a defendant's private investigator at my home. I considered it off-limits for them and chased them away. I felt their visit was more an act of intimidation. Besides, it was a waste of their time. I wasn't going to answer any of their questions.

Like many defense attorneys, Genson and his law firm were big political contributors. State campaign records showed he and his firm contributed over three thousand dollars to Ryan's campaign. Howlett knew Genson because of his many notorious clients. I was afraid that there might have been a connection between the reprimand I received and the fact that Genson was Bauer's attorney.

Fortunately it did not matter, because Genson made a plea agreement offer. The case did not go to trial, and I did not have to testify. One of the counts in Bauer's indictment included an obstruction of justice that was predicated on the fact that Bauer told a Secretary of State's Office employee, who was also an FBI informant, to get rid of two sensitive documents in October 1999, including a 1994 memo that revealed his office knew about Ricardo Guzman. Bauer agreed to plead guilty to one count if all other charges were dropped.

I was still in Patrick Collins's office when I was told this news. Collins told me that the U.S. Attorney's Office was going to have a press conference to announce the plea. He invited me to participate. I did not want to stay. I was dressed in blue jeans. All the prosecutors and federal agents would be in suits. I felt I would look foolish on camera in the sea of suits. I knew there were specific television reporters—Andy Shaw of WLS-TV and Phil Rogers of WMAQ-TV—who had wanted to interview me for over a year. I was not prepared. Not to mention the fact that I had been anxiously awaiting this day since the series of Bauer's obstructions in 1994, and I needed time to process the news.

The next morning Collins called me at my office. He said reporters from WLS, WBBM, and WMAQ were asking about me. He asked if I would call them. He said it was now okay to discuss the Bauer case, and he'd appreciate it if I would give them a call. He did not want them bugging him about me. I said I would call.

Like most cops, I was apprehensive about media people. I believed they were capable of interviewing a person and then purposely spinning the story and making the interviewee look foolish. I, however, had had good luck in the past with both newsprint and television reporters. It was a matter of preparation. Know the facts and then you will be able to answer all the questions professionally. This was slightly different. It was personal. Bauer was more than a boss to Sonneveld and me. He was a criminal, and we were victims.

I first contacted Chief Howlett. I did not want to violate department policy, and I wanted all TV interviews cleared by him. He said it was okay, but I was not to discuss current department business. Howlett also ordered me to call Elizabeth Kaufman, Jesse White's press person, and advise her that I was doing the TV interviews. I took it one step further: I asked if I could use her office in the Thompson Center in downtown Chicago. That way, she could watch the whole process.

I called Mike Flannery of WBBM-TV first. I had previously met him at a high school swim meet. His son and my son were on opposing teams. I introduced myself to him at the meet with the intent of developing a reporter/cop acquaintance. From my observations at the meet, he was gentlemanly and a caring father. I felt comfortable with him. Through his producer, we arranged an interview at one thirty the next afternoon in Kaufman's office. I then called Phil Rogers of WMAQ-TV. I had done a previous interview with him on the hot topic of identity theft. He knew my background with the Department of Inspector General, and on that day, he left me his card and asked me to call when I could talk. He never contacted me after that. I arranged for him to do his interview immediately after Flannery's. I then called Andy Shaw of WLS-TV. Shaw had called me a year earlier and asked to do an interview. I told him the U.S. Attorney's Office had requested that I not speak to the media. He responded by saying they could not tell me not to speak to the press. I told him that I was a grand jury witness and was not going to discuss the ongoing Bauer case. When I called Shaw, I was told that he was out of town and someone else from WLS-TV would get back to me. No one did until the following Monday, when John Garcia came to do the interview.

I did the WBBM and WMAQ interviews on January 19, 2001. I was in my blue Secretary of State Police uniform. WMAQ took a shot of me walking through the hallway of the Secretary of State offices in the Thompson building. Beth Kaufman watched as each of the reporters conducted his interview, concentrating on questions related to Bauer's act of obstruction and the connection to former Secretary of State George Ryan. The news reports that evening summed up the interviews by stating if Bauer had gone to trial, I would have testified to his hiding cash and fund-raiser tickets during a bust of the Libertyville driver's station; Bauer's closing the Naperville facility theft investigation upon learning the money was stolen to buy Ryan fund-raiser tickets; and Bauer's closing the Guzman case, which involved the investigation of the crash in Milwaukee resulting in the deaths of the Willis children.

After completing the interview with Phil Rogers, Kaufman asked me if I'd like to meet Jesse White. I had met him on at least one prior occasion when he visited the Bellwood SOS Police headquarters, where

I was assigned. When I walked into White's office, he politely stood up from behind his desk and shook my hand. I stood in front of his desk in a military stance called parade rest. White commented that I looked very military to him and asked if I had served. I told him no, but that my father, who had served in the infantry in World War II, raised me with military style, whistling reveille to get me up in the morning and bouncing quarters on my bed to see if was made with tight military corners. White, who often talked about his service in the army, seemed impressed and invited me to sit down. His office was large, with a wide wooden desk and a long sofa running along the wall perpendicular to his desk. I took a seat there while he sat at his desk. We talked some more about family and my career. He then thanked me for my service with the State of Illinois.

The next thing White asked me I had anticipated and hoped he would ask. White asked, "Is there anything I can do for you, Lieutenant Hammer?"

I anxiously responded, "As a matter of fact, there is. My partner, Russ Sonneveld, was fired by George Ryan for no reason other than doing his job. I'd like to see a public letter of apology from the Secretary of State's Office to him."

White neither said yes nor no. What he said made me realize that it doesn't matter whether an Illinois politician is a Democrat or a Republican; they have a strong political bond with each other that goes beyond party membership or ideologies. White replied, "You know, George Ryan and I have been friends for a long time."

I remained quiet for a few seconds then stood to leave. We shook hands and I thanked him for inviting me in to speak with him. As I walked out, I recalled what Chief Howlett said to me about all the Ryan people being gone, after I notified him that I had been subpoenaed to testify at a federal grand jury. It was not true. Jesse White had just proclaimed his allegiance to Ryan.

Tina Prose was Ryan's director of personnel and remained there under White. Howlett, who was made director of the SOS Police by Ryan, remained in the same position under White. Also, Howlett's family was close to the Ryan family. Steve Rutledge, an SOS Police deputy director, was appointed under Ryan and remained under White. They also had a common denominator: they were all contributors to Republican George Ryan's campaign. Even White, the Democrat, had contributed. Dennis DiGiore, the SOS Police captain promoted two weeks before my meeting with White, was a contributor to Ryan. Dave Poeshell, the sergeant who conducted the internal investigation on me, was not a contributor to Ryan, but his wife contributed to Judy Baar-Topinka, the Republican state treasurer and Ryan ally. I, however—the demoted Department of Inspector General special agent, the lieutenant who was not promoted, the lieutenant who was a witness for the prosecution in a federal corruption case against Dean Bauer, Ryan's buddy—was not a contributor to Ryan. As a matter of fact, I was receiving a disciplinary job action by that same group of Ryan contributors.

The night, I watched the TV interviews I had done just outside White's office. I was home alone that evening. My son was away at college and my wife was out shopping with my two daughters. About ten p.m., a neighbor across the street called and said that a Commonwealth Edison truck was parked in front of my house. The driver exited the vehicle and walked behind the house. I went to the front door to see what he was doing, and as I stepped out of the house, the truck drove away. I immediately called customer service and asked what was going on. The Commonwealth Edison service representative told me that I had called for service. I hadn't and was now worried. My wife and daughters would be home soon. It was too coincidental that a bogus service call was made for my house exactly as I was detailing corruption about Illinois' most powerful politician on the ten o'clock news. I called Postal Inspector Basil Demczak, who said he would have the U.S. Postal Police watch the house. Postal inspectors and I attempted to track the source of the bogus telephone call, with no luck. According to state election records, Commonwealth Edison, not including corporate officers and lobbyists, contributed over $6,500 to Citizens for George Ryan.

Investigator Dobbins grieved his suspension through the procedure outlined by the Fraternal Order of Police contract. The department dropped the charges against Dobbins and the resulting suspension. I, on the other hand, did not have the benefit of a union contract because, as a lieutenant, I was management. I grieved the written reprimand through a three-step procedure outlined by the Secretary of State Office's employee policy. Although the reprimand seemed like minor personnel action, I believe it cost me a deserved promotion, and I was concerned it could cost a chance at any future promotions.

The first step of the grievance went to the new captain, DiGiore. Upon receiving the written reprimand, I verbally notified him I was grieving it. He was then required to verbally respond within five days. He never did. A memo written by the newly appointed chief deputy, Brad Demuzio, stated that my first step of the grievance was denied because he never received notice of the grievance in writing. The employee policy on the first level of the grievance required that I verbally notify the first person in my chain of command, DiGiore. Demuzio, the son of Democrat state senator Vince Demuzio, was appointed chief deputy by Jesse White. In my opinion, Brad Demuzio lacked sufficient experience in administration and law enforcement to be the chief deputy of a police department with 140 officers. I was now getting the bureaucratic runaround—or, better said, the political polka.

The second step was a written memo to Chief Howlett requiring a written response from him within five days. My memo outlined several points justifying a retraction of the reprimand, the most important being that the written reprimand was an act of retaliation and intimidation against me based on my status as a witness in the Dean Bauer criminal trial. I further grieved that certain employees within the Office of the Secretary of State had a political association with George Ryan, Bauer's longtime friend. I was asking that the reprimand be removed from my personnel record. This step of the grievance was denied by Chief Howlett.

The final step in the grievance was my request for a review by Prose, the Ryan appointee. In my written request for review, I again outlined the politically motivated acts of retaliation and intimidation. Prose decided to appoint a designee in her place to review it, Jeanette Stroger, the deputy director of personnel and a White appointee. She was also the daughter-in-law of John Stroger, the politically powerful president of the Cook County Board. Several weeks had passed since my meeting with Jesse White in his office and Bauer's guilty pleas, not that that mattered. I met with Stroger and outlined my argument to remove the reprimand from my record.

She denied my request, ending her meeting with me by stating, "You know, Mr. Hammer, this is a political office."

I know that now, for sure. It was so political that if one of the political "in" group was charged with a crime, they all banded together behind that person and harassed those that stood up to do the right thing. In this case, the right thing was to take evidence of bribery, theft, and cover-ups to the United States attorney. Despite the harassment of me, my former boss was going to do time in federal prison.

It was Secretary's Day 2001, and I invited JoAnn Robertson and Carolyn Miller, the former secretaries for Bauer, to lunch at Berghoff's Restaurant in Chicago. Bergoff's was just east of the Dirksen Building, where the federal courts are housed. Bauer's sentencing was scheduled that same day, so all three of us attended the hearing. As we exited the elevator and began walking toward the courtroom, we saw Bauer sitting on a bench in the hallway. He was slumping forward, but looking up. He saw us and, to my surprise, he waved. We did not return the greeting, but as we approached the courtroom we discussed it. We wondered if Bauer thought we were there to offer him our support.

The three of us entered Judge Charles Norgel's courtroom and sat three rows behind the defendant's legal team. Looking to my right, about two o'clock, I saw the jury box was filled with both print and TV reporters. Many I knew personally, like Phil Rogers and Andy Shaw. I also recognized the *Chicago Tribune* columnist John Kass, who often wrote scathingly about Ryan, Bauer, and their shady group. I was on an emotional high. My heart was racing anticipating the judge's announcement.

The row in front of us was empty until a middle-aged couple walked in and sat down in front of us. It was Scott and Janet Willis. I had never met them before, so I tapped the reverend on the shoulder. He turned and I offered my hand as I introduced myself. Scott Willis began to cry. He introduced Janet and told me how thankful he and Janet were to Russ Sonneveld and me for all we had done. I never felt that I did that much, but his reaction touched me. I knew then more than ever that what I had done was the right thing to do.

Norgle sentenced Bauer to one year and a day in federal prison, two years supervised releases, and a ten-thousand-dollar fine. There was some discussion about where Bauer was going to do his time. Although Bauer looked healthy on this day, Edward Genson, his attorney, argued that Bauer needed medical attention while in custody to treat a case of bladder cancer he had been battling since 1994.

Judge Norgle responded that a federal prison in Duluth, Minnesota, had a good medical staff. He knew because he had sent many local convicted politicians there who also had medical issues when they did their time. The agreement was Bauer would do his time at a federal prison in Terre Haute, Indiana, closer to his home in Kankakee. Up to this point, thirty-two other people were convicted in the federal case called Operation Safe Road. Bauer was the highest-ranking official in Ryan's inner circle to do time.

The day Bauer was convicted, Ryan released a statement saying, "I respect the rule of law," and "I have empathy for a sick friend." Now his longtime friend would be receiving medical care courtesy of the United States Bureau of Prisons and the time he deserved.

CHAPTER 15

The Walls Came Tumblin' Down

Man is the only kind of varmint sets his own trap, baits it, then steps in it.

—John Steinbeck

On April 22, 2002, almost eight years after Tatro and Sonneveld swept Ryan's Rosemont campaign office, U.S. Attorney Patrick Fitzgerald announced the indictment of Citizens for Ryan. The campaign was the first organization of its kind in the nation to be indicted. The federal racketeering law was intended to go after the Mob. To me, there was no difference between Al Capone's business and Ryan's organization. They both employed the Mob modus operandi of shakedowns, bribery, and cover-ups. Ryan's lust for power had even resulted in deaths.

Criminal law allows corporations or entities to be charged with a crime. You cannot send an entity to the penitentiary, but if it is found guilty, it can receive a penalty of heavy fines. It is possible to deplete the entity of all assets. Doing this often might be a prosecutor's strategy, especially in a public corruption investigation. Indicting and convicting George Ryan's campaign, Citizens for Ryan, was one more step toward eventually getting Ryan himself.

The indictment alleged that Scott Fawell, Richard Juliano, the Citizens for Ryan campaign organization, and others known and unknown operated a racketeering enterprise. Fawell was Ryan's chief of staff in the Secretary of State's Office from 1992 through 1999. He also ran the Citizens for Ryan organization, becoming the full-time campaign manager in the gubernatorial race in 1998. The line of separation between the Office of the Secretary of State and the political campaign organization barely existed. In 1998, on one occasion the campaign handed out press releases to reporters that were printed on the back side of the Office of the Secretary of State letterhead.

Richard Juliano held various positions in the Secretary of State's Office under Ryan from 1991 through 1998. He also served during the same time period as the campaign manager and then assistant campaign manager of Citizens for Ryan. Like Fawell, Juliano's dual position made it difficult to distinguish between public service and the politics. He answered directly to Fawell. In my opinion, there was no public service. It was all about getting Ryan into the governor's mansion. Juliano cooperated with the government in the Operation Safe Road case in exchange for a guilty plea on one count of mail fraud.

The Citizens for Ryan organization and Fawell were charged with two counts of mail fraud, one count of racketeering, and one count of conspiracy to obstruct justice. Fawell was also indicted on separate counts of theft of government funds, perjury, and tax fraud. Racketeering originally meant an organized conspiracy to commit extortion. A more current meaning of the federal law is to eradicate the unlawful activities of organized crime. Extortion, a traditional Mob crime, is the illegal use of one's position of power to obtain property. Conspiracy to obstruct justice is two or more individuals plotting to prevent the administration and due process of law; i.e., an official federal government investigation. Perjury is the willful giving of false testimony under oath. Of course, theft of government funds and false tax returns are self-explanatory. Reading the federal indictment of Ryan's campaign fund was like reading from a book titled *Mafia Management for Dummies*.

Specifically, the racketeering count included the allegations that Fawell, Juliano, and the campaign fund conspired between 1991 and 1999 in a scheme to defraud the people of the State of Illinois; Secretary of State's Office employees and resources were diverted from their proper use to work on Ryan's campaign and other state political campaigns, including that of a state senator. Pay raises and other benefits were promised and given to SOS employees for campaign work. Fawell mandated and enforced fund-raising goals for Office of the Secretary of State departments. He was accused of directing and encouraging SOS employees to break the law and violate agency policy.

The indictment also alleged that in December 1994, Fawell and other high-ranking SOS officials became aware that special agents of the Department of Inspector General were conducting investigations into fund-raising misconduct. Those IG investigations included the 1993 Libertyville driver's license facility case, where employees were accused of accepting bribes from unqualified driver's license applicants and the motivation appeared to be fund-raising for the CFR; the 1994 case of the Naperville driver's license facility manager accused of stealing facility money for CFR fund-raising purposes; the deaths of the Willis children case, where an unqualified truck driver linked to the fatal crash allegedly bribed a McCook CDL facility employee whose motivation appeared to be fund-raising for the CFR; and other similar cases of bribery involving the same CDL facility. With knowledge of these investigations and the potential harm they could cause to Ryan and the Citizens for Ryan organization, Fawell and others conspired to dissolve the Department of Inspector General by terminating or reassigning its employees. The indictment further alleged that Fawell created documents falsely justifying the resolution to dismantle the department responsible for investigating the unlawful conduct, using budgetary cutbacks as the excuse. Fawell's motive was to prevent further attempts by the agents of the Department of Inspector General to perform their sworn duty.

In February 1995, Fawell personally carried out the obstruction conspiracy with the termination of IG Deputy Director Joe Jech. In June 1995, the action against the agents responsible for conducting the specifically named investigations was completed. Special Agent Russ Sonneveld was terminated. Special Agent Pat Dowdle and I were reassigned. Prior to that date, Special Agent Mark Lipe requested reassignment. With these agents and others out of the picture, the Department of Inspector General, through the authority and power of Ryan's number-one crony, was rendered incapable of damaging the George Ryan campaign for governor.

The indictment included other unlawful acts after June 1995, including kickbacks on vendor contracts, the destruction of evidence, and lying to a grand jury while a federal investigation into the conspiracy was ongoing. Although I never investigated vendor kickbacks or witnessed the destruction of evidence, during my several meetings with prosecutors from 1995 through 2001, I told them I had a gut feeling that stuff was occurring.

In the last several years, the national media has reported that the FBI and U.S. Attorney's Office have conducted federal investigations into white-collar crimes and public corruption that have resulted in perjury charges. The perjury is predicated on lying to the grand jury or to a federal agent. Two that come to mind are Martha Stewart and Scooter Libby. The difference between those examples and Scott Fawell is that the other two were not indicted or convicted of the actual crimes that initiated the investigations resulting in the perjury. Fawell was indicted and convicted of the predicated crimes and the perjury.

On March 19, 2003, after a nine-week trial and six days of deliberation, a jury found Ryan's campaign guilty of racketeering. The same jury found the campaign manager, Fawell, guilty of racketeering, as well as mail fraud and obstruction of justice. I was often told by Secretary of State's Office co-workers that Ryan would never go down on criminal charges. Many of them believed he was too powerful in the Illinois circle of politics to be indicted, let alone convicted. The more cynical described those who were already indicted in the Ryan scandal as scapegoats to satisfy the feeding frenzy of the prosecutors. Throwing them an occasional Ryan underling was supposed to satisfy the hunger. It even got back to me that Jim DeRicco, my former captain, asked another investigator, "Why did Eddie Hammer do something like that? It could hurt him."

DeRicco was alluding to my interviews on the evening news after the 2001 Bauer conviction. He felt that my outspoken crusade against the corruption could hurt my last chance of promotion to captain. He might have been right, but I was going to fight for both the exposure of Ryan's corrupt organization and the promotion. I wanted both. It turned out he was wrong. I was promoted to captain in 2001 despite my public clamoring.

I, however, never expressed my inner anxieties about the Ryan case. I hid my fear that Ryan's power would reach out far enough to quash any chance of him being indicted, resulting in my public humiliation accompanied by an "I told you so" that I would hear from all the naysayers. I've been a political optimist most of my life; however, twenty-five years as a cop in the Cook County system of justice negatively impacted my attitude. I feared I would become more cynical than I already was.

More important than my feelings was the effect this would have on the voters. Years of repeated corruption by many Illinois politicians had been wearing away voter confidence in the system. Ryan walking away unscathed from Operation Safe Road would only further darken the Illinois political walk of shame. Worse yet, there would be no closure to the heartrending story of the deaths of the Willis children.

The conviction of the highest-ranking official in the Ryan organization cooled down those fears. Convicting Ryan's organization meant the prosecutors stripped Ryan of his power, the campaign funds. Thomas Breen, the attorney that represented the fund, referred to the charges as "common in politics." Referring to the conviction, U.S. Attorney Pat Fitzgerald stated, "It was not political reform, it was prosecuting a crime." I was now confident that Ryan was next on their list. Once the USPIS postal inspectors busted the Secretary of State's Office employees selling commercial driver's licenses out of the Melrose Park Driver Services facility, the investigation into corruption by George Ryan and his cronies went full speed ahead. The 2003 conviction of Ryan's chief of staff and the CFR proved the investigative efforts were not in vain.

Beginning with the 1998 bust and working through to the Fawell conviction, a team of tenacious professional prosecutors now had me convinced they would eventually reach Ryan. Some Ryan cronies who were the subjects of investigations, indictments, and convictions might have described these professionals as zealots or politically biased. To me, they were committed public servants dedicated to putting an end to Illinois' long history of public corruption.

In the fall of 1998, under U.S. Attorney Scott Lassar, the federal case became known as Operation Safe Road. It had been three years since my meeting with AUSA Scott Mendeloff when I laid out the corruption and cover-ups in his office. During the fall of 1998, while Ryan ran for governor, news of corruption and bribes appeared almost daily in the Chicago papers and on the local TV news programs.

Lassar, appointed by President Bill Clinton, was a graduate of Northwestern University School of Law. He led the investigation into Illinois' most powerful Republican. On public television station WT-TW's evening news show, *Chicago Tonight*, Lassar had stated he was a Democrat. This was no surprise considering he was a Clinton appointee. However, U.S. attorneys must remain free of political bias. During the fall of 1998, Lassar did his best not to allow politics to interfere with the Operation Safe Road investigation. During his last two years as the top federal prosecutor in Northern Illinois, thirty-eight people were indicted or arrested as part of the Safe Road case on charges of extortion, mail fraud, obstruction of justice, and racketeering. However, just prior to the November 1998 gubernatorial election, Lassar publicly announced that Ryan was not a subject of the federal investigation. I believe Lassar's statement was made in good conscience so as not to have a federal investigation affect voters' decisions. Ryan was elected by a margin of only two percentage points. Had Lassar identified Ryan as a subject, I wonder to this day whether the election would have gone the other way and Democrat Glenn Poshard would have become Illinois' governor.

Then, on September 1, 2001, with vocal opposition by the Illinois old-school Republicans, the newly elected maverick Republican U.S. senator for Illinois, Peter Fitzgerald, nominated Patrick Fitzgerald to replace Lassar as the U.S. attorney for Northern Illinois. Although the two Fitzgeralds shared the same common Irish surname, they were not related. On October 24, 2001, the U.S. Senate confirmed the nomination.

Born in Brooklyn and educated in New York parochial schools, Patrick Fitzgerald's personal principles and work ethic were unquestionable. He earned his juris doctor from Harvard Law School in 1985. This Brooklyn kid with working-class values had a resume filled with an impressive list of successful prosecutions. He worked on the case of John Gotti, the godfather of the Gambino Mafia family. Fitzgerald prosecuted Sheikh Omar Abdel Rahman and eleven others charged in the 1993 World Trade Center bombings. He served as chief prosecutor for the 1998 bombings of the United States embassies in Kenya and Tanzania while working with a team of U.S. Department of Justice attorneys investigating Osama bin Laden. Illinois now had an experienced, dedicated prosecutor of mobsters and terrorists poised to go after the force destroying Illinois government: corrupt politicians.

I first met Patrick Fitzgerald at the Chicago Fraternal Order of Police Lodge in January 2002. I was attending the annual corned beef and cabbage dinner for the graduates of the FBI National Academy. Fitzgerald was the guest of my fellow graduate and longtime friend, Don Norton. I arrived before they did and was flattered that Norton introduced him to me as soon as they arrived. Fitzgerald thanked me for my part in Operation Safe Road and said in a subtle Brooklyn accent, "I can't believe you still have your job." Dean Bauer had pled guilty only the week before, and I had appeared on three Chicago news shows a few days earlier. I liked Fitzgerald immediately. He was much more a regular guy than most high-level public officials. I sensed a humility that is taught in many Irish Catholic homes. I admired him even more for his dedication to public service that followed during the next six years.

Patrick Collins and Patrick Fitzgerald are like two peas in a pod. Collins also is a man with working-class roots and Irish Catholic values. He is the son of a union printer who lost his job due to automation. Graduating magna cum laude from Notre Dame, he went on to earn a law degree from the University of Chicago. His reputation at the U.S. Attorney's Office was one of steadfastness. Long-term investigations were his style. He was the perfect choice to lead the team investigating the George Ryan organization. Some agents in federal law enforcement agencies were opposed to the investigation in its early stages, but Collins convinced them to devote the time and manpower to take on Illinois' culture of corruption.

After my experience in 1995 with AUSA Scott Mendeloff, I had a bad taste in my mouth for assistant United States attorneys. Mendeloff had treated me like a snitch and then done nothing with the information I furnished. When Collins called me in 1998, I was resentful and distrustful. In his first telephone call to me, he said, "I understand you have information about corruption inside the Secretary of State's Office."

I told him, "I already talked to the U.S. Attorney's Office," not knowing that Mendeloff neither wrote a report nor advised his boss about my visit.

Collins reassured me that they were starting over and would listen to what I had to say. Our meetings over the next several years were not without conflict. We sometimes disagreed on issues, especially when it came to releasing information to the press. Collins believed that certain facts should be held back from the media to ensure success in prosecution. I understood his perspective; however, I believed in the public's right to know. If people know more facts, they are better able to make decisions during elections, or, for that matter, pressure their representatives to move on impeachment when the malfeasance is at its worst. Beginning in 1998, the Operation Safe Road case was constantly in the news. Collins did his best to manage the stories by only releasing information that would not jeopardize the prosecution. He was one of the reasons the net result of the long-term federal prosecution was seventy-five convictions.

Tall, blond, clean-cut, and all-American best describes Zack Fardon, the AUSA who eventually would prep me and conduct the direct examination of me in Ryan's trial. Receiving his juris doctor from Vanderbilt University in 1992, Fardon has a long list of criminal trial experience. He worked both sides of the courtroom, serving as a public defender and a prosecutor. Fardon was part of the team under former Attorney General Griffin Bell that represented President George H. W. Bush in the Iran/Contra investigation.

In his opening statement at Ryan's trial, Fardon said Ryan "used his stated office for his personal gain, even at the risk of the public good." *Tribune* columnist Eric Zorn wrote that Fardon's use of the word "risk" was his way of sparking the memory of the Willis family accident without specifically referring to it. Judge Pallmeyer banned any direct reference to the crash. Be that as it may, Zack Fardon was a genius.

After convicting Fawell and the CFR, the long-term efforts of this combined team of dyed-in-the-wool attorneys would bring Ryan to justice. They would give Russ Sonneveld and me a public forum to vent our grievances and expose the corruption we witnessed firsthand.

CHAPTER 16

Indecent Public Exposure

I think that one of the most fundamental responsibilities is to give testimony in a court of law, to give it honestly and willingly.

—Adlai E. Stevenson

George Ryan's history of alleged political corruption is as long as his history of government service. While he was Illinois' speaker of the house, a six-week-long investigation by the Better Government Association and the *Chicago Sun-Times* uncovered that he had received thousands of dollars of business for his Kankakee pharmacy after he interceded on behalf of nursing homes accused of resident neglect. Ironically, Ryan called the allegations, "an outright damnable lie." What was more interesting was the U.S. Attorney's Office in Chicago was unable to uncover sufficient evidence to pursue a criminal indictment. The investigation was assigned to then Assistant U.S. Attorney Dan Webb, the man who later would become Ryan's chief legal apologist.

The corruption of George Ryan, his administration, and his political campaign organization lasted from the time he took office as secretary of state in 1991 until he completed his one term as governor in 2003. Russ Sonneveld and I reported a four-year pattern of corruption to the U.S. Attorney's Office in 1995, just two months after the fatal traffic crash in Milwaukee. I have thus far described the events I personally observed, most of which were obstructions of justice performed by members of his staff or reported to me by fellow workers. All that time, other hardworking and honest state employees also observed the corruption. Some reported it to their supervisors. Some reported it to the Department of Inspector General. All had their outcries against malfeasance go ignored. Some employees battled ridicule and retaliation from their supervisors.

Likewise news outlets exposed shakedowns and fund-raising abuses. In 1994, WMAQ-TV captured a Secretary of State's Office employee selling Ryan fund-raising tickets during working hours to an auto body shop, a business regulated by the Secretary of State's Office. The same series of WMAQ stories interviewed Secretary of State's Office employees who claimed they were pressured to sell Ryan tickets or face reprisals. Following WMAQ's series, Terrence Brunner, then the executive director the Better Government Association, testified before an Illinois House of Representatives committee, "Supervisors at driver's license facilities called in state employees and gave them large numbers of fund-raising tickets for George Ryan fund-raisers, which they were expected to sell for one hundred dollars each. The employees also observed certain individuals and businesses that contributed to Ryan's war chest being given special treatment and an easy time on driver's license exams." Brunner alluded to the fact that the continuance of these acts while Ryan publicly stated that he had told his employees to stop might constitute the federal crime of extortion.

Then, in early 1999, the BGA and attorney Robert Plotkin sued Ryan and his campaign fund in federal court for violating the rights of voters and SOS employees for coercive fund-raising. Ryan was represented by former Governor Jim Thomson and the then Attorney General Jim Ryan. The federal courts ruled that the plaintiffs had no standing. Later in 1999, the BGA alleged that SOS employees at the Elk Grove Village state truck licensing facility were pressured to get donations for Ryan's gubernatorial campaign from truck driving applicants. The BGA and Chicago attorney Bob Atkins then filed a lawsuit on behalf of an Illinois taxpayer to recover money unlawfully obtained from Ryan, his campaign, and several of his close associates. The Illinois Supreme Court eventually ruled against the suit, claiming that taxpayers had no right to demand accountability from corrupt public officials in court. In 2000, WBBM-TV announced that a Ryan family member and a regional manager in the Secretary of State's Driver Services Department asked a Pontiac facility employee to buy Ryan fund-raiser tickets and to work a political campaign on her own time. When she refused, she suffered job-related reprisals.

After all the allegations, arrests, litigation, and testimony, George Ryan's position as the captain of the culture of corruption was revealed in a federal indictment. On December 17, 2003, the U.S. Attorney's Office of the Northern District of Illinois announced that Ryan was being indicted for racketeering and fraud while he was both Illinois' secretary of state and governor. I remembered thinking that the indictment was a great Christmas gift for many people, me included. Don Norton, my friend and investigator at the U.S. Attorney's Office, called me and asked if I felt vindicated.

To me, vindication meant that I was clear of any blame. I was not accused of any wrongdoing, so for what was I to be vindicated? Some of Ryan's loyalists called me a disgruntled employee. Others said I was politically motivated. Neither was correct. Vindication seemed not to apply. When a police officer investigates a case, arrests the suspect, and the suspect is subsequently indicted, it is a feeling of accomplishment, and that is what I felt. The cliché "chalk one up for the guys" even better describes the feeling.

During the five-year process of preparing and waiting for this indictment, I had several conversations with Patrick Collins, the lead prosecutor for the federal case called Operation Safe Road. During one of the earliest conversations, he once asked me what outcome I would have wished to see from this case. I told him the eventual conviction and imprisonment of George Ryan. That was the cop in me talking. All the corruption in the Secretary of State's Office, the culture of corruption, was not only intentionally ignored by George Ryan it was encouraged and even nurtured. It was a series of serious criminal offenses. It went beyond administrative incompetence or ethical violations. Criminal law requires an act and intent—*actus reus* and *mens rea.* Ryan did both. He engaged in a criminal conspiracy, racketeering, and did it intentionally in order to ensure his election as governor. Now it was up to the federal prosecutors to prove the charges on the indictment.

Patrick Fitzgerald, the U.S. Attorney for the Northern Illinois District, stated at a press conference on December 17, 2003: "I submit that the citizens of this state expect honest government from the secretary of state or the governor. They deserve nothing less." The long process for Patrick Collins, Zack Fardon, and other members of Fitzgerald's staff was just beginning. At the same time, Scott Willis, Janet Willis, Russ Sonneveld, me, and many state employees anxiously waited for the trial that proved that the honest government we expected and deserved had been neglected for the ill-gotten gains of George Ryan and his close associates.

The indictment was ninety-one pages and twenty-two counts, most of which accused Ryan of awarding lucrative contracts and using the State of Illinois to benefit family, friends, and business associates. In the history of Illinois politics and its culture of corruption, this seemed innocuous to many—politics as usual. The criminal acts and intents that went beyond politics as usual were stated in count two of the indictment, as follows:

By December 1994, shortly after the 1994 reelection campaign, Fawell and defendant RYAN were aware that agents of the IG Department had been or were investigating alleged official misconduct by employees of the Drivers Services Department and the Vehicle Services

Department motivated by, or involving, the sale and distribution of Citizens For Ryan fundraising tickets.

It was further part of the scheme that, in December 1994, in an internal memorandum not intended for public disclosure, Fawell recommended to defendant RYAN that certain IG Investigators be terminated and reassigned, in order to discourage investigations into improper political fundraising activities and related official misconduct benefiting defendant RYAN and Citizens For Ryan.

It was further part of the scheme that, in one or more face-to-face meetings between Fawell and defendant RYAN following the distribution of the December 1994 memo, defendant RYAN agreed to Fawell's recommendation in the December 1994 memo as to the IG Department and thereafter authorized the termination or reassignment of the majority of IG Investigators.

It was further part of the scheme that, in or about January 1995, Fawell directed a memorandum to defendant RYAN summarizing the results of their meetings, including the decision to reassign IG Investigators who were "trouble."

It was further part of the scheme that Fawell drafted and distributed written memoranda falsely justifying the decision to terminate

IG Investigators and reorganize the IG Department as being based on budgetary cutbacks at the SOS Office.

It was further part of the scheme that, from February 1995 through June 1995, most of the IG Investigators, including those who had made inquiries into allegations of official misconduct linked to fundraising ticket sales, were terminated or reassigned. As a direct consequence of these actions, defendant RYAN and Fawell disabled the IG Department and substantially hindered it from fulfilling its duties to, among other things, investigate all allegations of SOS Office misconduct, including allegations linked to fundraising efforts of Citizens For Ryan.

There it was, the official government document after a long, exhaustive investigation by the Justice Department, FBI, Internal Revenue Service, U.S. Postal Inspection Service, and Department of Transportation, stating in legal mumbo-jumbo that Russ Sonneveld and I conducted investigations, upheld our public oath, reported crimes to a prosecutor, and got screwed by the man in charge. This was not politics as usual. This was the crime of obstruction of justice. We investigated employees of the Secretary of State's Office for criminal violations. Ryan conspired with others to stop us from investigating those crimes so that the public's awareness of them would not impact his election as governor. Several of those investigations occurred prior to November 1994, the day of the tragic crash in Milwaukee. Sonneveld and I could only speculate that we might have been able to prevent the tragedy. We did, however, attempt to investigate the aftermath, but the Ryan conspiracy stopped us.

On December 23, 2003, Russ Sonneveld and I attended Ryan's arraignment. The arraignment is the court procedure where the official charges are read aloud to the defendant. The defendant also states his plea. If he pleads guilty, no trial is necessary. Sonneveld was under the weather both physically and emotionally. I figured if I could get him to attend the arraignment, it would lift his spirits and benefit his health. Besides, criminal procedures are often entertaining. Ryan was represented by Dan Webb, the same attorney who was a former federal prosecutor that investigated House Speaker Ryan. Sonneveld knew Webb personally when they worked together in the Illinois State Police. Webb was its director then, and Sonneveld was a commander of internal affairs. They respected each other on a personal level. I knew Sonneveld would enjoy watching Webb representing one of the bad guys.

Ryan had a co-defendant, Larry Warner. Warner was indicted with Ryan because he benefited from many of the illegal kickbacks and contracts. Warner often was personally involved in the negotiation of illegal contracts and made governmental decisions even though he was not a state employee. Warner was represented by Edward Genson, a notorious Chicago criminal defense attorney. When I was a rookie cop, Genson represented Mob chop shop proprietors. I had a plethora of experience on the witness stand being cross-examined by Genson from my early days of policing. Genson later became a defense counsel for drug dealers and corrupt politicians in the federal court system. He was engaging to watch. Due to a chronic medical condition, he limped and often used a cane. He was previously both Dean Bauer and Scott Fawell's attorney. You would often see Genson and Bauer on the evening news leaning on each other as they exited or entered the Dirksen Federal Building. I believed this was done to generate public sympathy for Bauer, who was old and ill. Genson's courtroom persona is highly animated and goes with his magnetic personality. He is often well liked by prosecutors, judges, and cops. Watching Webb and Genson in court attempting to justify their motions to delay was going to be entertaining and worth the price of the ticket.

We knew that, despite the government's overwhelming evidence, Ryan would plead not guilty, and he did. Warner too pleaded not guilty. My experience with defendants that have high-priced attorneys is they drag out the trial for as long as possible, even though the evidence might be overwhelming. Witnesses move, change their mind, forget, or die. In public figure cases with endless media accounts, the story gets old and the public loses interest. Many of these cases are organized crime figures, white-collar criminals, or corrupt politicians. Many of the defendants, unlike street criminals, are past middle age. The longer the case drags on, the older the defendant gets. Older defendants draw public sympathy because of their age, compounded by the typical health issues that come with it. It was a sure thing that Ryan was going to plead not guilty, followed by his defense team requesting a distant date to begin the trial.

Sonneveld and I, along with our old friend Don Norton, sat in the back row. Genson motioned for a separate trial for Larry Warner, arguing that much of the evidence was on Ryan and trying the two together would be highly prejudicial to Warner. The motion was denied. Webb asked for a trial date in fifteen months. He stated that he had a multimillion-dollar tobacco case in Washington, D.C., and that would take up most of his time during the next year. When I heard that, I thought, *Too bad for you. Either Ryan can hire another high-priced, politically connected attorney from your firm or the client in D.C. can get another attorney.*

Genson argued that the government had been spending countless hours and dollars to prepare for this trial and he had only recently received the case. He needed at least a year to prepare a proper defense. I thought that the people should not wait any longer for justice to prevail. Patrick Collins argued what I was thinking. As Collins spoke, Ryan was standing to his left, about seven feet away, and staring at Collins. Ryan's face did not show emotion, but it definitely was an intense, obtrusive stare. I am sure Ryan felt contempt. After all, he was a veteran public servant, and this handsome, well-dressed young attorney was going to do everything within his power over the next several months to put Ryan in prison.

The trial date was set by Judge Rebecca Pallmeyer for March 2005, fifteen months away. I was disappointed but not surprised. The trial did not begin until September 2005. Again, it was no surprise.

The long ordeal of jury selection began on Monday, September 19, 2005. Potential jurors spent as much as forty minutes being questioned by the two defense teams and the prosecution. The method is arduous to ensure that each juror selected has no biases for either side, but it is mainly intended to guarantee the defendants a fair trial. A pool of more than one hundred jurors was questioned. Not until ten days later did the trial begin. This was an omen of things to come.

The government would have two hours for opening statements. The teams for the defendants also would have two hours for their respective opening. After opening statements, the prosecution presented its case first. During the next several months, an endless list of political allies and business associates of George Ryan, as well as state workers, sat on the witness stand. The trial fluctuated from intriguing to dull and back to intriguing. It was reported on daily in the newspapers, on Internet blogs, and on television. The Chicago media was consumed with the trial, and rightfully so. The Scopes Monkey Trial over evolutionary theory in the early 1920s was named the trial of the century. As far as Illinois history goes, this would be the trial of the twenty-first century.

Until November 2005, neither Sonneveld nor I had heard if we would be called to testify. We both knew we were on the government list of witnesses. We also knew it would take a day of preparation to ready us as witnesses. Then, in early November, I received a call from Basil Demczak, the postal inspector who was the federal government's case agent. He told me I might testify in late December. Sonneveld received similar notification. It was not until January 4, 2006, before we each took the stand. Although we shared a witness room across the hallway from the courtroom, we purposely did not discuss any of the trial for fear of being cross-examined over issues of corroboration. We read books, talked about family, and worked crosswords while we waited to be called.

Sonneveld went first. He told the story of how Dean Bauer, Ryan's trusted friend and inspector general, continuously warned him that our job was to protect George Ryan and not to embarrass him. Sonneveld described how Bauer told him not to investigate the fatal Milwaukee crash and to "let the Milwaukee authorities handle the matter." He also testified to the telephone conversation he had with Ryan, briefing him on the theft of money from the Naperville license facility by the manager, and how Bauer quashed the investigation after the telephone conversation. Sonneveld described how he was used to check the Ryan campaign offices for electronic bugging devices. He then told how he was fired from his job as a special agent. His language became coarse during the testimony as he described his frustrations of dealing with the Ryan administration. He later told me the language was harsh because he felt helpless in 1995 and now all that anger was being vented in front of the jury.

Dan Webb, Ryan's main defense counsel, did not do the cross-examination due to the personal history Sonneveld and Webb had. Instead, Tim Rooney questioned Sonneveld. Rooney, a senior partner with Winston and Strawn, was known for representing high-profile clients. Two of his clients were James Heiple, an Illinois Supreme Court justice who faced impeachment before the Illinois legislature, and former U.S. Representative Dan Rostenkowski, the Illinois Democrat who was convicted of mail fraud.

Sonneveld's testimony was split in half because of a lunch break. He went to eat in the cafeteria on the second floor of the Dirksen Building. After purchasing his meal and sitting down, Ryan and his wife, Lura Lynn, entered the same cafeteria. Mrs. Ryan, with one of the attorneys, sat down only two tables away and stared at Sonneveld. He saw Ryan standing with his lunch tray, hesitating as if he did not want to sit at the table chosen by his wife. Sonneveld told the attorney he would move so no one would feel uncomfortable.

By the afternoon, Sonneveld felt relieved that this chapter in his life was coming to an end. Throughout his testimony, he made eye contact with Ryan. Every time he did, Ryan looked away. That had to hurt Ryan. If the jury saw it, they had to wonder if Ryan's inability to look his accuser in the eye was due to guilt.

I took the stand later that afternoon. I remembering walking in the courtroom and the eyes of almost every person in the room were on me. Lawyers, reporters, spectators, and federal agents all focused on me, analyzing every detail. I had testified in many trials before, but nothing so public. I felt like everything about me was being analyzed— my clothing, size, and age, my expressions, and my walk to the witness stand. I was nervous, but not any more nervous than I usually was before testifying. It was my chance to vent in a courtroom the truth about George Ryan and his shady administration. I carefully looked at the jury to see if they were analyzing me too. Curiously, they all had pens and pads. Although jurors may take notes during criminal proceedings, I never noticed this in previous trials. They needed to take notes, with the massive amount of testimony they had heard over the last four months.

It impressed me because it demonstrated that this was a jury genuinely concerned with the duty of finding the truth in a very complicated trial. I considered that historical issues of power and corruption were at stake for all of Illinois—or, for that matter, all of American democracy. The decision by this jury would impact the political morale of voters for generations. In my opinion, a finding of not guilty would have further alienated an already cynical citizenry. On the other hand, a verdict of guilty would give new life to our less-than-perfect system of government and criminal justice. My observations of this jury encouraged me to be the best witness I was capable of being.

Assistant U.S. Attorney Zack Fardon did the direct examination on me. I focused on him as he asked the questions. I casually turned to the jury to answer each question and attempted not to appear overly zealous. Most of the direct examination was about cases specifically shut down by Ryan's buddy Dean Bauer. I also discussed the Naperville facility theft investigation and how Bauer ordered that case closed after Sonneveld's conversation with George Ryan. The prosecution team was instructed by Judge Pallmeyer that they could not refer to the details of the fatal crash in Milwaukee. Fardon, however, could ask me about a traffic accident in Milwaukee and its connection to commercial driver's licenses issued for bribes in Illinois. I testified how Sonneveld attempted to investigate the matter but was ordered to shut the case down by Bauer. I also testified how former Cook County Assistant State's Attorney Pat Quinn told me that Ryan blurted out an expletive at then State's Attorney Jack O'Malley prior to a news conference about a bust we made on Secretary of State's Office employees. Quinn had made a comment about how Ryan could fix the corruption within the Secretary of State's Office, and it seemed to anger Ryan.

My most important testimony was about the June 1, 1995, dissolution of the Secretary of State Department of Inspector General. I described how I was told that I had a choice between being fired or agreeing to a demotion and returning to my position as a sergeant with the SOS Police. Fardon asked if I was told why the department was being dismantled. I answered that I was never given an explanation. This part of my testimony linked the conspiracy to obstruct justice—to rid the state of the investigators whose duty was to uncover corruption. Scott Fawell, Ryan's chief of staff, and Ryan began that conspiracy with a memo in December 1994 and finished it on June 1, 1995.

I believe my direct examination lasted about two hours. I no longer felt nervous. I was now exhilarated. Cross-examination began immediately after. Andrea Lyon did the cross. Lyon is an assistant dean of the law school at DePaul University. She made her reputation as a public defender, taking on clients that faced the death penalty. She was part of Ryan's defense team because of Ryan's anti-death-penalty stance. Why she took on the task of cross-examining me, I don't know. She stood in front of Judge Pallmeyer, blocking my vision of Ryan. I wanted to look Ryan in the eye as I answered Lyon's questions. Unlike many trial attorneys—Edward Genson for instance, who paces the courtroom for dramatic effect—Lyon stood at a podium the entire time she questioned me. I was disappointed that I could not look at Ryan. Lyon probably did this intentionally, but I did not show my disappointment and continued to answer the questions coolly and concisely.

Lyon questioned me about the Naperville facility theft and a memo I prepared after questioning Russell Nisavaco, the facility manager and suspect. Dean Bauer ordered Sonneveld and me to write separate memos, an unusual request since case reports were written detailing the investigation. Bauer told us he wanted us to write what questions we each asked Nisavaco and why we asked those questions. I felt Bauer's demand was so highly irregular that my response would justify my actions. The Department of Inspector General, the agency for which I worked, sent me to professional interrogation training at the John Reid School of Interview and Interrogation. The school teaches techniques to identify lying through body language, facial conveyances, and verbal expressions. It also teaches how to elicit a confession from a guilty party. I described in my memo how Sonneveld and I used the Reid technique to determine if Nisavaco was lying to us and actually had stolen the facility's money. A subsequent polygraph examination proved he was lying. However, Nisavaco never confessed.

Andrea Lyon held the book *Criminal Interrogation and Confessions*, the textbook of the Reid technique, in her hand as she questioned me about the interrogation technique, referencing specific passages in the book. Each time, I affirmed that I used the tactic to which she alluded. It was not making sense to me. I looked good because I went by the book. Time ran out and court was recessed until the next day.

Postal Inspector Demczak escorted me to a private exit so I would not be hounded by reporters waiting in the main lobby of the Dirksen Building. That night, the news reports on the trial were about Sonneveld's testimony. He did not comment to reporters after testifying, so all they had to go on was what he had said on the stand.

That night, I looked over my copy of *Criminal Interrogation and Confessions.* I had used the technique successfully over the years, but it had been a long time since I reviewed the book. I was more confused. My review reassured me that I was following the technique outlined in the text. Lyon's line of questioning still was not making sense.

The next morning, I arrived at the witness room about eight thirty. It was not until about nine thirty when I walked back into Judge Pallmeyer's courtroom. This time I did not feel like all eyes were on me. Andrea Lyon continued the cross. After about another forty-five minutes, it was clear where she was going. Her point to the jury was that Sonneveld and I did not get Nisavaco to confess; therefore, we were incompetent. If we were incompetent, then it was Ryan's prerogative and duty to fire us. She did not say that in so many words, but the point was inferred.

I was humored by the attempt. Not all interrogations result in a confession. State employees are especially difficult. They not only fear they will lose their job if they confess, they fear they will embarrass and expose their political clout. As bizarre as it sounds, I had a few past bribery cases where the employee was willing to go to jail, as long as he could keep his job with the state. I only wish I could have explained that further. I later discussed the cross-examination with NBC 5 reporter Phil Rogers. He felt the cross-examination was an attempt to bore the jury and downplay the significance of my testimony. It did not matter; Zack Fardon's redirect was even better than the direct examination.

During cross, Lyon asked me a question about a private corporate executive's right to deal with internal corruption without seeking the police or prosecution. I agreed that the executive had that right. I was anticipating Fardon's redirect referencing that issue. He asked if public officials were different. I answered that they were, ending my statement with, "The people have a right to know the truth." I looked at Collins as I answered. Collins very rarely showed emotion, but I could see his eyes get bigger, as if affirming that we had just scored a point for the good guys.

I was done with my testimony around eleven thirty a.m. on January 5, 2005. Mark Lipe, the former special agent from the Springfield office of the Department of Inspector General, came next. Lipe recounted how Bauer short-circuited criminal investigations and even hid evidence that linked driver's licenses issued to illegal aliens to Ryan fund-raising at the Libertyville Driver Services facility. Lipe also testified that he heard Bauer contact Ryan by telephone, a conversation Ryan was accused of lying about when questioned by federal agents. Ryan's lie was part of the twenty-one-count indictment. At the end of the day, Collins said the government would rest its case "by the end of two weeks." Several months later, in a conversation with Sonneveld, Lipe, and me, Collins said the jury had begun to look bored as the Christmas holidays approached, and the post-holiday testimony seemed to bring life back to the jury.

While the Feds were winding down their case, there was a lot of media speculation about whether Ryan would take the stand. I was keeping my fingers crossed that he would. My observations of him at news conferences were that he was okay as long as he had a prepared script. Once reporters began asking him questions, he would become frustrated and often agitated. Direct examination by Webb would be his prepared script. Ryan would crash and burn under cross-examination by AUSA Patrick Collins. Ryan's team played it smart by keeping him off the stand.

The Ryan defense team put a variety of witnesses on the stand. They included a U.S. attorney from southern Illinois, a forensic accountant, a nun, and a television actor. It wasn't enough. After the closing arguments of both sides and the lengthy and detailed jury instructions, the jury went into deliberation on March 12, 2006. The jury had unprecedented problems. One juror refused to deliberate and argued with other jurors. One juror failed to disclose an arrest. Another juror failed to disclose her divorce. Judge Pallmeyer did all she could to ensure the deliberation would go on and Ryan received a fair trial. On April 19, 2006, the tired and battered jury of George Ryan's constituents found him guilty on all counts. One hundred percent guilty!

Ryan was now facing time in a federal prison. Sentences are not handed out immediately at the time of the verdict. Many things are considered before the judge hands down a sentence, including the defendant's age, criminal history, public service, and the impact of his criminal actions on his victims. Both defense and prosecution prepare their arguments. The defense will argue mitigating circumstances. In Ryan's case, his age, health, and public service were issues. The prosecution argued that the aggravating circumstances, the cost of corrupt actions to taxpayers, nationwide highway deaths, and the fatal Milwaukee crash would play in favor of a long sentence.

Ryan's team of lawyers said Ryan was ill. He suffered from Crohn's disease and diabetes. Likewise, Lura Lynn Ryan, his spouse, was said to be frail and depended heavily on him. His lawyers even argued that he had already been punished by the adverse publicity and humiliation from the investigation and trial.

The Rev. Scott Willis, father of the six children killed in the November 1994 traffic crash in Milwaukee, wanted to testify before Judge Rebecca Pallmeyer prior to her handing down Ryan's sentence. The government's attorneys told the honorable judge that they wanted Willis to testify. In a *Chicago Tribune* interview, Joe Power, the Willis family attorney, said, "Scott Willis just wants the court and the public to know how they've paid the ultimate price for corruption. There's nothing more precious in society than our children."

In a hearing before Pallmeyer, Collins argued, "Reverend Willis was a victim [of Ryan's corruption] in the sense that he was entitled to a good-faith investigation."

On September 1, 2006, Judge Pallmeyer announced her decision: "The court declines to hear Reverend Willis's testimony at George Ryan's sentencing hearing but will accept a written submission from him or from any additional witnesses."

Scott and Janet Willis promptly responded with their own heart-felt letters to the court. Janet Willis described her feelings as a mother before, during, and after the tragedy that took her six children away from her. She stated how she had voted for Ryan in 1994, unaware that one year earlier investigations about illegal licenses being issued had been reported to Ryan and he did nothing. Scott Willis added in his letter that Ryan should have been a champion of justice for the six Willis children. As a father, he should have understood the meaning of the loss of six children. Instead, he covered it up. The Willises did not ask for punishment. They asked for justice.

On September 6, 2006, Pallmeyer sentenced Ryan to six and one-half years confinement in a federal penitentiary. He was allowed to remain free on bond until a federal appellate court heard an appeal. It did not really matter what the appellate court decided. He deserved a longer sentence, but that did not matter either. What mattered was that a jury composed of Illinois voters unanimously voted to convict him on all counts. What mattered was that the very public trial of Ryan exposed to Illinois citizens the self-serving, corrupt man he was. If the verdict was to be overturned, cynics could call it politics as usual and rightfully so. No matter what the outcome, Ryan would go down in Illinois history books as a typical fat-cat politician with a long career of cheating the taxpayers. The people have a good reason to be cynical.

CHAPTER 17
Mercy for Some, Justice for Others

There are three things in the world that deserve no mercy, hypocrisy, fraud, and tyranny.
—*Frederick W. Robertson, nineteenth century British evangelical minister*

Many people were hurt by George Ryan and his corrupt organization. Competent professional people were fired because they attempted to do their jobs and expose public corruption and cronyism. Special Agent Russ Sonneveld was one of them. People like Scott Fawell and Dean Bauer conspired to rid the Secretary of State's Office of the do-gooders. Some state workers lost their jobs simply because they did not participate in the George Ryan political organization, either through fund-raising or campaign work.

Some were transferred to new assignments or demoted, like me. During the time I was working the corruption investigations, I felt stressed. For over a seven-year period, my blood pressure was elevated to dangerous levels despite medication. I was moody and nervous. Those close to me suffered from my anger and distrust. I've changed since those days. Losing weight combined with serious exercise has helped me deal with the stress and wean myself from medication. Despite the setback of my demotion, I regained my rank and eventually retired from the Secretary of State Police at the rank of captain, with a great deal of pride for my career accomplishments.

Russ Sonneveld has not been so lucky. He has been fighting a serious illness since 2003. After being fired by Ryan in 1995, Sonneveld obtained a job as an insurance investigator in Minnesota. He investigated life insurance claims when there were questionable circumstances surrounding the policy holder's death. Sonneveld was the first insurance investigator to resolve a false claim connected to the September 11, 2001, World Trade Center bombing. He found the alleged deceased living in Atlanta. Sonneveld seemed to enjoy the work, and it paid well. Illness struck and he was forced to go on disability. I cannot help but believe the stress from his years of exposing Ryan's corruption contributed to Sonneveld's current struggle with his illness. If he had not been fired by Ryan, he would have been able to complete his years of law enforcement service with the State of Illinois and would now be receiving a generous police pension that includes a health insurance benefit. He is a quiet, humble man and does not want pity or sympathy. Sonneveld would be embarrassed by my writing about him as if he was a hero, but he is one.

Hundreds of illegal commercial driver's licenses were issued through acts of bribery and official misconduct. It was estimated by the United States Department of Transportation that twelve highway accident deaths occurred that were directly related to the Illinois licenses for bribes scandal. You must add the family, friends, and employers to the list of those hurt to see the full impact of those fatalities.

Then there is the Willis family. They lost six children in a horrific way. There is no comparison for their suffering. There is no compensation either. They will tell you their faith gives them their strength. If you meet them, you will have no doubt about their strength, their inner peace with God. However, something is missing. Ryan refused to take responsibility for the series of events that led to the accident in Milwaukee. He showed no remorse. There has been no closure.

Thirteen years after the six uncorrupted children were lost in the fatal crash, a box full of memories goes untouched. It is filled with souvenirs belonging to those kids. Scott Willis told me, "I have not gone through it. I know there would be a lot of tears. We don't dwell on it and try not to wonder how they would be now."

All human beings deal with life's traumatic events through coping mechanisms. Some people are hateful and bent on revenge. Others cope by abusing alcohol or drugs. Still others find peace through love and mercy.

In contrast to the Willises' former home in the Mount Greenwood neighborhood of Chicago is their current home. Twenty-five miles from downtown Nashville is the peaceful hamlet of Ashland City, Tennessee. Sitting on the Cumberland River, it is located in Cheatham County. There are abundant opportunities to boat, fish, and hunt.

Ashland City is in the Bible belt. With a population of 4,550 people, it has twenty churches. Like much of the rest of America, it also has McDonald's, Domino's Pizza, Taco Bell, Wal-Mart, and Dollar Store. It has been home to Scott and Janet Willis since 2004.

Their current house was purchased for $132,000. The nine-hundred-square-foot, green wood-frame home sits on thirteen acres at the end of a ridge. Scott Willis describes it as a little two-bedroom cottage, located in a peaceful and rustic environment. He walks about eight hundred feet up the ridge to pick up his mail. His closest neighbor is also at the top of that ridge.

It is the ideal place to have a dog and a cat. The Willises have one of each. Scott told me that they used to have three chickens, which he named after players on the Boston Red Sox, his favorite baseball team. The dog ate the chickens. I couldn't resist, and told him that his dog is probably a New York Yankees fan. He laughed and repeated the joke to Janet. It made me feel good that someone who has experienced such sorrow could laugh at my dumb joke.

The Willises' lives have been full since 1994. Life has included dealing with criminal and civil litigation. They have had to go to meetings, depositions, and trials. They have written letters and anxiously awaited verdicts and sentences. Then there was an almost daily barrage of newspaper and television stories of tragedy and corruption. All the media outlets wanted their opinions. When they appeared on the news, they looked strong and positive. However, there were emotional and physical setbacks. Scott contemplated suicide. Janet had breast cancer. Despite their troubles, they have come through it all with a heartening perspective.

They have three adult children: Amy, forty; Toby, thirty-eight; and Dan, thirty-seven. Those three have blessed Scott and Janet with twenty-seven grandchildren. Scott and Janet wanted to get away from Chicago's weather and politics. Scott wanted to move to Florida. Janet wanted to be close to the grandchildren. Some live in Chicago. Some are in Michigan. And others are near their home in Tennessee. Ashland City seemed ideal. It is warmer than Illinois and Michigan, but not as far away as Florida.

Janet had a lumpectomy shortly before moving. She is now cancer free. She recently won a prize with her exhibit at the Cheatham County Art Fair. She also wrote and illustrated a children's book titled *A Dad's Delight*. It is dedicated to their nine children. In 2007, Scott had bypass surgery. It slowed him down only a little. He loves to play baseball and played in hardball adult leagues prior to the surgery. He now works out on a treadmill and lifts weights three times a week. In 2008, he played in twenty-three ball games. Scott lightheartedly told me he feels he is a better baseball player at the age of sixty than when he was a teenager. He said he played on a team when he was a kid, but did not play very well. I guess that has now changed.

Janet's parents moved close to the Willises' home about a year ago. She spent almost every day helping with their needs. They still live nearby, but are now in assisted living. Caring for them remains a big part of Janet's life.

Scott and Janet planned a trip to Branson, Missouri. Scott called it the "senior thing." I don't know many seniors who play twenty-three hardball games a year and lift weights three times a week. Scott said he does not like the "grand" in grandpa. He joked that he is a "so-so grandparent." His grandkids call him "so-so-pa." Janet and Scott Willis are much more than "so-so" people. It is not just grandparenting, caregiving, art, writing, and baseball that fill their lives.

In 1999, the Willises won a one-hundred-million-dollar settlement in a lawsuit stemming from the Milwaukee accident. Two-thirds of the Willis family's settlement went to charitable gifts, interest-free loans to needy individuals, hospital bills for the uninsured, and a nonprofit foundation. Prior to that settlement, Scott Willis's annual income from teaching in the Chicago Public Schools and ministering at Parkwood Baptist Church in the Mount Greenwood neighborhood was never more than thirty thousand dollars. As allowed by law, the Willises now receive an annuity from the money that is left from the settlement, much of which continues to be used for charitable contributions.

Scott currently teaches Sunday school classes at their local church, First Baptist of Ashland City. The Willises have always lived a humble life, and they were determined to keep it that way. The couple felt that the money bestowed on them had to be used to help others in need and started a philanthropic organization called the Khesed Foundation. *Khesed* is the Hebrew word for mercy. Scott first heard the word from a professor while he was attending college. He says he always liked the word and its meaning. He told me there are many variations on its spelling and a Jewish friend gave him the version the Willises chose for the foundation.

Scott said that so far this year, the Khesed Foundation has given away $8.3 million. The foundation reported having $7.5 million in its fund in its most recent filing with the State of Illinois, and its primary purpose is inner-city and foreign missions. The Chicago-based Bible League is the largest recipient of Khesed Foundation money, getting $2 million in grants and another $2.9 million in loans, state records show. The Bible League is a ministry that distributes Bibles worldwide. They want those Bibles to be used for evangelism and church growth. This is accomplished by sending ministers out to hold Bible instruction and start new churches. Scott and Janet traveled to China, the Philippines, and Kenya to make sure the work of the foundation was being accomplished in those places. They saw things they had never seen before in Chicago or Tennessee. They witnessed people who had great physical and spiritual needs. It touched the Willises' hearts and they knew the Khesed Foundation would provide.

Closer to home, the foundation also gave money for a project in Chicago called the By the Hand Club for Kids. It tutors and mentors children on which the system may have otherwise given up. When they are referred to the project, their standardized test scores are below the twenty-fifth percentile and their behavior is problematic. With an annual budget of $2.3 million, the project's staff works with teachers and parents to see that the children reach their full potential. "The By the Hand Club for Kids works in the most impoverished neighborhoods of Chicago, like Cabrini Green and Altgeld Gardens," Scott said.

I personally connected to this philanthropy and discussed it in more detail with Scott. About a year ago, I began substitute teaching in the Chicago Public Schools and observed a particular seventh-grade boy that fit the criteria for the Club for Kids. I described to Scott the young man's classroom behavior, discussions I have had with the school's staff, and what I knew of his home life. The boy refused to do assigned work, roamed the classroom antagonizing other students, and was frequently fighting. I substituted in his class many times and had to keep the cop in me in check. Scott described with much concern how the Club for Kids could work with this child after school, developing his God-given talents and building his self-esteem. With a clear resolve in his voice, he suggested that I look up the Club for Kids on the Internet and recommend that the school refer this student to the program.

Other organizations the Khesed Foundation has served include the Jimmy Fund, which fights cancer in adults and children by helping Boston's Dan-Farber Cancer Institute. The Willises visited the institute and saw how it successfully treats what were once thought of as incurable childhood cancers. Another Khesed Foundation recipient is Joni and Friends International Disability Center in Agoura Hills, California, where people with disabilities are mentored to use their leadership skills for their church and community. Founded in 1979 by quadriplegic author and artist Joni Eareckson Tada, the ministry serves disabled people and their families throughout Asia, Africa, Europe, and North America. Another philanthropy the Willises' foundation has helped is Lee Memorial Health System in southwest Florida. Fifty percent of the children treated by Lee's Children's Hospital have limited medical coverage or are uninsured.

"We learned a lot by visiting places. It opened our eyes," Scott told me. He went on to say that there are people suffering from poverty and illness in places all over the world. We have anguish in America, but most people in the middle class don't see it. Many things we take for granted. You don't see basic plumbing and medical care everywhere. "Janet and I are grateful to God to grant us the capability to help wherever it is needed," Scott said. "It is easy to write a check. It is other people that do the hard work. Besides, it is not our money. We are stewards for the money God has endowed."

Not all of the Willises' generosity has been bestowed to groups promoting their religious beliefs. In a nod to Scott's love for Boston baseball and its most noteworthy Hall of Famer, the Ted Williams Museum in Hernando, Florida, received twenty-five thousand dollars in 2004, state records show.

The most recent conversation I had with Scott Willis lasted about an hour and forty-five minutes. He said Janet and he would visit with Russ Sonneveld and me the next time they come to Chicago. I am looking forward to it. Scott and I could have talked longer, but he was interrupted by voices in the background. Four of his grandchildren had just arrived at the house. "Hi, So-so-pa," they said.

(The Willis home in Tennesse)

With the obvious delight and love I heard in his voice as we talked on the phone, Scott said, "I gotta go, I just got busy."

While I was writing this book, Lura Lynn Ryan released a book titled *At Home With Illinois Governors*. Dan Monroe wrote the book with her assistance while she lived in comfort with her husband at the Illinois governor's mansion. In September 2007, Governor Ryan sat and autographed copies at the Pasfield House in Springfield, Illinois, while he awaited the federal appellate court's decision on his fate.

In the summer of 2007, a federal appellate court of three justices upheld his conviction in a two to one vote. Ryan's defense team argued at the appeals hearing that Ryan deserved a new trial because a juror was dismissed and replaced after the jury deliberation had begun. According to other jurors, she refused to vote for a verdict. They said it was difficult to find a case like that in the history of U.S. courts.

On the contrary, a Philadelphia federal appellate court recently upheld a guilty verdict in a public corruption case where a juror was let go when fellow jurors complained she would not deliberate. In a Miami police corruption case, three jurors were dismissed, one for refusing to deliberate and one for bringing in outside information. In both the Philadelphia and Miami cases, the appellate courts held that the trial judges articulated reasonable rationales for replacing the jurors. A juror in Ryan's case was also accused of bringing outside material to the deliberation proceedings. The appellate courts affirmation of Ryan's guilty verdict was reviewed and upheld by all the appellate justices in the U.S. Court of Appeals Seventh Circuit. I believe in the American criminal justice system. Despite his age and some public sympathy, I believe Ryan deserved time in a federal prison. He was convicted by a jury of his Illinois constituents, but has yet to express any admission of wrong-doing.

At the book signing, Ryan refused to meet with reporters and could be seen only after buying his wife's book. Mrs. Ryan met briefly with reporters on her husband's behalf and said, "My conscience is clear, and so is George's. We get on with our life." She added that their faith in God would sustain them in the future.

I am a self-decreed combined social scientist and cynic. A fusion of thirty years as a cop, criminal justice teacher, police academy instructor, and personal research warrants this label. My personal analysis of Ryan is the man has something pathologically wrong with him. It may be biological or it may be culturally based. That I'll leave to the more scholarly to debate.

Scott Willis is a devout Christian minister. He is neither an expert criminologist nor a criminal psychologist. Anyone who has met Willis knows he does not have a cruel or hateful bone in his body. Although bewildered by Ryan's failure to atone, Scott finds my analysis harsh. In my opinion, pathological is an accurate explanation for Ryan's inability to admit his part in the corruption that led to and followed the deaths of the Willis children. "Pathological" means uncontrolled or unreasonable: a condition that is not normal or a deviation from the normal. It is normal for people to feel guilt. It eats away at them. To set their conscience free from this guilt, they atone. Lura Lynn Ryan also said at the book signing, "When you've got a clear conscience and you're right with the Lord, I don't think too much bad can happen to you."

As I was nearing completion of this manuscript, I began discussing with friends a way to end this tragic story in Illinois history. I did not want to close with just George Ryan going off to federal prison. Many politicians have done that, only to return to their respective constituencies, remaining in the local spotlight as popular political elites. Congressman Dan Rostenkowski, convicted of mail fraud, returned to Chicago after serving his sentence and became a television political commentator. Even Lura Lynn Ryan's book holds praises for Joel Matteson, Illinois governor from 1853 to 1857. He was responsible for the construction of the governor's mansion, along with being the first governor to occupy it. After leaving the office of governor and the mansion, he built an elaborate home nearby and was known for his wealth and prestige in Springfield society. The town of Matteson, Illinois is his namesake. Yet he fled from Springfield to Europe with his family in disgrace. Matteson was accused of embezzling two hundred thousand dollars—a substantial amount in 1857—from the Illinois state treasury while he was governor. In an apparent attempt to atone for his illegal conduct, he paid the money back, but left behind a tarnished image. The words of convicted former Governor George Ryan's wife's book pay historical homage to Matteson, another of Illinois crooked politicians. Illinois' history is rife with these political heartbreaks. Many others U.S. states have similar pasts. It makes voters feel cynical and helpless against a system that consistently fails them. Ryan himself often referred to this system while his house of cards was crashing down around him as "the culture of corruption." So my discussion with friends concluded with the thought that George Ryan needed to be given one last chance at atonement. That would be the sweetness the story needed to kill the bitter.

I took it upon myself to attempt to ask Ryan directly if he was sorry for hurting so many people in so many ways while he was Illinois' secretary of state and governor. On October 4, 2007, I decided to drive to Kankakee. I asked Mike Hogan, a friend and former co-worker, to join me. Mike retired from the Secretary of State Police at the same time I did and was familiar with the struggle between corruption and public service that occurred in the Office of the Secretary of State. Hogan did not know the details behind the obstructions of justice regarding investigations of bribery, theft, and Ryan campaign funds that led to the deaths of the Willis children, but he was familiar with the federal investigation that began in 1998 and culminated in Ryan's conviction. I felt Hogan was an ideal companion to take to Ryan's home turf. I did not want a confrontation with Ryan. I also feared that if I appeared at his front door, false accusations might be made against me. I wanted a credible witness who would verify that I did nothing more than ask the former governor a couple of questions. Hogan's professional background and gentlemanly demeanor made him the perfect choice.

Kankakee is an old Illinois city and the town where Ryan was raised. Located fifty miles south of Chicago, with a population of slightly over one hundred thousand, it is an interesting blend of urban and rural. It is the town where Ryan met his wife, Lura Lynn, his high school sweetheart. Ryan's father operated two Kankakee drugstores where Ryan worked after attending pharmacy college. He and Lura Lynn reared five daughters and one son in the house the Ryans still call home. Ryan served as a member of the county board and as a state representative, eventually becoming the speaker of the house. From there, his power continued to grow as he became lieutenant governor, secretary of state, and finally governor. Kankakee is the town where he was trained in his style of politics.

Far removed from the concrete and steel of a federal prison is the Riverview Historic District of Kankakee. The Ryan family home is located there. Within a block of their home are two Frank Lloyd Wright homes. One is the Bradley House, one of the first Wright homes of the prairie school of architecture. Next door to the Bradley house is the Hickox House, often described as a Tudor-style home with a prairie house layout. These two landmarks were built in the early part of the twentieth century, like most of the homes in the district. There is a public park across the street from the Kankakee River less than one block from Ryan's house. The park has several tennis courts, a gazebo, and a playground shaded by old oak trees. There is a concrete pier extending into the river for the neighborhood fishermen. All in all the district looks like a comfortable and safe place to live.

Some of the homes are dilapidated and need serious repairs. Others have been renovated and are as picturesque as a photo from *Architectural Digest*. The home directly behind Ryan's is one of the latter, with a wraparound porch and an attached greenhouse. Ryan's is a dark brick American foursquare, two and one-half stories high with a full-width front porch and wide stairs.

Paint was peeling from the wooden trim of the Ryan house. Some of the roof's shingles were loose and separated. The house needed some exterior cosmetic repairs, but looked structurally sound. If not for the colorful shrubbery and flowers, as well as the autumn decorations, a child looking at the peeling paint and square architectural style might assume it was an old haunted house.

That morning, I wore Izod blue jean shorts and a lavender polo shirt, covered by a dark blue hooded sweatshirt with the zipper left open. On my head was a baseball cap with a "Police Torch Run" logo on it. I covered my eyes with a pair of lightly tinted sunglasses. I carried in my right hand a copy of *At Home With Illinois Governors*. Over the last several years, news reporters had flooded the neighborhood to get stories about George Ryan. I wanted someone to answer the door. I did not want to be taken for a reporter, nor did I want Ryan to recognize me immediately as a government witness who had testified at his trial. I dressed to fit the neighborhood.

It was ten a.m. when I decided to approach the house. My plan was to ring the doorbell and ask for Mr. Ryan. Based on recent news events, I couldn't imagine that he would answer the door. No matter who answered, once I was recognized, the person would demand that I leave. I had no problem with that. I would simply leave and accept the fact that I would not get an opportunity to put my questions to the former governor. I got out of my car and Mike Hogan remained behind. He would watch my back and make sure that all went well. He wasn't going to let someone trick bag me. I could feel my heart beat faster as I climbed the steps of the front porch. I passed a scarecrow and two geese statues decorated with brown and orange capes for the autumn season. After I rang the doorbell, I turned around and saw another scarecrow lying on the porch with its head half falling off. I waited for what seemed like five minutes for someone to answer the door. It took exactly twelve seconds.

(Hammer at the front door of Ryan's house, October 2007)

339

The wooden inside door opened, but due to the glare from the windows of the storm door, I could not see who it was. I was looking down because I was expecting a tiny older woman, Lura Lynn Ryan. The person inside then opened the storm door and came out on the porch, face-to-face with my six-feet-four-inch frame. He was wearing a blue bathrobe. His size and hair color made me think of my father in his bathrobe. Before he died, we had many conversations with one another on weekend mornings while we stood eye to eye. But it wasn't Dad; it was George Ryan, the federally convicted politician, only weeks from going to prison.

He spoke first. "Hi!"

"Mr. Ryan?" I asked.

"Yeah," Ryan said.

"Do you know who I am?" I said.

"No," he responded.

"I am Ed Hammer," I told him.

"Ed Hammer?" he said, seeming unfamiliar with me.

"Right, former Secretary of State Investigator," I said, taking off my sunglasses.

He looked at my face, but still did not seem to recognize me. "Come on in. I am just getting ready to go out and gonna take a shower," Ryan said.

I apprehensively followed him into the foyer of his home. I hadn't wanted to be out of Hogan's sight. But the combination of being stunned by the fact that he answered the door, followed by his invitation for me to come in his house, got the best of me.

I said to Ryan, "Did not mean to get you up."

"Come on in," he said again.

"I just wanted to ask you something," I said.

"Yeah."

"You know, I was demoted when I worked for the inspector general, Dean Bauer," I said.

"Yeah!" he said. At this point, he turned toward me and seemed to recognize me. His jaw dropped.

"And my partner, Russ Sonneveld, was fired," I added.

"Yeah?" he said, walking into a room immediately to the left of the entrance.

It was a small parlor with a fireplace on the north wall. A beige couch located at the entrance of the room stylishly faced the fireplace. I remained in the foyer and looked into the parlor as Ryan sat down on the couch, with his back to me.

Although I was a welcomed guest at first, I sensed that would change after I asked the question I was there to ask. I did not want to go any farther into the house.

I then asked it. "And I was wondering if at this point in time in your life you have anything to say to us, an apology or anything to the other Secretary of State employees?"

With his back to me, he responded, "If I have what?"

He now was clearly annoyed and his voice was gruff-sounding in the typical Ryan manner so frequently heard on the late-night news and in his clashes with the media.

"Do you have an apology or anything like that you wanted to say?" I asked.

"For what?" he asked, sounding more aggravated.

I did not want to be involved in a debate, but I needed more. "Me getting demoted for doing my job or Russ Sonneveld—"

He interrupted me before I completed my statement as he stood up in the parlor. "I really don't know a hell of a lot about it," he said, seemingly struggling for words.

He was hospitable when he answered the door, but now I was challenging his long career of government service.

"You don't know anything about Russ getting fired?" I asked him.

"I know about Bonneveld getting hired," Ryan said, mispronouncing Russ's last name and looking up at the old home's ceiling as if searching his memory.

"Uh-huh," I responded, with little patience for this once proud man in his bathrobe.

"I think somebody came to me and asked me to help hire him. No, I am not familiar with him being fired," he answered.

"Not with him being fired?" I responded.

"And I don't know about you being demoted. I mean, I don't know what you're talking about," he bellowed in his well-known baritone voice.

"You don't know what I am talking about? Well, I just wanted to ask. I do have your book. I have it signed already." I pointed to the book in my hand. "What about the Willis family?"

"I had nothing do to with the Willis family. I don't remember back then," he answered.

At this point, I began walking to the door. George Ryan then held it open for me.

As I walked out, I turned back to look at the old man in the blue bathrobe, my once all-powerful boss, and for a brief moment felt pity.

"Well, I wish you good luck," I said.

"Yeah, I got screwed," Ryan growled as he looked away from me.

My feeling of pity disappeared instantly at his caustic remark.

I asked him how his health was, the concern his lawyers had raised in court to reduce his sentence. He answered with one word, "Good."

"Yeah, well, good luck then, and thank you," I said, wondering if my tone of voice revealed the cynicism I felt.

Ryan followed me outside onto the porch. I stopped and shook his hand for the first and last time.

The whole conversation lasted about three and a half minutes. George Ryan did not offer an apology to me, to Russ Sonneveld, or to Scott and Janet Willis.

I have learned a lesson from the Willis family. As I walked away on this warm October day, with the sun shining on this old house in this cozy, Middle America neighborhood, I silently thanked God for his blessings and prayed for George Ryan's soul.

EPILOGUE

He did a lot for the community and whatnot, but you've got to follow the rules, just like everybody else.

Resident of Kankakee, Illinois

Some might call this poetic justice. On November 6, 2007, the United States Supreme Court rejected Ryan's last request for bail. The next day, Ryan, accompanied by his family, left his comfortable home in Kankakee, Illinois, and rode in his van to Wisconsin. At noon, inmate 16627-424 checked into the federal medium security prison located in Oxford, Wisconsin.

Inexplicably, prison officials granted him a courtesy not shown to most other new inmates. Ryan was allowed to enter the facility from the rear, away from cameras ready to capture the indignity of an Illinois governor going to jail. Ryan's family would then return home to Illinois without him.

(Oxford federal prison, Ryan's home after leaving Kankakee)

Almost exactly thirteen years earlier, Scott and Janet Willis likewise drove to Wisconsin, with six of their children in the family van. Later that day, Ben, Joe, Sam, Hank, Elizabeth, and Pete Willis died in fiery crash on a Wisconsin interstate. Scott and Janet Willis would return home to Illinois without their children.

On February 28, 2008, Ryan was moved to the federal prison in Terre Haute, Indiana. The official reason given by the Federal Bureau of Prisons was that the Terre Haute facility was better equipped to handle geriatric medical issues.

(Terre Haute federal prison, Ryan's home since 2008)

Then, on May 27, 2008, the United States Supreme Court rejected Ryan's last bid for appeal on his conviction for fraud and racketeering. His only chance to get out of prison would be a presidential pardon or clemency.

Illinois Senator Dick Durbin announced on December 2, 2008, that he was sending a letter to President George W. Bush, asking him to commute the sentence of Ryan. Citing both Ryan's and his wife's health,

Durbin said, "Further imprisonment will not, in my opinion, serve the ends of justice."

With the thought of Christmas in the hearts of all, on December 12, 2008, Ryan made a written public apology. He said, "I want to make things right in my heart with God. My heart will always go out to the Willis family."

Internet comments by *Chicago Tribune* readers were scathing.

David P. wrote, "The system is poisoned. There must be repercussions for vile acts—and an understanding that the corruption is not victimless or benign."

Michael V. said, "This criminal needs to serve his full sentence, regardless of the suffering he has caused his family."

In an allusion to Ryan's opposition to the death penalty, a reader named Shamus wrote, "Sounds a lot like a death row inmate finding Jesus when he gets near execution so he can be commuted to life…Too little, too late—serve the time, you scumbag—you did the crime."

Scott and Janet Willis also responded to Ryan's message. In a *Chicago Tribune* column by John Kass, Janet is quoted as saying, "The burden was put on us. And because Ryan was vague and unclear, we were left in a no-man's land."

Referring to a potential meeting with Ryan, Scott went on to say, "This is not for our sake. The kids aren't going to come back. I don't want to make things emotional here. Really, this is for his benefit. He talked about a clear conscience. But I don't understand how you can have a clear conscience and live with a lie. So if we meet, it's for his sake, to clear his conscience. Not for our sake."

In a final yuletide season cry for compassion, Lura Lynn Ryan sent a letter to Bush asking him to let her husband out of prison. She pleaded to the president that she needed her husband because of her health. She said that she had suffered from dizzy spells since she had an aneurysm four years earlier. She wanted him home by Christmas with her, their children, and their grandchildren.

Christmas came and went without a clemency announcement from Bush. Meanwhile another gubernatorial scandal was brewing with Rod Blagojevich, Ryan's successor. He was arrested by the FBI on December 9, 2008, and Illinois politicians became fodder for all the late-night comedy shows. There was speculation that Bush would never grant Ryan clemency due to the Blagojevich scandal. Then, on January 9, 2009, the governor was impeached by the Illinois House and was facing a trial by the Illinois Senate.

Finally, on January 19, 2009, his last day in office, President Bush commuted the sentences of two Border Patrol agents convicted of shooting a Mexican drug dealer. Ryan's sentence was not commuted. The consequences of Ryan's actions were that he must serve out his sentence. He is scheduled to be released on Independence Day 2013.

In August 2009, Scott and Janet Willis moved from their house in Ashland City to another home in Tennessee.

CHARACTER APPENDIX

Ansel, Harvey, chop operator

Atkins,Bob, Chicago attorney

Autullo, Dante, car thief and drug dealer

Baar-Topinka, Judy, Illinois State Treaqsure, Ryan ally, gubernatorial candidate

Bauer, Dean, Secretary of State Inspector General, close friend to Ryan, convicted felon

Beal, Mary, Secretary of State Police investigator

Bell, Griffin, United States Attorney General

Berlin, Tony, secretary of state employee, whistleblower

Bickel, Roger, Secretary of State General Counsel, Ryan confidant

Boyle, John "Quarters", convicted felon, owner of Public Armored Car

Brennan, Bill, FBI special agent in charge Chicago office

Brunner, Terrance, executive director, Better Government Association

Burke, Jim, Secretary of State Department of Inspector General, deputy director

Burns, Jim, former United States Attorney, Secretary of State Inspector General, appointed by Jesse White

Bush, George H.W., 41st President of the United States

Bush,George W., 43rd President of the United States

Cacciatolo, James, former Chicago police officer, brother of JoAnn Robertson

Capone, Al, famous Chicago mobster

Carpentier, Charles, 29th Illinois Secretary of State

Catuara, Mary, wife of Carl Catuara

Catuara, Jimmy "the Bomber", hitman, father of Carl,

Catuara, Carl, vehicle and driver's license facility manager

Chan, Waitung "Tony", owner of Advance Driving School, plead guilty of extortion

Christopher, John, alias John DeVito, FBI mole on "Silver Shovel" investigation, obtained fictitious driver's license

Cipowski, Larry, Secretary of State Police investigator

Collins, Patrick, assistant United States attorney

Consentino, Jerry, state treasure, convicted felon

Coley, Robert, mob attorney, FBI informant

Cox, Rick, Secretary of State Inspector General special agent

D'Arco,Johnny, state senator, convicted of extortion

Dauber, Billy, chop shop enforcer, mob hitman

Davis, Jim, FBI special agent

Demczak,Basil, United States Postal Inspector

DeVito, John, alias for John Christopher

DeGiore, Dennis, Secretary of State Police, captain

Dixon, Alan, 34th Illinois Secretary of State, US Senator

Dobbins,Cardell, Secretary of State Police investigator

Dobrosavljevich,Miodrag, owner Brookfield Truck Repair, pleaded guilty racketeering

Dowdle, Pat, Secretary of State Inspector General special agent and police sergeant

Dvorak, Mary Ann, Secretary of State, employee

Dvorak, James, Cook County under sheriff, convicted, felon

Dzjiercinski, George, convicted driver's license counterfeiter

Edgar, Jim, 35th Illinois Secretary of State, 38th Governor

Ettinger, Micheal, criminal attorney

Fajdich,Carmen, retired driver's license facility employee, pleaded guilty of racketeering

Fardon, Zack, assistant United States attorney

Fawell, Scott, Secretary of State Chief of Staff, convicted felon

Finnely, Ross, Secretary of State Police investigator

Fitzgerald, Patrick, United States Attorney

Fitzgerald, Peter, US Senator

Flannery, Mike, WBBM-TV political reporter

Gabuzzi, Joe, Secretary of State Police, sergeant

Garcia, John, WLS-TV, reporter

Genson, Edward, criminal attorney

Gibbs, Ron, Secretary of State Inspector General, appointed by George Ryan

Gillman, Dan, Secretary of State Inspector General special agent

Goldwater, Barry, Republican candidate for president in 1968, Arizona US Senator

Gotti, John, New York mafia godfather

Goudie, Chuck, WLS-TV reporter

Guzman, Ricardo, unqualified licensed truck driver

Hanzar,Larry, Secretary of State employee, pleaded guilty for accepting a bribe

Hartman, Arthur, Secretary of State Police major

Hartzler, Joe, assistant United States attorney, special prosecutor

Hickman, Robert, Secretary of State Deputy Secretary, convicted of felony while director of Illinois Tollway Authority

Hogan, Michael, Secretary of State Police sergeant

Holmes, Kelly, Secretary of State Inspector General special agent

Hooks, Kirk, Secretary of State Police, investigator

Howlett, Robert "Bob", Secretary of State Police Department Director

Igoe, Phil, Secretary of State attorney

Jackson, Walter, Secretary of State Inspector General special agent, Police investigator

Jackson Sr., Jesse, community activist

Jech, Joe, Secretary of State Inspector General Deputy Director

Johnson, John, former Will County Sheriff, Secretary of State Inspector General special agent

Juliano, Mike, Secretary of State lieutenant

Kass, John, Chicago Tribune Columnist

Kaufman, Elizabeth, Secretary of State Jesse White's press secretary

Kissinger, Gary, FBI special agent

Klasing, Tony, Secretary of State Inspector General special agent

Krause, Ed, FBI assistant special agent in charge Chicago office

Krzyzak, Janusz, instructor for Mega Driving School, pleaded guilty for racketeering

Lagrow, Jerry, Secretary of State Police, chief deputy director,

Lake, Keith, Secretary of State Police investigator

Lassar, Scott, United States Attorney

Leak,Spencer, Secretary of State Inspector General Deputy Director

Lewis, John W. 32nd Illinois Secretary of State

Lipe, Mark, Secretary of State Inspector General special agent

Luna, Tony, alleged to have furnished fake social security card

Lux Sr., Joe, uncle to Ed Hammer

Lux, Jr., Joe, Chicago police officer, cousin to Ed Hammer

Lyon, Andrea, criminal attorney, DePaul law professor

Manning, Kenton, Secretary of State Police sergeant

Margolis, Jeremy, former Illinois State Police director, attorney

Mastrodomenico, Mary Ann, driver's license examiner supervisor, pleaded guilty to racketeering

Mattesom Joel, 10th Illinois Governor

McCarthy, Tim, Orland Park Chief of Police

Mendeloff, Scott, assistant United States attorney

Mendoza, Gonzalo, License for Bribes' middleman, plead guilty to racketeering

Miller, Carolyn, administrative assistant, Secretary of State Inspector General

Monroe, Dan, Illinois author

Motton, Nathaniel, Orland Park Police patrol officer

Murcerino, Sal, Chicaog mob associate

Murphy, Frank, Secretary of State Inspector General special agent

Nisavaco, Russell, manager of driver's license facility

Nixon, Richard, 37th President of the United States

Norgel, John, federal judge

Norton, Donald, former Illinois State Police captain, US Attorney investigator

O'Malley, Jack, Cook County State's Attorney

O'Brien, Timmy, chop shop operator

O'Grady, James. Cook County Sheriff

Olgivie, Richard, 35th Illinois Governor

Ostrowsky, Richard, chop shop operator

Pallmeyer, Rebecca, federal judge

Pecoraro, Giacomo "Jack", Secretary of State Police Department Director

Philip, James "Pate", Illinois State Senate President

Poeshell, Dave, Secretary of State Police sergeant

Poshard, Glenn, U.S. Representitve, candidate for governor

Powell, Paul, 31st Illinois Secretary of State

Powers, Rob, Secretary of State assistant general counsel

Prendergast, William, Cook County judge

Prose,Tina, Secretary of State Director of Human Resources, appointed by Ryan and White

Quinn, Patrick, former Cook County assistant state's attorney, Illinois Appellate Court Justice

Quinn, Patrick, 45th Lieutenant Governor, 40th Governor

Rahman, Sheikh Omar, convicted terrorist

Raynor, Tammy, driver's license examiner, whistleblower

Redenbo, Jim, Secretary of State Inspector General appointed by Edgar

Richter, Ralph, Secretary of State Inspector General special agent

Robertson, Eric, husband of JoAnn Robertson

Robertson, Joann, administrative assistant, Secretary of State Inspector General

Rogers, Phil, WMAQ-TV reporter

Rutledge, Steve, Secretary of State Police, deputy director

Ryan, Lura Lynn, wife of George Ryan

Ryan, George, 36th Illinois Secretary of State, 39th Illinois Governor, convicted felon

Ryan, Nancy, daughter of George Ryan

Schwartz, Barbara, administrative assistant, Secretary of State Inspector General

Seibel, Marion, driver's license examiner supervisor, plead guilty to racketeering

Serafini, Dennis, Secretary of State Police sergeant

Shaw, Andy, WLS-TV reporter

Shirkey, Charles, target of undercover operation

Sneigowski,Mark, Secretary of State facility zone manager

Sonneveld, Russ, Secretary of State Inspector General special agent, key witness in Ryan trial

Stanley, Roger "the Hog", Ryan crony, plead guilty to mail fraud and money laundering

Streder, Steve, Secretary of State Inspector General special agent

Stroger, John, President Cook County Board

Stroger, Jeanine, Secretary of State Equal Employment Opportunity Officer, appointed by White

Swanson, Ronnie, son of Ron Swanson, Sr., Secretary of State property manager

Swanson, Sr., Ron, lobbyist and Ryan crony, convicted felon

Tatro, Elwyn, Secretary of State Inspector General special agent, appointed by Ryan

Thompson, Debbie, Secretary of State Inspector General special agent

Thompson, James, 37th Illinois Governor, attorney for Ryan

Tikus, Dave, Illinois State Police lieutenant

Tocco, Albert, Chicago Heights mob boss

Townsend, Jack, Illinois State Police master sergeant

Trainer, John, fake name used by CDL applicant

Twiss, Susan, manager of Citizens for Ryan campaign office

Vasconcelles,Bob, Secretary of State Inspector General special agent

Velasco, George, driver's examiner supervisor, pleaded guilty racketeering

Vogt, Liz, Secretary of State assistant general counsel

Volpe, Phyllis, driver's license facility manager, pleaded guilty racketeering

Warner, Lawrence, Ryan crony and codefendant, convicted felon

Watkins, Dave, Secretary of State Police Director, appointed by Edgar

Webb, Dan, former assistant United States attorney, former Illinois State Police Director, defense attorney for Ryan

White, Jesse, 37th Illinois Secretary of State

Williams, John, WGN Radio talk show host

Willis, Ben; Elizabeth; Hank: Joe; Pete and Sam, victims of a fatal vehicle accident

Willis, Janet, mother of victims

Willis, Scott, father of victims

Woods, Gerry, Secretary of State Inspector General special agent and Secretary of State Police investigator

Wright, Frank Lloyd, Illinois architect

Zorn, Eric, Chicago Tribune columnist

COMPLETE TEXT OF SCOTT AND JANET WILLIS' LETTERS

The Rev. Duane "Scott" Willis and Janet Willis submitted written statements to U.S. District Judge Rebecca R. Pallmeyer before former Gov. George Ryan was sentenced Wednesday to 6 1/2 years in prison for racketeering conspiracy, mail fraud and other offenses. The Willises gave their letters to the Chicago Tribune, which published them in Friday's editions:

From Janet Willis:

To the Honorable Judge Pallmeyer:

On Nov. 8, 1994, I voted to re-elect George Ryan as secretary of state to be in charge of road safety. I am a mother. I loved my children, home-schooled them, and with God's help, poured my heart into trying to be the best mother I could be. We were very close. A few hours after that vote was cast, I watched as my children were trapped in an inferno. I have had to ask God to help me to forget the sights and thoughts of that day and all that occurred. However, I think now maybe for this one time, if I would be willing to share some things, it might down the road, benefit others.

That day I thought (death) was instant for the little ones in the back. It wasn't. An accident report delivered to our home some weeks later related that there was some evidence of a struggle. Months later, the fire chief who was at the scene told me as gently as he could, "In this type of case it's never really instant."

As the weeks and months passed, little by little other pieces of information about that day have come our way unbidden. One of the first persons on the scene happened to be the brother of the boyfriend of my husband's best friend's daughter. He related to me that he ran from his car and saw our 13-year-old son, Ben, climbing out of the van right after me, his clothes aflame. He ran in a panic, but this man ran after him yelling, "Stop, drop and roll." He caught up with him and grabbed his hand yanking him to the ground. Ben then began to roll.

I saw my son moments later lying on the street as people tried to help him. He hardly looked like my Ben. His hair and eyebrows were gone, his burned lips made it hard for him to talk. But I was grateful to be able to talk with him, a brief sentence or two. He asked about the others, then said, "My feet are hot." People were trying to quickly but gently pull off the remaining burned clothes. One man asked me if I would mind if he put his T-shirt over Ben's body. He had moistened it with a water bottle. As I stood there, I suddenly was aware of searing, blinding pain in my burned hands; I could not imagine what my son who was burned over much of his body was going through. Ben was put into a helicopter and the paramedic later told me our son was relatively calm and lost consciousness before landing.

Over a year later, I found out that Ben was very much alert in the emergency room. I had the opportunity to talk to the attendant who was at his side. In pediatric cases, she was in charge of simply being an emotional support to young patients who had no parent available. She told me, "I believe he knew he was dying. He asked me to pray with him. He asked if someone would hold his hand; I couldn't because of his burns."

I feel it is my obligation, on behalf of my children, to make these facts known to the court and to Mr. Ryan. Here was a violent end to a violation of the public trust.

In the years since, both my husband and I have struggled with depression. While my husband battled thoughts of suicide, I battled to keep my sanity. My parents have also had their battles. My mother taught the four boys piano so we went to their house twice a week. She has battled depression ever since the accident.

My husband and I have prayed and asked God to keep us from bitterness and to help us be faithful to him and he has. We tried to honor God by not complaining.

But there is a time to speak. I am sharing these facts only because I believe if justice rules, wrongdoing will be deterred. I have learned "when (God's) judgments come upon the earth, the people of the world learn righteousness. Though grace is shown to the wicked, they do not learn righteousness; even in a land of uprightness they go on doing evil." (Isaiah 26:9, 10)

That Election Day, in 1994, I was unaware that in 1993, dishonest and unsafe procedures in driver's licensing facilities had been reported. I was unaware that in spite of some investigations into those activities, Mr. Ryan had allowed illegalities to continue. I was unaware that Mr. Ryan had his sight on the governor's seat and was using these activities to build his campaign funds.

Incredibly, even after our accident, he permitted the fundraising scheme to continue. But I was fully aware of these things when Mr. Ryan ran for governor and won. It was extremely hard at that point not knowing whether justice would be served.

Although we are very grateful for the prosecution of Mr. Ryan, it must be said that he made our heavy grief even heavier. This has affected our whole family: a great-grandmother, three grandparents, three older siblings, our grandchildren, and many nieces and nephews. Many of us have had to see our burned-out van on TV repeatedly over the past 12 years. Had there been an admission of guilt from Mr. Ryan, right from the start, the air would have been cleared. All of us have waited patiently for justice.

Respectfully submitted,

Janet Willis

From Scott Willis:

Gov. George Ryan is a father and a husband. He seems to have a close, loving family. My wife Janet and I are aware of his years of public service for the State of Illinois. Because of this, it makes the issues of this case so difficult.

First, six young children from Illinois are killed in a fiery explosion in Wisconsin caused by a mud-flap assembly (falling) off an Illinois truck driven by an Illinois Commercial Drivers Licensed driver. These deaths would strongly necessitate an investigation by the Illinois Department of the Secretary of State, overseer of public safety on the roads. Besides discovering why the accident happened and who might have caused it, the investigation could have provided insight (on) how to prevent similar future tragedies. When attempts to investigate were made, they were ignored, then suppressed.

Eventually evidence was uncovered pointing toward buying fundraising tickets for Secretary of State Ryan in exchange for CDL licenses. The driver had received his license illegally and was unqualified to drive a truck on the road. Warnings from other truck drivers about the piece of metal dangling went unheeded. The driver could not understand English. Thus, six children were innocent victims resulting from a political scheme to raise campaign money. Now a decision had to be made. Either allow the truth to come out giving understanding and justice for the children's deaths, or cover it up to protect the scheme and the one who benefited from the money.

What was required was a person of integrity and compassion to champion justice for the six children. The secretary of state, George Ryan, should have been the one to take that responsibility. Because it was his campaign that benefited, it would have been the mark of a compassionate and honest man to admit the truth. But under his watch, the investigation was suppressed to protect him, even to the closing down of the inspector general's office so no one could look further.

Our family's unanswered questions compelled us to look to other options to bring to light the facts surrounding the accident and its follow-up. (Attorney) Joseph Power pursued the investigation and uncovered the facts, and, it should be noted, took great abuse publicly from Mr. Ryan for doing so.

Secondly, Gov. Ryan must have understood as a father what the loss of six young, innocent children meant to Janet and me, yet no personal contact or written contact concerning the accident was ever made. Instead the investigation was terminated and suppressed, and our efforts to investigate were criticized.

Because he was the secretary of state and because of the massive publicity following the accident, he cannot claim ignorance. Thus he bears the ultimate responsibility in the suppression of the investigation.

How could this happen? How could a man, a father, a public servant allow this? What was done was a crime, according to the rule of this court. But the question remains as to the motivation. (Ryan defense attorney

Dan Webb) correctly answered this: "It was politics." Thus, decisions concerning life and death were not decided on principle but on politics.

Janet and I are ordinary people. Not powerful, not forceful. Our children brought great joy to us. Benjamin, Joseph, Samuel, Hank, Elizabeth and Peter were like anybody else's kids: playful, happy, mopey, energetic. The boys loved reading and sports. Elizabeth was her mom's shadow and her doll's mom. We love them. We miss them. We do not despair. We live with a God-promised hope in Jesus Christ.

Almost 12 years have passed since Nov. 8, 1994. The heartache remains but has softened. Janet and I have prayed to not have a bitter or revengeful spirit. These feelings have only occasionally flared up but have not consumed or dominated our thoughts and are not the motive for this letter.

Our thoughts are not on punishment. That is for the court to decide. The real tragedy is that no reconciliation has yet been attained between George Ryan and Janet and me. My wife and I have a strong desire to forgive Gov. Ryan but it must be on an honest basis: sorrow and admission. Even a 6-year-old boy knows when he's done wrong he needs to be truly sorry, and admit it. Then forgiveness and mercy can be graciously offered. That would be our joy.

Respectfully submitted,

Scott Willis

From Scott and Janet Willis:

As (has) been said so often, corruption has consequences; in this case they were severe. It can happen again. We are not going to go away. This is a battle about right and wrong, good and evil. It's a battle worth fighting. Evil tries to win by wearing us down. We deeply appreciate the tenacity of all those who have worked on the side of truth. They have done so with respect and honor. We are grateful to this court for its patience in hearing this case.